Change Your Career: Transitioning to the Nonprofit Sector

Shifting Your Focus from the Bottom Line to a Better World

Laura Gassner Otting

KAPLAN

PUBLISHING

New York

Change Your Career: Transitioning to the Nonprofit Sector

Shifting Your Focus from Bottom Line to a Better World

Laura Gassner Otting

KAPLAN)

PUBLISHING

New York

Editorial Director: Jennifer Farthing
Editor: Megan Gilbert
Production Editor: Caitlin Ostrow, Julio Espin
Production Artist: Virginia Byrne
Creative Director: Lucy Jenkins
Cover Designer: Carly Schnur

Published by Kaplan Publishing, a division of Kaplan, Inc.
888 Seventh Ave.
New York, NY 10106

Printed in the United States of America

May 2007
10 9 8 7 6 5 4 3 2 1

ISBN-13: 978-1-4195-9341-3
ISBN-10: 1-4195-9341-2

For information about ordering Kaplan Publishing books at special quantity discounts, please call 1-800-KAP-ITEM or write to Kaplan Publishing, 888 Seventh Ave., 22nd Floor, New York, NY 10106.

Dedication

This book is dedicated to Eli J. Segal, a great man who taught me that increasing the bottom line means nothing if you aren't also building a better world.

Contents

Contents

PART TWO   Ready, Set, Search!

About the Author

Laura Gassner Otting is the founder and president of the Nonprofit Professionals Advisory Group, a search firm working exclusively with nonprofits and nonprofit job seekers, that is dedicated to building the capacity of nonprofit organizations, associations, institutions of higher education, the public sector, and the professionals who make them run smoothly. Since 2002, her firm has offered services for people nationwide who seek employment in the nonprofit sector—résumé writing, cover letter editing, and job search consulting—and for nonprofits themselves—strategic hiring, search, training, planning, and communications. The firm has been recognized by the Bill and Melinda Gates Foundation and the Center for Philanthropy at Indiana University as one of the best resources for nonprofit job seekers.

Prior to 2002, Laura served as the senior vice president of ExecSearches.com, which she helped build into the Web's leading site for mid- to senior-level nonprofit job postings and search services. Laura has served as vice president at Isaacson, Miller, one of the largest search firms in New England and one of the most highly respected nonprofit executive search firms in the country. Previously, Laura served as a presidential appointee for the White House Office of National Service, a program officer for the Corporation for National Service, and as a member of the Clinton-Gore transition team and 1992 election team.

Laura sits on the boards of Camp Starfish and chairs the board of Strong Women, Strong Girls. She has served as a member of the Alumni Board of the Graduate School of Political Management at the George Washington University and as the founding board chair of the Boston Choral Ensemble. Laura holds a master's degree in political management from the George Washington University and a bachelor's degree in government from the University of Texas at Austin.

Laura lives in Newton, Massachusetts, with her husband, Jonathan, their two young sons, Benjamin and Tobias, and their 13-year-old Dalmatian, Annie.

KAPLAN

Preface

- Is now the right time for me to transition into the nonprofit sector?
- What do I want to do, and where do I want to do it?
- Will my skills transfer to the nonprofit sector?
- What is working in the nonprofit sector really like?
- How do I deal with the financial ramifications?
- Where do I even begin?

These are among the many questions I get asked in my executive search practice by individuals looking to transition from the for-profit to the nonprofit sector. This book answers all of those questions and more.

The nonprofit sector is burgeoning with opportunities for career changers. Students are graduating from colleges and universities with bachelor's or master's degrees in nonprofit management. Midcareer professionals are looking around for a better work-life balance in careers that matter to them. Retiring baby boomers are finding that they are not so retiring after all. And the nonprofit sector is changing to accommodate the enormous richness of experience all of these individuals can bring with them. This book endeavors to help each of them find a place in the new nonprofit sector.

This book is divided into three parts. Part One will help you assess whether the nonprofit sector is right for you and where in this vast sector you can find your place. Part Two explores the finer details of how you should conduct your search, with specific tips and tools to enable you to network effectively, write a better résumé, craft more enticing cover letters, and interview as though you've been in the sector for ages. Part 3 is a compendium of helpful resources, including job-posting Web sites, education programs, and knowledge tools.

Chapter 1 describes the types of people who transition into the nonprofit sector. It walks you through a short diagnostic test to determine whether the nonprofit sector is right for you at this time in your career. It reviews the advantages and disadvantages of working in the sector and discusses both the great opportunities that currently exist and those that are quickly emerging. It presents some recent research pointing to success for career changers like you. Finally, it outlines the three-tiered method by which you can find your next career in the nonprofit sector.

Chapter 2 gives you an eagle's eye view of the nonprofit sector. First, it starts with a short but technical definition of the sector. Second, it divides the sector by issue area, such as education, environment, or health care. Determining your driving social concern—the issue area about which you are passionate—is the first step in finding your next career. The second and third steps are figuring out where your skills fit best and which type of nonprofit fits your personality.

Chapter 3 examines both of these things. First, it delves more deeply into trends in the nonprofit sector that have begun to use skills that are in diminished supply but great demand in nonprofit organizations. Corporate career changers like you often have many of these skills in abundance. Then it walks you through the tactical methods by which a specific nonprofit might get its work done (e.g., direct service versus advocacy). Third, the chapter covers which stage in the nonprofit lifecycle fits your specific personality. Finally, the chapter demystifies nonprofit job titles, many of which bear no resemblance to their corporate counterparts and, as such, can be confusing to career changers.

Chapter 4 addresses special considerations for career changers by tackling myths and stereotypes that corporate employees hold about nonprofit employees, and vice versa. It offers tips to determine your readiness factor for making this move and for dealing with the transition's economic reality. Finally, Chapter 4 will help identify the right nonprofit for you by pointing out characteristics that make them friendlier to jobseekers whose résumés are weighted more toward business than nonprofit experience.

KAPLAN

Chapter 5 launches your job search. Here, we assess your skills, experience, education, and interests and set you on your networking journey. Chapter 5 also walks you through the plethora of resources you have at your disposal, all of which will make you smarter, more efficient, and ultimately more successful in your search.

Chapter 6 assists you in building your nonprofit résumé. Nonprofit résumés differ in ways both large and small from your typical for-profit résumé. In this chapter, you will learn about the pros and cons of different traditional résumé formats and hear about a better format that is perfect for the career changer. You will learn about specific techniques, tips, and tools to rewrite your résumé right the first time—and use that rewriting process to hone your networking and interviewing prowess.

Chapter 7 teaches you how to write cover letters that get interviews and how to ace the interview once you're in the door. It puts lists of likely questions in your hands and gives you the correct answers—even to the pesky salary question. Finally, this chapter teaches you how to master post-interview etiquette, including thank-you letters and offers and negotiations.

Throughout the book, you will meet others who have made this transition before you. In each chapter, you will read two profiles of career changers who have thoughtfully—and sometimes accidentally—found themselves in the midst of a new and challenging career in the nonprofit sector. Many of them describe their transition as the best decision they ever made. You will, too.

Welcome to the nonprofit sector! We're glad you are here.

—Laura Gassner Otting
Nonprofit Professionals Advisory Group
November 2006

Acknowledgments

This book could not have been written without the help and support of so many friends, colleagues, and loved ones. Heaping amounts of gratitude go to Linda Babcock, Jason Finestone, Jack Goldsmith, Leslie Williams, Jameila Haddawi, Jess Brooks, Amy Goldstein, Mark Miller, John Gomperts, Deb Berman, Paula Dodds, Caren and Jon Krumerman, Walter and Shelly Gassner, and Butch and Barbara Otting for helping me launch this project and for their sage wisdom, relentless support, and unending patience throughout. Special appreciation belongs to Megan Gilbert, who brought me this book idea and then held my hand through each draft. Mostly, though, I owe a debt of gratitude to my children, Ben and Toby, who every day inspire me to make the world a better place, and to my husband, Jon, my wings and my safety net, who always remains my true north.

PART ONE

Nonprofits and You

CHAPTER 1

Is a Nonprofit Career the Right Move for You?

"I enjoy my job, but what really drives me is the volunteer work I do on the weekends...I wish I had more time for that."

"I've finally reached my financial goals, but I know that I have one or two more big jobs in me...and I want them to matter."

"I am returning full-time into the workforce...As much as I need a job, I want one that makes a difference."

"I just realized one day: I want more."

Does this sound familiar? It might be the right time to consider a new career in the nonprofit sector.

From every walk of life, at every age, and from every professional background, employees in the nonprofit sector wake up each morning to promising, fulfilling, and demanding careers, working for issues in which they deeply believe or on behalf of causes they truly love. Some have spent their entire careers in the nonprofit sector. Some, like you, considered the change in midcareer. No longer satisfied just to increase the bottom line, they also want to build a better world.

While the transition from the for-profit sector to the nonprofit sector may seen natural, logical, or even easy in theory, many career changers find that it is quite tricky in practice. Some find themselves flummoxed by foreign lingo, unfamiliar yardsticks of success, or drastic differences in the pace of the work, while others are simply overwhelmed by the sector's vastness and mission-driven culture. However, with a little assistance in their transition, most find the move into the nonprofit sector to be one of their best life decisions and have wondered, as will you, why they didn't do it sooner.

The desire to make a change in your life—and in your local community or the larger world—will outweigh any difficulties you may face along the way. It will become the overall driving force behind your transition, but going into it with eyes open is still important. This book aims to do just that—open your eyes—helping you to explore the answers to your questions in more detail, providing guides to which type of nonprofit will be right for you at this time in your life and your career, and giving you tools to make this change a reality.

TRANSITIONING INTO THE NONPROFIT SECTOR

The nonprofit sector is experiencing an influx of corporate career changers. Their personal motivations, their chosen pathways, and their challenges and successes may surprise you. Bridgestar, a nonprofit organization providing talent-matching services, content, and tools to help organizations build strong leadership teams and help individuals pursue careers as nonprofit leaders, performed a June–September 2006 study of sector transition. Here are some key points to consider from that research:

- More corporate transitioners come to nonprofit work out of a general desire just to *do good* rather than to *do good for a specific cause.*
- Most for-profit types found their nonprofit job through personal networking, while others relied on more traditional sources like classified ads or executive search firms.
- Those looking to transition from the for-profit sector to the nonprofit sector volunteered at a rate of about twice that of other Americans.
- The quality of people in the sector and the passion they bring to their work are seen as the best aspects of the transition, while financial constraints and the challenges they cause are seen as the worst.
- The nonprofit sector is experiencing growth and turnover, creating opportunities for new talent to drive innovation and change. While some areas of functional expertise transfer better than others, this overwhelming demand for talent opens the window wide for transitioners at every level of nonprofits across the sector.

EXPLOSIVE SECTOR GROWTH = GREATER JOB OPPORTUNITIES

Growth in the nonprofit sector has radically outpaced growth in the private and government sectors over the past 20 years. In fact, between 1987 and 2005, the number of nonprofits in the United States grew at nearly triple the rate of the business sector.[1] As anyone in the for-profit sector knows, growth means opportunity. But where does this growth come from, and what does it mean to your career change?

First, the baby boomer generation is responsible for creating and leading many of the nation's nonprofits, and as this group retires over the next decade, the rate of nonprofit executive transition is expected to climb 10 to 15 percent, meaning that three to four out of every five executive director jobs will be vacated between now and 2010.[2] This will produce a leadership vacuum unparalleled in the history of the nonprofit sector, leaving nonprofits scrambling for experienced managers. More than just causing change at the top, leadership vacuums create ripple effects, sending waves of turnover throughout every level of the organizational chart.

Second, to respond to this leadership deficit, nonprofits will need to address three difficult but critical imperatives, most of which are also prevalent in the for-profit sector:[3]

1. Invest in leadership capacity
2. Refine management rewards to attract and retain top talent
3. Expand recruiting horizons and foster individual career mobility.

This is very good news for career changers, particularly the last item. As the staffing needs of nonprofits multiply, hiring corporate employees coming into the sector at all levels will become a common practice.

---

1 Independent Sector, "Facts and Figures about Charitable Organizations," (Washington, D.C.: Independent Sector, June 20, 2006, and updated September 20, 2006), *www.independentsector.org/programs/research/ Charitable_Fact_Sheet.pdf* (accessed November 26, 2006). Report relies heavily on statistics from the Internal Revenue Service *Data Book*, various editions.

2 Denice Rothman Hinden and Paige Hull, "Executive Leadership Transition: What We Know," *The Nonprofit Quarterly* 9 (Winter 2002): 24.

3 Thomas J. Tierney, "The Nonprofit Sector's Leadership Deficit," (Boston: The Bridgespan Group, March 2006), *www.bridgespangroup.org/kno_articles_leadershipdeficit.html* (accessed November 26, 2006).

Most nonprofits have neither the historical record of accomplishment nor the current resources to develop top-level senior management from within their own ranks. Further, they often lack the funds necessary to hire top-flight recruiting consultants who scour the Earth for perfect candidates. Yet filling this overwhelming leadership vacuum will force the nonprofit sector to take a long, hard look at the types of staff it employs and retains. Nonprofits will need to be much more flexible about the types of candidates they interview and the skills they bring on board. Candidates with experience in rapid-growth environments, expertise in management that is nurturing while still results-driven, and histories of actively grooming internal staff will thrive in the nonprofit sector. This includes, in large part, job seekers from the for-profit sector.

More Opportunities in Nonprofits

Explosive sector growth has meant a sharp increase in opportunity for those choosing to pursue society's betterment through nonprofit work, as the following Bridegspan statistics show:[4]

- Over the next decade, nonprofits will need to attract and develop some 640,000 new senior managers—2.4 times the number currently employed.

- If the sector experiences significant consolidation and lower-than-forecast turnover rates, the above number might fall to 330,000. On the other hand, given historic trends, the total need could well increase to more than one million.

- By 2016, nonprofit organizations will need almost 80,000 new senior managers per year.

WHO TRANSITIONS INTO THE NONPROFIT SECTOR?

With 11.7 million employees, it is fair to say that the nonprofit sector employs just about every kind of person you know. People from all walks of life and in different stages of their careers transition into the nonprofit sector. Here are five of the most common types of career changers:

---

4   Ibid.

1. *Young professionals wanting to get ahead.* Rather than waiting around as the assistant to the assistant to the assistant on an exciting project, young private sector professionals are leaping into the nonprofit sector to get their break. Those in their 20s and 30s are given more opportunities earlier in their careers than they might get in the for profit sector, allowing them to make a splash at a younger age. Whether they leave the corporate world because they are unfulfilled in their day-to-day work, or they are unsatisfied with the overall goal of their nameless, faceless corporation, they usually find the nonprofit sector a breath of fresh, and highly charged, air.

2. *Professionals looking to gain new skills.* The "generalist professional" nature of the nonprofit sector means that each staffer handles more responsibilities. The nonprofit sector simply does not have the luxury of hiring as many specialists. Therefore, corporate professionals who once were pigeonholed as "just finance," for example, can take on roles in the nonprofit sector that include finance, operations, and administration. Likewise, transitioners who serve on a nonprofit board can use this experience as an opportunity to diversify their background before starting their search. Taking on the program committee chairmanship of a board, for example, is a perfect way to reposition a skill set and a résumé.

3. *Experienced executives looking for work-life balance.* Nonprofits appreciate the whole of a person, not just the small fraction that contributes to increasing shareholder value. New parents enjoy the more family-friendly atmosphere in the nonprofit sector, where they can trade flexible hours for less pay while feeling better about spending time away from their children. Businesspeople who have spent ten years living in airplane clubs in distant airports, too, are thrilled that they can attend soccer games, participate in community activities, and not be exhausted and jet-lagged when it comes to "date night" with their significant other. Nonprofit employees get to contribute to society in their day job as well as get encouragement to take time off to pursue other worthy endeavors complementary to the mission of the nonprofit, important to the individual, or, in particularly demanding jobs, their emotional and mental health.

MICHELLE GISLASON PROJECTS DIRECTOR, EXECUTIVE LEADERSHIP,
COMPASSPOINT NONPROFIT SERVICES, SAN FRANCISCO, CALIFORNIA

In 2000, Michelle became very sick from an anti-malarial drug while honeymooning in Thailand and Vietnam. She had been working as a marketing director for an educational Web site in the boom-and-bust dot-com world and came back from her illness to find that she was the last one standing at work after a series of layoffs. "It sounds like a cliché, but it was a soul-searching time," she says. Michelle left her job, took some time off, and started to look around.

Her transition to the nonprofit sector was somewhat unintentional, a by-product of her habit of following the content of her work rather than the environment in which she did it. "My real interest was organizational development, and I found that I always gravitated toward committees or assignments where I could be working across departments," she says. "I liked trying to get teams to work together, finding redundancies, and training and coaching staff." She was asked by a former colleague to do some consulting for a nonprofit and found herself drawn toward the sector. Some of her nonprofit friends noticed her interest and told her that she should check out CompassPoint, a local nonprofit doing exactly what she enjoyed but in the nonprofit sector.

"I took a position as a conference director, because I had experience in marketing and events management," she says. "I didn't want to make a career of it, but I used it as an entry point to an organization that was doing the kind of work I was interested in." Over the years, Michelle started slowly transitioning into CompassPoint's leadership development program. She also began a master's program in organizational psychology and was certified as an organizational coach. "All I do now is everything that I love:

training, facilitation, and coaching around leadership," she says. "It was a very slow process for me, but it was worth every minute to be doing what I want to be doing now."

What biases did Michelle encounter in the nonprofit sector?

Michelle encountered certain biases from some of her peers when she came to CompassPoint. "Some people didn't understand why I wanted to be in the nonprofit sector," she says. They didn't think my for-profit experience would translate, even though I had experienced some very similar issues. They also didn't always relate to the for-profit jargon I unconsciously carried over. "I had be mindful of saying things like, 'Let's take this conversation offline,' or referring to the 'return on investment.'" Although Michelle had volunteered for nonprofits before starting at CompassPoint, she notes that if she had spent more time as a board member, she would have learned sooner about the different dynamics and board governance structure found in the nonprofit sector.

Will Michelle's next job be in the nonprofit sector?

Even though she came upon this new career by accident, Michelle expects to stay in the nonprofit sector. "It is a bonus for me that I get to do what I love in the nonprofit sector," she says. "Before, I was jumping from job to job after just a few years," she says, "but I've been here for five years and counting. There's a reason people stick around nonprofits longer." For Michelle, that reason includes the dual bottom line of profitability and mission, the personal values around social change that she feels she can fulfill, and the variety of people she gets to work with on a daily basis. "I work with some of the most intelligent, thoughtful, committed, and humorous people I have ever met in my life. It's difficult to find that elsewhere."

Michelle's Key Lessons Learned:

■ "Nonprofits have a lingo all their own. Do a lot of reading about the sector and talking to people in the sector to make sure you get the language right. That will go a long way toward alleviating any biases."

■ "It's a myth that nonprofits need to be more businesslike. In reality, many nonprofits are managed extremely well, while others struggle (just as they might in the for-profit world). In my interviews, people

didn't assume that because I have worked in the dot-com world, or run a $1.5 million educational center, or am getting a master's degree, that I could save their nonprofit. In fact, it would have been presumptuous of me to think that I could."

■ "Many nonprofits can have a deficit or 'scarcity' mentality. They come to the table thinking everything is wrong or broken and that they have to fix it themselves. They can also have underdeveloped infrastructure but may be unable or unwilling to pay for services and unwilling to seek outside support from peers. That way of thinking can lead to burnout."

4. *Baby boomers searching for a more fulfilling retirement.* Each day, 7,918 baby boomers turn 60.[5] Many of them are retiring, eagerly anticipating years of free time without the constant worry of financial pressures. This free time allows them to travel, play golf, spend quality time with their grandchildren, and volunteer. But for many, these activities are not enough. Rather than leading a retiring life, these children of Martin Luther King Jr., John F. Kennedy, and the Vietnam War are finding within themselves the need to give back, to continue to live a life of purpose, and get back to their younger and idealistic dreams of changing the world. Seasoned and wiser, they now know that bringing their formidable skills to bear within the nonprofit sector is a worthy outlet for that energy.

5. *The outraged, the unfulfilled, and the disappointed simply wanting more.* At any and every age, the desire for more out of life encroaches on us all. It's found you, or you wouldn't be holding this book. The nonprofit sector is filled with people from all walks of life—whether they started in the private sector or not—who want a more fulfilling professional experience, a way to blend their work with their world, and a road that feels more comfortable for the long haul. These individuals have chosen their nonprofits as the tool by which they are making that change, and the world is richer for having them there.

---

5 U.S. Census Bureau, "Facts for Features," (Washington, D.C.: January 3, 2006), *www.census.gov/Press-Release/www/2006/cb06ffse01-2.pdf* (accessed November 26, 2006).

ADVANTAGES AND DISADVANTAGES OF WORKING IN THE NONPROFIT SECTOR

Just as when working in the for-profit sector, you will encounter things in the non-profit sector that will alternately excite or frustrate you. Some, like fulfilling work and kind coworkers, can be expected. But many, especially increased bureaucracy and burnout, take career changers by surprise. Knowing about both the advantages and disadvantages of nonprofit work *before* you make your move will better prepare you for success. With everything else in the world, there is good news and bad news here. Let's start with the bad news; you'll find it easily trumped by the good.

Disadvantages

Working in a nonprofit can be both fulfilling and maddening, all at the same time. The industry has its own way of doing things, and insiders know how to navigate the negatives. Here are some of the most common complaints of nonprofit workers.

Concrete Results or Clear Benchmarks of Success Can Be Difficult to Spot

It is often hard to judge the success or failure of daily actions in pursuit of a broader goal. For example, it is easy to know how much a stock price rose, but it is impossible to know that a third-grade girl from the inner city went on to become a physicist because she learned about Marie Curie in an after-school mentoring program. Employees in nonprofit organizations sometimes have to "take it on faith" that the work they are doing day to day is contributing to a larger, more important goal.

Work Environments Can Be Frustrating

From antiquated technology to bureaucratic red tape, working in a nonprofit can be downright exasperating. Employees are asked to do more work with fewer resources, create miracles on a daily basis, and satisfy competing interests. The pace of change is often slower than in a for-profit environment, given that so many opinions must be considered and the bottom line is not as clear. Personal sensitivities can often impede progress, and predilections and idiosyncrasies must be taken into consideration in any decision. The reward system is as much emotional as monetary, lending itself to pats on the back and inflated job titles. From strategic program direction to the color of the napkins at a fundraiser, no decision can be considered minor in the nonprofit sector.

The Level of Burnout Is High

Those who enter the nonprofit workforce with a specific mission and goal in mind do so with great purpose. This great purpose often places a heavy weight—and even, sometimes, a chip—on the shoulders of those doing the work. Every decision made has deep consequences, and the work is taken extremely seriously. When a worker feels a personal responsibility to the individuals whose life he is affecting, he is likely to get burned out faster than if he spends his days crunching numbers on a spreadsheet.

The Bottom Line Is Not Always the Bottom Line

Nonprofits base decisions on many important factors, not just the numerical bottom line. In fact, many nonprofits decide to move forward with a program, even though they know it will hemorrhage money. They do this because it is simply "the right thing to do." It may seem like common sense in the corporate world to replace a live person at the front desk with an engraved list of offices and extensions or to cut down personnel costs by closing the intake office on Saturdays, but to many nonprofits, this sort of personal touch represents their heart and soul.

The Stakes Are Higher

A bad day in your corporate job is unlikely to resemble a bad day in your nonprofit job. Consider the difference between losing a few percentage points off your stock price and losing a kid to drugs. Consider the difference between closing down a franchise and firing ten employees and closing down a community center that was the centerpiece of a revitalized neighborhood. Compare being told that you can't introduce your products to a new country because they won't be profitable there and being told that you can't bring immunizations to Africa because of a glitch in U.S. foreign policy. The stakes are simply higher when you are dealing with a cause close to your heart.

There Is a Constant Focus on Fundraising

Nonprofit executives wake up every morning and go to bed every night worrying about the location of their next dollar. This constant pressure leads to certain internal issues going unaddressed until a crisis emerges, takes the chief executive away from the office for long periods of time, and can promote mission drift. Further, most funders prefer to pay for the more tangible costs of program implementation—the actual shots administered to children or meals delivered to elderly shut-ins—and not the far less sexy operating needs—a database, a salary survey, or a desk. Therefore, nonprofits often are forced to ignore vital infrastructure issues until a crisis emerges.

Advantages

Now let's talk about the good stuff, because it is in great abundance and is highly rewarding. While they may be emotional, personal, mental, physical, and spiritual, the advantages of working in the nonprofit sector far outnumber the disadvantages. Perhaps the best advantage, though, is that it simply feels right to you, right now, to work for something in which you believe deeply and hold close to your heart. With your eyes on the prize, the potentially debilitating disadvantages will fade from deterrents to distractions.

Nonprofits Employ Interesting People

A common misconception is that nonprofits must settle for only those employees willing to work long hours for low pay. On the contrary, nonprofits often get to choose among the best and the brightest candidates and can afford to be picky. As a result, your nonprofit coworkers likely will be exceptionally intelligent, warm, passionate, and caring people, there because they believe in the mission of the organization. There is something to be said for working with people who have self-selected to work toward a higher goal. While they certainly aren't all saintly, you may enjoy them a bit more than your average corporate coworker.

Unparalleled Growth Opportunities Exist

While three corporate employees may be assigned to one project, one nonprofit employee may be assigned to three projects. Money is scarcer, so fewer are asked to do more. This leads to faster career development and more varied job responsibilities for those looking to get ahead quickly. Employees in nonprofits can find themselves taking on responsibility for budgets, staffs, and portfolios of larger and more complex work at earlier stages of their career than do their for-profit counterparts. In addition, many career changers move back and forth between the sectors, taking advantage of the crash courses obtained in the nonprofit sector each time to achieve more senior positions in the corporate world, only to find themselves ultimately drawn back yet again to the nonprofit sector at an even higher level of responsibility.

Employees Can Shift Skill Sets Quickly

The nonprofit sector loves a generalist. With fewer staff slots than necessary for the work to be done, nonprofits look to employees to multitask and multitask big-time. Therefore, nonprofits offer the opportunity for employees to learn new skills and gain experience in new areas. Those making a career change can use nonprofit experience to shift slowly into a new line of expertise, leaving behind their corporate pigeonhole for a broader nonprofit portfolio.

A Common Vision Makes for a More Compelling Workplace

In the nonprofit you choose, you will find yourself surrounded by coworkers who have made the same decision as you: to work for a cause, this cause in particular. Being surrounded by other "true believers" can be invigorating, energizing, and exciting. Keeping your eyes on the prize becomes easier when it is something you truly value, and getting input and buy-in from coworkers who feel the same way lessens the frustration that comes with late nights and grueling deadlines. In fact, many nonprofit employees are happy to work long hours on a special project for the small price of a few free slices of pizza and a hearty handshake.

The Universe Gets Smaller

Employees at large for-profit corporations rarely get to interact with the top brass, either to show their stuff, learn from the best, or simply get reinvigorated on a regular basis. Not so in nonprofits. In fact, because many employees are generalists and organizational structures are often less hierarchical, nonprofit employees can take advantage of a smaller—whether in reality or just in culture—internal community. Further, the nonprofit often approaches the external community similarly, not just allowing but actually inviting more junior staff to take part in community-based activities and events, meet community leaders, and broaden their professional and personal horizons.

The Opportunity to Change the World Is Around Every Corner

It used to be that nonprofits universally had seven-year-old computers and insular management thinking. Not anymore. Most nonprofits have become more sophisticated, no longer resembling the dinosaurs of the past but, instead, eagerly and nimbly responding to market opportunities. Whether it is a natural disaster half the world away or a donor down the street who wants the organization to "think bigger" about its programs, many nonprofits have employed new thinking, technology advances, and a more entrepreneurial approach to become more agile, adept, and prepared.

There Is Great Innovation in the Nonprofit Sector

Each year, nonprofits are responsible for some of the newest and most exciting thinking around. They look for creative ways to solve the world's most vexing problems, those that were deemed too unprofitable by corporations or too dicey by governments. They bring together public-private partnerships and introduce solutions where none existed before. And they do it while competing for scarce dollars and attention.

Nonprofits Value Business Skills

The nonprofit sector is being flooded with people just like you, who have spent a day, a year, or a whole career in the for-profit sector but have decided that now is the time for change. The lines between corporate and community are shrinking, and each sector is rapidly understanding and capitalizing on the value of people from the other. Ten years ago, nonprofits would have looked at a corporate résumé with utter confusion, perhaps even a bit of mirth, but now they see skills and talent that can enable them to accomplish bigger and better things.

DETERMINING IF A NONPROFIT CAREER IS RIGHT FOR YOU

The nonprofit sector has its own personality and its own quirks. For some, this culture is wonderful; for others, it is downright maddening. Whether or not you fit neatly into one of the categories of transitioners just discussed, or if you are blazing your own path, knowing whether the nonprofit sector is right for you demands a critical examination of your personal and career goals, the practical implications of the transition, and your individual motivations.

Questions to Consider

What does this move mean to you on a personal level?

- What change do you want to make in your community, your country, your world?
- If someone gave you $5,000 a month to do whatever you wanted, what would it be?
- Would you rather work for a company or for a cause?
- Would you work harder or longer hours if what you did mattered to you more?
- In what ways are you lacking personal and professional fulfillment in your current work?
- How do you want to give back to the community?
- Do you have a clear sense of how you think the world should be? What would you change?
- Do you want your work to be more personally meaningful?
- Would a job in a nonprofit connect you more deeply to your passion, purpose, or spiritual needs?
- At the end of the day, do you feel that something is missing?

Does a career in the nonprofit sector fit with your personal and career goals?

- What social good would you like to serve, or what change would you like to see in the world?
- How passionately do you feel about this cause? Passionate enough to change your life?
- In what ways would a better work-life balance serve your personal and professional interests?
- What is driving this transition to a nonprofit job?
- Are you running away from your current career or toward a new one?
- Is your current company taking advantage of the full breadth and depth of your skills?

- How would your job satisfaction change if you were working with people more invested in the ultimate outcome of their day-to-day tasks?
- Do you want to work with intelligent and motivated people who are driven by the same mission as you?
- What do you enjoy more, your volunteer work or your regular job? Why?
- What do you want to have done in your career and in your life? What do you want to be remembered for?

What practical impact would a transition into the nonprofit sector have?

- What would be the ramifications of a possible pay cut?
- Would you be satisfied making less money if the work you did was more important to you?
- Why are you looking for a better work-life balance?
- What parts of your current work cause you stress? What would you like to change? What would you like to keep?
- In what ways do you need greater freedom or flexibility in your work environment?
- Is there a place for your skills in the nonprofit sector? Where?
- How much do you need in the way of office resources and staff support to reach your goals?
- Do your family needs, at this time, allow or require that you take this chance?
- What intangible rewards would you want in exchange for, or in addition to, your current career's monetary rewards?
- What time, energy, and resources do you have to develop the skills necessary to be successful in your new nonprofit career?

Reflecting on Your Answers

Each of your answers, if thoughtfully rendered, reflects your readiness to transition to the nonprofit sector and the direction your job search should take. You may find that you are prepared to start your search today. Or you may realize that your transition is three, five, or ten years away, or even that the nonprofit sector fits more into your after-work life. Rest assured, there are no wrong answers.

Now, let's find your place in the nonprofit sector.

FINDING YOUR PLACE IN THE NONPROFIT SECTOR

Now that you have determined that the nonprofit sector is right for you, you must find your place among the sector's many opportunities. Doing so requires a three-tiered decision-making making process:

1. What is your motivating social cause?
2. What approach would you take to solve this cause or this problem?
3. What skills and experience do you bring to the table?

Pinpoint Your Cause

Do you care about saving the whales or teaching children to read? Would you rather fund economic development in villages in sub-Saharan Africa or develop a food bank in your own community? Are you more passionate about creating opportunities for increased access to education or discovering an alternative fuel source?

These are big questions, but your gut and your heart already know the answers. While many people come to the sector wanting generally "to do good," you likely have a preference among the vast number of needy causes. In Chapter 2, you will learn about the variety of work being done in the nonprofit sector and read about some specific examples of innovative nonprofits. This information may help solidify your choice to work for a cause you know or pique your interest in one that is still unfamiliar.

REVELL HORSEY   DIRECTOR OF STRATEGY AND DEVELOPMENT, SPORTS4KIDS, SAN FRANCISCO, CALIFORNIA

After 18 years of taking companies public as an investment banker, Revell decided that he'd had enough. He took his family on a cultural adventure to Paris for two years while he sorted out what he wanted to do with the rest of his life. Financially able to retire but not at all emotionally, physically, or mentally ready, Revell sought to do something different. "I started reading books like *How to Change the World* by David Bornstein and *The Cathedral Within* by Billy Shore," he says, "and began to wonder, 'What would it look like for me to be in the nonprofit world?'"

When he returned to San Francisco, Revell joined the Full Circle Fund, a nonprofit engaged in philanthropy that invests expertise and money in other nonprofits to build their capacity to do more of the work that they are already doing well. Having always volunteered and sat on various boards, like that of his old boarding school, Revell joined the education impact circle as a way to learn more about what was happening in the area that interested him most. "I quickly found myself leading the teacher professional development team," he says. "It gave me the most intensive exposure to nonprofit management and allowed me to see just how many smart people there were in the nonprofit field."

How did Revell determine which nonprofit was right for him?

Revell went about his search with a three-tiered approach: "exploration, skill mapping, and network building." As a former investment banker who'd been around a spreadsheet or two and raised several billion in capital for public and private companies, he knew that he would be seen as an ideal candidate for a chief financial officer or director of development position at a secondary school, but he wanted to make an impact on a bigger scale. "Through my informational interviews and exploratory conversations," he says, "what became exceptionally clear to me was that I wanted to work at a higher elevation, taking a proven but small nonprofit to scale in a sustainable, demonstrable way." That realization also led him to make the difficult decision and turn down an opportunity to be the CFO at a boarding school in the Northeast, where he would have worked with a close friend and former teacher, and eventually brought him to Sports4Kids, a nonprofit poised for radical expansion.

How is Revell contributing in his work with Sports4Kids?

"In some ways," he says, "I'm frustrated that I have had little opportunity to focus on what I was hired to do: to craft a strategic plan to drive our expansion and to develop a long-term sustainability model." In a start-up, high-growth environment where fires are burning everywhere you look, whether in the nonprofit or for-profit sector, staying focused on the big picture is a constant challenge. "I find that I am spending much of my time developing and refining internal systems and processes that are building blocks to our success." Revell is working

harder than he ever has, but having more fun too. "Instead of being in business with a focus on driving a profit margin," he says, "I'm now in a business with a heart where the margin is defined by social impact."

Revell also brings to bear his vast connections from the hundreds of companies he has taken public over the years. "In order to expand into a new city, Sports4Kids needs corporate champions and high-profile individuals who are leaders in their communities," he says, "and I just happen to know people everywhere whose businesses I helped launch. Being a connector to them is among the greatest values I bring to Sports4Kids right now."

Revell's Key Lessons Learned:

■ "I expected that this experience would be a one- to two-year extensive schooling on the nonprofit world, but I got traction faster than I thought I would. The issues facing a high-growth nonprofit were surprisingly similar to the issues facing the hundreds of companies I took public over the years. It's really all about finding good people, skill matching, communication, and access to financial capital to fund growth."

■ "In the nonprofit sector, it's not only important to get the right people on the right seats on the bus but to recognize that the benches are longer and that people may slide around as the needs of the organization and its growth demand."

■ "Management in the nonprofit sector is much more of a legislative process. Intimidation can force outcomes, but these are typically short term and lead to dissatisfaction and a lack of unified vision. People need to be inspired to perform."

Determine Your Approach

Nonprofits approach the world's problems in many ways. Consider the problem of the teenage mother. A nonprofit might do direct service, such as running nutritional counseling workshops or prenatal health care. Another nonprofit might advocate on behalf of young mothers, perhaps lobbying state governments for greater food stamp distribution for those purchasing infant formula. Or a nonprofit might raise or distribute money to be used directly by its constituents, such as giving out day care vouchers for high school mothers working toward their GED or funding programs that teach mothering skills. Finally, a nonprofit might act as a membership association, gathering together groups of similar individuals for something mutually beneficial, such as pooled health insurance premiums or diaper collections and toy exchanges.

The tactical approach of a nonprofit defines both how it raises and how it spends money. It determines the personalities and skill sets of the employees needed as well. It is reflected in both its mission and its tax status. These implications are described in Chapter 3 in more detail.

Assess Your Skills

Finally, exactly what are you qualified to do? This is where a lot of job seekers fail. They rely solely on how others have defined them in terms of their day job but forget to look at the broader picture. You likely have gathered skills at work that are readily inventoried, but what about the rest of the hours in your day? What have you done for your child's school? How have you volunteered in your place of worship? What have you learned along the way through your involvement in neighborhood committees? Have your hobbies or leisure activities lent you expertise relevant to your new career?

Nonprofit job titles tend to be different and may be an amalgam of several jobs you have come to know in the corporate sector. Assessing your skills—from both the paid and unpaid hours in your day—will allow you to see the whole you and enable you to target the right job title for you in the nonprofit sector. Finding the right job will be discussed further in Chapter 3.

EXAMPLE #1—JADE   PUBLIC RELATIONS EXECUTIVE → STAY-AT-HOME MOM → INTERNATIONAL TEEN HEALTH CARE MISSION DIRECTOR

Jade spent her corporate career developing public relations campaigns for private, for-profit hospitals in Texas. She started her career at large corporations, but after being laid off, struck out on her own. Having had a successful but stressful run, she realized that she missed her young children and wanted to spend more time with them at home and volunteering as a room parent and a fundraiser at their school. She often travels with her children, because raising citizens of the world is important to her.

Jade's children have grown and are now in school all day, and she finds herself at a crossroads. Rather than jumping back into the high-paced world of corporate public relations, Jade now seeks fulfilling work within an interesting organization that values her skills and allows a better work-family balance.

Passions

- ☒ Education
- ☒ Children and family
- ☒ Health care
- ☒ Travel

Tactical Approach

A hands-on person, Jade enjoys developing and implementing actual projects rather than broader, less tangible ideas. She would be more comfortable in an organization that provides direct service. But because of her corporate contacts, she has access to high-net-worth individuals, so she could easily raise money as well.

- ☒ Direct service
- ☒ Philanthropy and fundraising

Qualifications

Jade has a varied background from both her corporate work and individual volunteering.

- ☒ Communications and public relations
- ☒ Fundraising
- ☒ Logistics and coordinating of details, multitasking
- ☒ Start-up and entrepreneurship
- ☒ Substantive knowledge of the health care arena and world travel

Jade's Place in the Nonprofit Sector

Jade might consider becoming an event planner or trip director for a start-up nonprofit that promotes international travel and health care–related humanitarian missions for teenagers, teaching them both the importance of raising funds and an awareness of their place in a responsible society. Her hands-on approach, ability to raise money for travel expenses, knowledge of public relations campaigns to promote trips, and experience with travel and health care enable her to be a real asset to such an organization. Besides, what better way to raise true citizens of the world?

EXAMPLE #2—MARSHALL   CORPORATE ATTORNEY → SOCIAL ENTREPRENEUR

Marshall is a patent attorney by training and an outdoorsman by passion. While he has received many accolades for his work at his law firm, he knows that he is only there to pay the bills, biding his time until the weekend comes and he can once again retreat into the woods for a weekend of camping and fishing. He has from time to time taken on some public advocacy work in his community. On his last camping trip, he noticed that a factory, aiming to expand its operations, was encroaching upon his beloved trails. What had once been an annoyance became an all-consuming passion. Once he returned from his trip, Marshall could see nothing but the need to stop this factory in its tracks. His research led him to learn that legions of others are fighting the same war but without the proper battlements.

Passions

- ☒ Environmental protection
- ☒ Sustainable development
- ☒ Access to trails and woods

Tactical Approach

As an attorney, Marshall's first focus is always to work through the courts. He sees solutions in terms of new legislation and increased enforcement. He also understands that once people get out on the trails, they will be unlikely to let such beauty be ruined.

- ☒ Lobbying and advocacy
- ☒ Direct service

Qualifications

Marshall brings experience from his corporate work as well as passion from his weekend camping excursions.

- ☒ Public advocacy
- ☒ Substantive knowledge of the legal system
- ☒ A hands-on knowledge of the effect of corporate encroachment

Marshall's Place in the Nonprofit Sector

Marshall might consider becoming an attorney for an environmental defense organization that encourages the active use and protection of public lands. He could use his legal knowledge to wage a campaign in the court system or his advocacy background and personal passion to wage the battle in the court of public opinion. Either way, he's likely to enjoy his day job much more if he's surrounded by people who gather around the water cooler to discuss the great new private camping spot they found, rather than his old crew concerned only with the latest developments in intellectual property transfer.

CONCLUSION

Today's nonprofit sector is growing rapidly, and opportunities exist around every corner for making important changes in the world. While the idiosyncrasies of the sector might cause minor annoyances from time to time, the fulfillment and enjoyment you derive from your work will carry the day. The key to success is in finding not just the right sector but your personal place in that sector. Learning about the sector as a whole and the roles of its employees will help you to make smart choices that will ease your transition. Now, let's find your next career.

CHAPTER 2

Overview of the Nonprofit Sector

We all remember the days when our mothers would walk around the neighborhood collecting money for juvenile diabetes or when our fathers would head off in the evenings for their local civic league meetings. We think about soup kitchens and homeless shelters, libraries and schools, or museums and zoos and think we know the nonprofit sector. Think again.

The nonprofit sector today is a dynamic, vibrant, and vast place, filled with every conceivable kind of person and organization and addressing any need you might imagine. Its employees hold PhDs, MBAs, and GEDs and perform work that spans the highly lucrative to the drastically underpaid. The mothers and fathers we remember are still doing their important volunteer work—volunteers are the lifeblood of many nonprofits, after all—but they are now more of an army mobilized to accomplish annual campaigns, not the office staff relied upon for daily support and strategic direction.

Approximately 1.9 million nonprofit organizations are registered with the Internal Revenue Service. Millions more probably exist that are either too small or too informal—those with an annual budget of less than $5,000—to be counted. In total, nonprofits have a combined revenue of $621.4 billion, which represents 6.2 percent of the nation's economy. An estimated 11.7 million people, or nearly 9 percent of working Americans, are employed in the nonprofit sector.[1]

Innovation is the name of the game in nonprofits. Sure, they still serve the tired, the poor, the huddled masses yearning to breathe free, but today's nonprofits no longer resemble the organizations of yore. In an exceptionally competitive market for scarce fundraising dollars, nonprofits increasingly leverage resources for double or even triple plays. Providing beds to a tired and cold family in the middle of winter is a great and noble endeavor, but teaching the mother or father of that family to bake and run a small but profitable café—then funneling those profits back into the purchase of beds and food to benefit more families—is entirely another. This "triple bottom line"—feeding and housing the poor, job skills training, and earned-income generation—is the emerging trend in the nonprofit sector, and career changers will likely find their easiest transitions in nonprofits that have embraced this approach.

WHAT IS A NONPROFIT ORGANIZATION?

Technically speaking, a nonprofit organization is a nongovernmental entity formed to benefit its members or a specific population or cause, according to the Internal Revenue Service:[2] Every exempt charitable organization is classified as either a public charity or a private foundation; in both cases, directors are concerned with a betterment of society and not the generation of personal profits.

Public charities have an active program of fundraising and receive contributions from many sources, including the general public, governmental agencies, corporations, private foundations, or other public charities. They also receive income from the conduct of activities in furtherance of the organization's exempt purposes, and they may actively function in a supporting relationship to one or more existing public charities.

---

1 "Facts and Figures about Charitable Organizations," (Washington, D.C.: Independent Sector, June 20, 2006, and updated September 20, 2006), *www.independentsector.org/programs/research/Charitable_Fact_Sheet. pdf* (accessed November 26, 2006). Report relies heavily on statistics from the Internal Revenue Service *Data Book*, various editions.

2 Internal Revenue Service, "Publication 557: Tax-Exempt Status for Your Organization," revised March 2005, *www.irs.gov/pub/irs-pdf/p557.pdf* (accessed November 26, 2006).

Private foundations, in contrast, typically have a single major source of funding (usually gifts from one family or corporation), and most primarily make grants to other charitable organizations and to individuals rather than directly operating charitable programs.

DETERMINING YOUR MOTIVATING CAUSE

As discussed in Chapter 1, finding your place in the nonprofit sector means making three important choices: your motivating social cause or societal problem, the approach you would like to take to aid this cause or solve this problem, and the skills and experiences you bring to the table. We will start with a discussion about the vast number of causes you can serve and then move on to the tactical approach you might take. Chapter 3 will cover how your skills and experience might fit into your new nonprofit career.

Let's start with your motivating cause. Most nonprofits fall into eight major categories.[3] As we walk through them, you will learn about different nonprofits operating within each category, read about some traditional programs that you may recognize, and learn about exciting, cutting-edge work you may not. In this latter type of organization, where new business thinking permeates daily operations, career changers may find the friendliest transitions.

> ### By Any Other Name...
>
> The nonprofit sector is also known as the not-for-profit sector, the voluntary sector, the charitable sector, the independent sector, the social sector, or the third sector. Internationally, nonprofits are called nongovernmental organizations (NGOs).

Arts, Culture, and the Humanities

Are you interested in history, music, photography, or painting? Do you attend historical reenactments? Do you enjoy cultural performances and exchanges? Are you part of a singing society or community theatrical group? Do you frequent your local museum or planetarium, library, or monuments? If so, you already know a great deal about the arts, culture, and humanities segment of the nonprofit sector. What you

---

3   National Taxonomy of Exempt Entities classification system, a project of the National Center for Charitable Statistics, housed at the Center on Nonprofits and Philanthropy at the Urban Institute, *http://nccsdataweb. urban.org.*

may not know is that this segment also includes publishing activities; radio or television broadcasting; film production; discussion groups, forums, panels, and lectures; and nonscientific study and research as well as organizations supporting all of these arts, cultural, and humanities nonprofits.

Arts, Culture, and the Humanities

The arts, culture, and humanities category of the nonprofit sector includes the following interests:

- *Arts and culture.* Organizations that promote cultural awareness, folk arts, or arts education; also arts and humanities councils
- *Media and communications.* Film and video, television, printing and publishing, Internet, and radio
- *Visual arts.* Painting, drawing, and photography
- *Museums.* Art museums, children's museums, historical centers, natural history museums, private homes, and science and technology museums
- *Performing arts.* Performing arts centers and all the art that they present, from ballet to opera to musical theater, as well as performing arts schools
- *Humanities.* Organizations that archive or promote the study of history, literature, philosophy, folklore, historic preservation, archaeology, jurisprudence, or comparative religion
- *Historical organizations.* Societies or other groups that support commemorative events
- *Arts services.* Theater education, financial management support, or networking opportunities

While this category may seem large, it makes up less than 3 percent of the entire nonprofit field.[4] Further, only 5 percent of U.S. museums have operating budgets in excess of $7 million,[5] meaning that they must be particularly picky about hiring new staff. Still, there are many jobs for businesspeople.

There are finance, operations, and administrative jobs throughout the nonprofit sector. However, corporate transitioners might take advantage of a new trend in the arts, culture, and humanities sector. Major cultural production nonprofits, like the Metropolitan Opera or the Houston Ballet, are increasingly dividing the leadership post in two, placing all artistic decision-making responsibilities with an artistic director and all business decision-making responsibilities with a business director. Further, these nonprofits also do a brisk business in merchandise, tickets, and reproduction rights, so each organization encompasses revenue-generating models that are perfect for business minds to run.

Let's take a look at a few arts, culture, and humanities nonprofits.

National Geographic

Yes, that's right. National Geographic is a nonprofit, and it has been for more than a hundred years. From the beginning, National Geographic was created to inspire people to have a lifelong appreciation for the planet and its people, and that mission hasn't changed one bit. National Geographic supports its mission through dues from more than 9 million members and revenues from the sale of its products, all of which align with its mission. While it could assert that the sales of these products create nontaxable revenue given their mission-supporting nature, National Geographic chooses to pay taxes on this piece of its business to ensure the most flexibility with the revenue.

Opera New England of the Boston Lyric Opera

Opera New England (ONE), Boston Lyric Opera's education and community programs division, engages and educates people of all ages about opera by bringing

---

4 Independent Sector, *National Almanac of Nonprofit Statistics in Brief*, (Washington, D.C.: Independent Sector, 1998): 5.

5 Stephanie Lowell, *The Harvard Business School Guide to Careers in the Nonprofit Sector*, (Boston: Harvard Business School Press: 2000): 33.

inspirational and often first-time experiences to many who might not otherwise have such exposure to any arts, let alone opera. Each year, ONE reaches 25,000 students, educators, and families across New England with a fully staged, one-hour English version of a popular opera for the whole family to enjoy. By reaching out to schools and families in diverse and underserved communities, ONE makes opera accessible and available to people of all backgrounds and provides role models for children with its inspirational, multicultural performers. It helps to fill the gap created by cuts to music and arts education and offers young people and families access to stimulating, interactive experiences away from the standard educational environment.

Contemporary Arts Center

Museums aren't just hushed hallways of stuffy artifacts. In fact, the Contemporary Art Center (CAC) in Cincinnati is just the opposite. For more than 67 years, the CAC has been a forum for progressive art ideas; it is one of the oldest, most active, and most adventuresome museums of contemporary art in the United States. Founded in 1939 as the Modern Art Society by three visionary local women, the CAC was one of the first institutions in the United States dedicated to exhibiting contemporary art. Always groundbreaking, the CAC became one of the first American institutions to exhibit Picasso's *Guernica* (1937) and has continued this pioneering tradition by featuring the work of hundreds of now-famous artists early in their career, including Andy Warhol, Jasper Johns, Robert Rauschenberg, Nam June Paik, I.M. Pei, and Laurie Anderson. In 1990, the CAC pushed the envelope even further, throwing itself into the center of an important First Amendment legal case, when it successfully defended the right of Cincinnati's citizens to view an exhibition of the photographs of Robert Mapplethorpe.

Education

Do you want to promote access to education across diversity and disabilities, build better programming or richer cultural understanding in the classroom, or support faculty and administrators. Have you developed an expertise you would like to teach to a particular population? Education, one of the largest parts of the nonprofit world, might be for you.

Composing about 18 percent of the nonprofit sector,[6] education includes schools, colleges, and trade schools; special schools for the disabled; nursery schools; faculty groups; alumni associations; parent or parent-teachers associations; fraternities or sororities; student societies; school or college athletic associations; scholarships, student loans, and other aid; student-housing activities; and foreign exchange programs. Transitioning into this segment may be as easy as transferring your skill set into a supporting administrative role, or it may require additional coursework to gain the required licensure for a hands-on experience.

Education

The education component of the nonprofit sector includes:

- *Elementary and secondary education.* Preschools, primary and elementary schools, secondary and high schools, special education, and charter schools
- *Vocational and technical schools*
- *Higher education.* Two-year and four-year colleges and universities
- *Graduate and professional schools*
- *Adult education.* Continuing education, certification, and licensing
- *Libraries.* These may be found in communities, schools, foundations, and other public access areas.
- *Student services.* Scholarships and student aid, student sororities and fraternities, and alumni associations
- *Educational services.* Remedial reading and encouragement; parent-teachers groups

Contrary to popular opinion, the education sector is not filled with educators. In fact, there are more nonteachers than teachers in the field. Opportunities exist for administrators, student-life coordinators, counselors, and entrepreneurs. The charter school movement alone houses a great deal of innovative, start-up thinking. Indeed, some of the most interesting work being done in education today is performed by people from the for-profit sector, including school start-ups, endowment management, town-gown relations, or teacher recruitment and retention.

---

6   Independent Sector, *National Almanac of Nonprofit Statistics in Brief,* (Washington, D.C.: Independent Sector, 1998): 5.

ANDREA KIMMEL   ASSOCIATE DIRECTOR OF MARKETING, HARVARD BUSINESS SCHOOL, CAMBRIDGE, MASSACHUSETTS

Andrea grew up in Revere, Massachusetts, a working-class town outside of Boston where few graduate to an Ivy League education or a *Fortune* 500 professional pedigree. Yet Andrea had dreams and worked hard to fulfill them. An athletic scholarship to Brown University transported her from a conservative, religious community to a bastion of liberalism, where she had to compete with classmates who had prepped at the world's best schools. "When I got there," she says, "I was light years behind. These students already had what I considered to be a college experience at their private boarding schools. In response, I put my head down and copied what they did." For them, and her, that meant going to Wall Street to become an investment banker.

Andrea put in her requisite three years on Wall Street and then followed the pack to business school. "That's where my path began to diverge," she explains. Upon graduation, Andrea looked for a job in a nonprofit but had a hard time convincing anyone to take a chance on her. She ended up back in the for-profit sector at Best Buy in Minneapolis. Even though business school got her out of finance, it didn't get her into the nonprofit sector as she had hoped.

As a member of the strategic marketing group, Andrea was able to turn out work she never thought possible. "I loved my job, and I loved the challenge," she says, "but my husband decided he'd missed his calling as a consultant, and his new job brought us back to Boston." When she inquired back at the business school, she learned of a marketing position that felt immediately right. "I now feel a purpose every day when I get out of bed," says Andrea. "I've had my share of frustrations, but I know that I am making a difference."

What have been Andrea's biggest surprises in the nonprofit sector?

"When I got here, nobody in the office had a corporate marketing mentality," she explains. Andrea immediately was forced to put on the brakes and slow down her approach. "I was surprised at how much I had to build up buy-in around decisions that seemed so intuitive from my corporate life." Now, her colleagues come to her and say, "Let's do this. It's an important idea."

Andrea learned that the nonprofit sector is very political. There is more give and take around each idea. "I found that I could contribute what I knew was a cutting-edge corporate marketing idea," she says, "but that it was worthless unless I learned how to operate in the nonprofit environment."

What has been Andrea's most significant reward?

At the end of the day, Andrea feels that she is accepted for who she is. "I was told early on that my colleagues felt threatened by my capabilities and how much I could get done in a month," she says. "So I started coming to meetings looking less prepared and working less hard, or at least trying to give that impression." She quickly realized how ridiculous that was. Instead, Andrea decided to invest in building relationships.

Working in the nonprofit sector, Andrea has found, is about the people. She feels that people care about each other much more than in the corporate world and that she has been much more comfortable being herself because she invested early in building those relationships.

Andrea's Key Lessons Learned:

■ "No one works just 40 hours work week anymore. If you are going to be married to your job, you might as well love what you do."

■ "Be prepared for change to occur more slowly and for more opinions to be weighed. Do not give up on your work goals, but be willing to change your approach to how you make them happen."

■ "Invest in personal relationships early for maximum long-term benefit."

Let's look at some education nonprofits.

The SEED Foundation

The SEED Foundation (Schools for Educational Evolution and Development) is a national nonprofit that partners with urban communities to provide innovative educational opportunities to prepare underserved students for success in college. The SEED Foundation developed the SEED boarding school model and opened its first school, The SEED School of Washington, D.C., in 1998. SEED's innovative model integrates a rigorous academic program with a nurturing boarding-student life program, which teaches life skills and provides a safe and secure environment. This boarding school model provides a comprehensive solution to the challenges facing inner-city youth—a whopping 100 percent of the class of 2005 was admitted to college—and serves as a prototype for expansion nationwide. Cofounded by two former management consultants who were determined to create a sustainable business and financing model, SEED applies business-planning techniques that are common in the for-profit world to its nonprofit model.

Building Excellent Schools

To some, charter schools hold the promise of changing public education for our most underserved children. While some impressive charter schools are beating the trends and producing impressive results, there is, at best, uncertainty and disagreement about the overall ability of charter schools to live up to their lofty promise. Building Excellent Schools supports the design and start-up of high-performing urban charter schools across the country, and its schools have consistently achieved sustainable, demonstrable success. At its core is the Building Excellent Schools (BES) Fellowship, an intense, year-long, full-time, comprehensive training program that prepares individuals (often from the private sector), organizations, and communities to create academically excellent urban charter schools. During its first year, the BES Fellowship resulted in 11 new charter school openings in Massachusetts alone. In 2007–2008, fellows will be chosen to start schools in 15 different cities.

Yale University From the hallowed halls of Ivy Leagues across the country comes a renewed focus on community, both internal and external. As it enters its fourth century, Yale is among the universities leading the charge. Focused both on the outside world and on its own population of staff, faculty, and students, Yale offers both free tuition for students from families with incomes under $45,000 a year and perks like child-elder care and a homebuyer program for employees. All the while, it remains a major research institution led by some of the most distinguished faculty in the world.

Environment and Animals

Are you worried about the state of the planet you are leaving to your children? Do you enjoy the exercise and the environmental benefits of riding your bike to work? Are you concerned about the ever-shrinking planet and the ever-enlarging hole in the ozone layer? Do you leap for joy at the first sign of spring, a telltale sign that you will soon be up to your elbows in new seedlings? Did the stories of pets lost during Hurricane Katrina bring tears to your eyes? You may want to consider a career in the environment and animals segment of the nonprofit sector.

These nonprofits support the traditional conservation and beautification efforts and animal shelters you may remember from your youth, including the preservation of natural resources, combating or preventing pollution, and animal safety programs. But they also incorporate advanced science and partner with big business to ensure sustainable development, land acquisition for preservation, soil and water conservation, and wildlife sanctuaries or refuges. So, too, have local communities gotten in on the act, with local garden clubs and community garden plots flourishing nationwide. Let's also not forget farming, farm bureaus, agricultural and horticultural groups, and cooperatives, a major piece of this sector.

Environment and Animals

The environmental segment of the nonprofit sector includes:

- *Pollution abatement and control.* Recycling education and support
- *Natural resources conservation and protection.* Land, water, energy, and forest resources conservation
- *Botanical, horticultural, and landscape services.* Botanical gardens, arboretums, and garden clubs
- *Environmental beautification*
- *Environmental education*

The animals component of the nonprofit sector includes:

- *Animal protection and welfare.* Societies to prevent cruelty to animals
- *Wildlife preservation and protection.* Endangered species protection, bird sanctuaries, fisheries, and wildlife sanctuaries
- *Veterinary services*
- *Zoos and aquariums*

The environmental movement is perhaps the subdivision of the nonprofit sector least recognizable from its previous incarnations. No longer filled only with hemp-clad hippies who chain themselves to trees and rally against the corporate sector as the last of the great, true evils—though they certainly still exist, and we can thank them for building the sector into what it is today—the environmental segment of the nonprofit sector relies on data-driven research, advanced marketing tools, and highly trained advocates. Those from the for-profit sector can find themselves at home leveraging public-private partnerships to make new discoveries about energy conservation, creating community investment in public land beautification, or even packaging education models for national distribution in schools.

Animals, too, are big business. Whether in managing the revenue-generating division of an aquarium, developing and marketing tourism packages for wildlife sanctuaries, or implementing a capital campaign to build a new monkey house, those with corporate backgrounds can find many opportunities.

Following are a few examples of nonprofits in the environment and animals sector.

Rare

For the past 30 years, Rare has been turning average citizens into lifelong advocates for the environment by giving communities a voice in conserving their natural resources and by helping individuals better their life through more sustainable livelihoods. Rare supports hundreds of grassroots conservationists around the world each year by providing them with training, technical support, and resources. They, in turn, inspire conservation among thousands of local residents, decision makers, and tourists in some of the planet's most important places for biodiversity. Sometimes these conservationists are traditionally trained biologists, park managers, and environmental educators. More often, they are homemakers, fishers and farmers, radio DJs, teachers, and small-town mayors—anyone who has a passion for the environment and a commitment to community, region, or country.

The White Dog Cafe Foundation

Over the last 20 years, the White Dog Cafe of Philadelphia has become a model enterprise, known nationally for its community involvement, environmental stewardship, and responsible business practices. Its foundation, founded in 2002, creates, strengthens, and connects locally owned businesses and farms that are committed to working in harmony with natural systems; providing meaningful, living-wage jobs; and supporting healthy community life. It supports this mission with two programs. The Sustainable Business Network of Greater Philadelphia is a network of local business people, professionals, social entrepreneurs, investors, nonprofit leaders, and government representatives who are committed to building a more socially, environmentally, and financially sustainable local economy. Fair Food builds wholesale markets for local farmers; improves distribution channels for locally grown food; increases consumer access to local food grown with care for people, animals, and the Earth; educates people about the value of locally and sustainably raised food; and increases the supply of humanely and naturally raised animal products in the Philadelphia marketplace.

The Bronx Zoo

As the number-one family attraction in New York City, with more than 4 million visitors per year, the Bronx Zoo and its related parks and zoos have a golden opportunity in their hands. The Wildlife Conservation Society, headquartered at the Bronx Zoo, has capitalized on this, taking the smartest branding and marketing thinking from the for-profit world and plunking it right in the middle of the lions and tigers and bears… oh my. Its highly successful corporate partnership program allows corporations to do anything from sponsoring a fun-filled family weekend at one of the five parks (Bronx Zoo, New York Aquarium, Central Park Zoo, Prospect Park Zoo, and Queens Zoo) to supporting educational and conservation programs around the world. With companies like Pepsi, Hess, Fisher-Price, Bank of America, Delta Airlines, Wendy's, ConEdison, and Norwegian Cruise Lines as customers, the Bronx Zoo has certainly become king of the sponsorship jungle.

Health

Do you loyally stand in line once a quarter to donate blood, race out and gather medical supplies for every natural disaster, run in your local 10K for cancer each year (or just wish you did)? Have you ever spent time translating overly technical insurance forms for a friend or colleague, wondering why it has to be so difficult for sick persons to access the care they need? Are you a steadfast believer that, with enough time and resources, we can find a cure to most anything that ails us? If you believe in the power of a healthy universe and want to do anything you can to make it a reality, a job in the massive health sector of the nonprofit world may be for you.

Generating almost 50 percent of the revenue of all nonprofits,[7] the health segment is certainly the largest segment in the nonprofit sector. This doesn't mean that your neighborhood primary care clinic has money; it just means that the nonprofit research giant down the street has lots more. Typically seen as hospitals, nursing homes, and public health clinics, these nonprofits also include rural medical facilities, blood banks, rescue and emergency services, visiting nurses, aid to the handicapped, pharmaceutical supplies, scientific research for cures to diseases, health insurance and group health plans, community health planning, and mental health care.

---

7   Ibid.

Health Care

Have you often wondered why those with the least money get the worst health care treatment? Are you frustrated by the legions of poor who are forced to seek general care in the emergency room? Do you want to find solutions that open the doors of health care for all, regardless of socioeconomic status, language barriers, or education? If so, transitioning from a direct service or administrative position in a for-profit setting into one in the nonprofit sector may be right for you.

Health Care

The health care component of the nonprofit sector includes:

- *Hospitals.* Community health systems, general hospitals, and specialty hospitals
- *Ambulatory and primary health care.* Group health practices and community clinics
- *Reproductive health care and family planning*
- *Rehabilitative care*
- *Health support.* Blood banks, emergency medical services and transportation, and organ and tissue banks
- *Public health*
- *Health support and financing*
- *Nursing facilities and home health facilities*

Many nonprofit health care providers, such as hospitals, operate in a manner similar to that of their for-profit counterparts. The major difference is that the revenues of the nonprofit are reinvested in the organization in the form of fee reductions, educational programs, and community outreach. Also, health care nonprofits tend to focus on preventative health measures, such as family planning or public education.

Let's look at a couple of health care nonprofits.

The Scojo Foundation The Scojo Foundation was established by the partners of Scojo Vision, LLC, which donates 5 percent of its profits to the foundation. The Scojo Foundation trains local women entrepreneurs—because studies show that when women have access to their own capital, they use it to feed, educate, house, and provide medical care for their children—to give basic eye exams and sell low-cost reading glasses in their communities. By providing people with the tools to see, Scojo Foundation improves their health and extends their working life by 50 percent. At the same time, they help raise the standard of living for local entrepreneurs and their families.

PlayPumps International Picture a playground in rural Africa filled with laughter. Now imagine that a merry-go-round in that playground, filled with spinning children, is powering a pump a few feet away that brings water to the entire village. It's a simple yet innovative idea. PlayPumps International, a nonprofit based in the United States and Africa, has installed nearly 700 PlayPumps in South Africa so far and aims to install thousands more, bringing clean water to 10 million people in the next three years and eliminating some of the more than 2.2 million deaths caused by water-related illnesses per year.

Mental Health and Crisis Intervention

Have you or someone you loved suffered because of mental illness? Have you seen the terrible effects of families torn apart because of a lack of support in a crisis? Do you approach all people with great empathy and understanding, believing that everyone can succeed if only given a chance to compete on equal footing? If so, you may find a career in a mental health or crisis intervention setting quite rewarding.

Mental Health

The mental health component of the nonprofit sector includes:

- *Substance abuse dependency, prevention, and treatment*
- *Mental health treatment.* Psychiatric hospitals and community and residential mental health centers
- *Hot lines and crisis intervention.* Domestic violence and depression help
- *Addictive disorders.* Eating disorders, smoking disorders, or gambling additions
- *Counseling services.* Either in one-on-one or group settings
- *Mental health disorders and associations*

Like the heath care segment of the nonprofit sector, organizations that deal with mental health and crisis intervention can offer smooth transitions for direct service providers and administrators from the corporate world.

Below are a couple of nonprofits that work with mental health and crisis interventions.

National Domestic Violence Hotline In 1994, Senator Joseph R. Biden and Senator Orrin G. Hatch coauthored historic legislation, the Violence Against Women Act, and Congress responded to the nation's high rate of domestic violence by enacting the legislation and creating the National Domestic Violence Hotline (NDVH), an independent nonprofit. Since then, the Hotline has become the vital link to safety for over 1.5 million families, responding to more than 16,000 calls each month. NDVH serves as the only domestic violence hotline in the nation with access to more than 5,000 shelters and domestic violence programs across the United States, Puerto Rico, and the U.S. Virgin Islands. The Hotline is toll-free, confidential, and anonymous and operates 24 hours a day, 365 days a year. Help is offered in more than 140 different languages through interpreter services, and a TTY line available for the deaf, deaf-blind, and hard of hearing.

Screening for Mental Health Screening for Mental Health, Inc. (SMH), first introduced the concept of large-scale mental health screenings with its flagship program, National Depression Screening Day, in 1991. SMH programs now include both in-person and online programs for depression, bipolar disorder, generalized anxiety disorder, posttraumatic stress disorder, eating disorders, alcohol problems, and suicide prevention. SMH's programs have been used by hospitals, mental health centers, social service agencies, government agencies, older adult facilities, primary care clinicians, colleges, high schools, corporations, and HMOs, reaching individuals from teens to older adults. SMH's programs have reduced the stigma that inhibits many individuals from seeking treatment and have helped people to identify mental illness and specific ways to access treatment for themselves or a loved one.

Diseases, Disorders, and Medical Disciplines and Supporting Research Organizations

Have you lost a loved one to a disease that could have been prevented or should have been cured long ago? Are you appalled by news of a disease that has obliterated whole populations of unsuspecting children? Are you convinced that we are "this close" to finding cures to diseases that our grandchildren will never have to fear? If so, and even if you have no particular medical training, look no further than the medical and research segment of the nonprofit sector.

Diseases, Disorders, and Medical Disciplines

The diseases, disorders, and medical disciplines and research segment of the nonprofit sector address the following issues:

- *Birth defects and genetic diseases*
- *Cancer*
- *Diseases of specific organs*
- *Nerve, muscle, and bone diseases*
- *Allergy-related diseases*
- *Digestive diseases and disorders*
- *Specifically named diseases*
- *Medical disciplines*
- *Research around any of these areas*

Diseases get cured through research, and research is expensive. Those with experience as a medical practitioner will transfer easily into this field, like teachers in the education subsector, relying on their interest in contributing to a greater purpose and their medical expertise. Those without a medical background can contribute through fundraising, operations, marketing, and public affairs and lobbying campaigns, facilitating efficient operations and garnering increased attention and funding from domestic and international governments.

Certainly you've heard of the multiple nonprofits organized around specific diseases, like multiple sclerosis, breast cancer, or HIV/AIDS. Let's look at other organizations in this segment that support the victims of disease and research cures.

PATH What if products and strategies meant to improve health in the developing world were designed expressly for the people who need them? Instead of tossing expensive answers at problems unique to poor countries, PATH's mission is to find and create effective, sustainable solutions that work best where they're needed most. These include health technologies that are appropriate for use in remote villages, immunization programs built side by side with the governments that administer them, and cultural projects that spark dialogue and social changes in communities at risk from HIV. The results are staggering: hundreds of thousands of women in Afghanistan, Ghana, and Mali are receiving PATH-developed tetanus toxoid vaccine; thousands of youth in Cambodia, Kenya, Nicaragua, and Vietnam access reproductive health services from pharmacy staff who have received training through PATH's programs and curricula; nearly a half-million individuals at high risk for HIV have received one-on-one information and counseling from 4,300 PATH-trained community workers in the Philippines; and thousands of girls in Kenya have participated in a PATH-sponsored rite-of-passage program that provides an alternative to female genital mutilation.

Partners In Health The world is focused as never before on averting millions of preventable deaths in the developing world and is throwing substantial funding at the problem. Yet for this massive investment to make a real impact on the twin epidemics of poverty and disease, a comprehensive, community-based approach is key. Partners In Health's (PIH) success has helped prove that allegedly "untreatable" health problems can be addressed effectively, even in poor settings. Until recently, conventional wisdom held that neither multidrug-resistant tuberculosis (MDR TB) nor AIDS could be treated in such settings. PIH proved otherwise, developing a model of community-based care used successfully to treat MDR TB in the slums of Lima, Peru, and deliver antiretroviral therapy for AIDS in a squatter settlement in rural Haiti. Today, elements of PIH's community-based model of care have been adapted by other countries and programs throughout the world.

Shop Well with You Serving as a body-image resource for women surviving cancer, their caregivers, and health care providers, Shop Well with You (SWY) was founded by a 25-year-old woman who watched her own mother's struggle through four bouts of breast and thyroid cancer. While cancer often alters a woman's body image or self-perception, SWY helps each woman move beyond being identified primarily by her cancer to being recognized by her other attributes—a mother, friend, wife, sister, daughter, mentor, artist, advocate, and so on. Through its Web site, SWY focuses on helping women improve their self-image and quality of life by giving them customized clothing tips arranged by cancer-related treatments and side-effects, compiled in a resource kit tailored to the client's size, financial resources, fashion preferences, and medical condition.

Human Services

In each and every city, local nonprofits exist to better the community for all. You've likely been asked for money for one of these, or read about a contentious not-in-my-back-yard (NIMBY) debate occurring between community members and local and state elected officials. If you have ever worked for the benefit of those in your neighborhood, wanted to become more invested in your community, or desired to create social justice for all (even those actually in your backyard), this may be the segment for you.

Human services nonprofits may focus on low-income and moderate-income housing, elderly housing and housing for the disabled, area economic development or renewal, homeowners' associations, business redevelopment, community promotion, or loans or grants for minority or woman-owned businesses. They also may help assist and support local safety officers in crime prevention or voluntary firefighter's organizations. In some communities, these nonprofits may include community chests, booster clubs, or other grant-making organizations.

Crime and Legal-Related Services

Do you have a law degree sitting around gathering dust, either because you never used it or never used it in the way you once had hoped? Those pesky student loans pushed many an aspiring public interest attorney into more lucrative corporate work, where the golden handcuffs proved harder to unlock than originally expected. Perhaps you have been touched by the stories of death row pardons after new evidence came to light? Or maybe you have seen ex-offenders contributing to society after paying their debt and want to find ways to facilitate reentry into society? If so, consider looking into one of the many crime, crime-preventon, and legal-related nonprofits.

Crime and Legal-Related Services

The crime and legal-related component of the nonprofit sector includes:

- *Crime prevention.* Youth violence and drunk driving prevention
- *Correctional facilities.* Halfway houses for offenders and ex-offenders
- *Rehabilitation services for offenders.* Prison alternatives and inmate support
- *Administration of justice.* Mediation and dispute resolution
- *Law enforcement.* Community policing
- *Protection against abuse.* Spousal, child, and sexual abuse prevention
- *Legal services.* Public interest law

The legal field has, perhaps, the largest historical track record of pro bono work. Many nonprofit leaders have long used lawyers and legal professionals who work full-time in for-profit endeavors. They already know the value that a lawyer from the private sector can bring and are able to readily envision your transition. For the job seeker, developing nonprofit experience will be relatively easy through providing hands-on assistance or creating programs that are implemented by others.

Let's take a closer look at one legal-related organization.

A Fighting Chance Poor people facing the death penalty typically receive inadequate representation at trial because of a lack of effective investigation and mitigation development. A recent study of Louisiana public defenders showed that only one witness was interviewed by the defense per 200 felony clients. Facts change outcomes, both in terms of guilt or innocence and in terms of a life or death sentence. A Fighting Chance is working to make sure that those facts come to light. In an experiment that provided thorough investigation from the point of arrest in 119 New Orleans death penalty cases, the conviction rate decreased dramatically, from 68 percent to 16 percent. One hundred defendants were released when charges were dropped.

Employment

Imagine a job seeker looking to start over, reaching into a new career in a new industry for a second chance to do something more. Sound familiar? Many people are attempting to start a new career, but criminal records, poor training, missing education, or simply a lack of mentors and role models can be major obstacles. Perhaps you can empathize with their plight? If so, working with nonprofits focused on employment preparation, procurement, rehabilitation, or security may be of interest to you.

Employment

The employment component of the nonprofit sector includes:

- *Employment preparation and procurement.* Vocational counseling and job training
- *Vocational rehabilitation.* Goodwill Industries; sheltered employment
- Labor unions

Whether it's workforce development, welfare-to-work partnerships, or skills training for youth, nonprofits that enable advances in employment provide a plethora of opportunities for those looking to move into the nonprofit sector. Individuals with human resources, training and development, or counseling experience will find that their skills have prepared them well for this type of work. The most innovative nonprofits working in this segment combine training, education, and safety nets with an intense understanding of community, client, and customer needs and emerging labor trends.

We'll look at a couple of organizations that prepare people for employment.

Citizen Schools Since 1995, Citizen Schools has built a creative, effective learning model that addresses community needs while building student skills through hands-on experiential learning activities. Citizen Schools operates a national network of apprenticeship programs for youth that connects middle school students with adult volunteers in hands-on learning. At Citizen Schools, students develop the academic and leadership skills they need to do well in school, get into college, and become leaders in their career and in their community. Citizen Schools currently enrolls 2,000 middle school students and engages 1,500 volunteers at 30 campuses nationwide, but it envisions a day when most of the nation's 88,000 schools reopen after school, on weekends, and in the summer for experiential learning opportunities that powerfully link children and schools to the larger community.

Working Today (The Freelancers Union) The Freelancers Union is a national nonprofit that represents the needs and concerns of America's growing independent workforce through advocacy, information, and service. Independent workers—freelancers, consultants, independent contractors, temps, part-timers, contingent employees, and the self-employed—currently make up about 30 percent of the nation's workforce. The Freelancers Union exists to provide them a safety net, including the health care benefits, workplace rights, and legal protections they so vitally need.

Food, Agriculture, and Nutrition

Do you get incensed when you see babies with apple juice in their bottles? Are you appalled by the lack of good nutritional choices in schools and see childhood obesity as the next public health epidemic? Do you frequent your local organic farmers' market each week—and buy extra for the family down the street? If so, you may enjoy a nonprofit career in providing more and better food choices around the block and around the world.

Food, Agriculture, and Nutrition

The food, agriculture, and nutrition component of the nonprofit sector includes:

- *Agricultural programs.* Farmland preservation, animal husbandry, and farm bureaus
- *Food programs.* Food banks, congregate meals, soup kitchens, and meals on wheels
- *Nutrition*
- *Home economics*

Without subject matter expertise, most for-profit transitioners come to this segment to manage a food bank or market nutritional programming in school. Others bring a commercial banking background, using their expertise to make microloans to small communities in emerging markets. Much of the exciting work in this area involves combining agricultural needs with the development of third-world countries.

Let's take a look at two such organizations.

The Agros Foundation Founded in 1984, the Agros Foundation is a nonprofit organization that enables poor rural families in Central America and Mexico to escape the cycle of poverty by purchasing their own land. Agros organizes communities and extends land loans, repayable over a seven- to ten-year period, to families to purchase farmland and then partners with these families in applying sustainable agricultural practices. Since 1982, Agros has helped nearly 4,000 people build a new life by facilitating land ownership and providing technical assistance, training, capital loans, village infrastructure, and volunteer service teams to support the work and vision of community members.

Heifer International Today, millions of people who were once hungry will be nourished by milk, eggs, and fresh vegetables. Families who for generations knew only poverty are building new homes and starting businesses. Children who once headed out to the fields to do backbreaking work are heading into schoolrooms to learn to read. And people who never thought they'd be in a position to help someone else now experience the joy of charitable giving. How is this possible? Because you have given them a cow, sheep, or pig. It's a simple idea: give an animal to an impoverished family, with the promise that it passes along any offspring of that cow to their neighbors. Through livestock, training, and "passing on the gift," Heifer has helped 7 million families and communities in more than 125 countries improve their quality of life and move toward greater self-reliance.

Housing and Shelter

Does the thought of a person living in a car make you wish you could do something to help? What about a whole family, without the car, in the dead of winter? Do you have skills in human resources, banking, or mental health counseling but aren't sure how to help? Do you believe in giving both a handout and a hand up? If so, you will find great rewards in the housing and shelter segment of the nonprofit world.

Housing and Shelter

The housing and shelter segment includes:

- *Housing development, construction, and management.* Low-income and subsidized rental housing, retirement communities, independent housing for people with disabilities, and housing rehabilitation
- *Housing search assistance*
- *Temporary housing.* Homeless shelters
- *Homeowners' and tenants' associations*
- *Housing support.* Housing improvement or repairs and cost-reduction support

Housing and shelter programs are intertwined with community banks, thus offering a natural transition point for many from for-profit banking, real estate, or financial services careers. The analytic and assessment skills and the understanding of community players enable the corporate career changer to bring along a ready-made tool kit of transferable skills. Further, many of these nonprofits have created social venture models to underwrite housing costs.

We'll take a closer look at two nonprofits in the housing and shelter segment.

Rubicon Programs Rubicon was established in 1973 in Richmond, California, by community members concerned about the closure of state psychiatric hospitals. The founders recognized the need to develop local services for people disabled by chronic mental illness who were returning to the community. Although finding solutions for this major social issue was in itself an ambitious job, Rubicon also took on the problems of poverty and homelessness, building and operating affordable housing and providing employment, job training, mental health, and other supportive services to individuals who have disabilities, are homeless, or are otherwise economically disadvantaged. Each year, Rubicon helps over 3,000 people in the San Francisco Bay area. Not your typical nonprofit, Rubicon's social enterprise initiatives—such as its bakery and landscape services—fund more than 50 percent of its $15.3 million budget.

Boston Community Capital Economic, social, and civic isolation among individuals and communities are barriers to healthy communities, economic independence,

KAPLAN

and wealth creation. Boston Community Capital recognizes this problem and has created a financial intermediary system that serves low-income and disadvantaged people and communities. Boston Community Capital connects them to the mainstream economy by providing a range of financial vehicles, services, and products and by acting as an investment banker in those communities. This nonprofit works through a loan fund, lending money to organizations and private developers to provide housing, community facilities, and social services for low-income people and neighborhoods. It also works through a venture fund, making equity investments in high-potential, emerging businesses that create a "double bottom line" of financial and social returns, thus strengthening businesses that build healthy communities.

Public Safety, Disaster Preparedness, and Relief

It's been hard to watch the news recently. Images hurtle toward us: babies in the arms of firefighters; grief-stricken mothers carrying dead children; families torn asunder by plague, famine, floods, or terrorism. Each is more horrible than the last. Have these events inspired you, like many, to make the sector switch? Or have you always been driven to help out during disasters? Do you find yourself scrambling to organize clothing, blood, or toy drives? Do you always line up first to support those who support us in times of crisis? Do you feel the best measure of protection is an ounce of prevention? If so, you may belong in a public safety, disaster preparation, or disaster relief nonprofit.

Public Safety, Disaster, and Relief

The public safety, disaster preparedness, and relief segment includes:

- *Disaster preparedness and relief services.* Search and rescue squads and fire prevention
- *Safety education.* Automobile safety and first aid
- *Public safety benevolent associations*

Corporate career transitioners can find a home for themselves at almost any level in these organizations. From project management to crisis intervention to fundraising and operations management, the tactical and strategic thinking honed in MBA programs and in corporate careers make for an ideal employee in this segment. While the nonprofit sector prides itself on valuing the experience of each human being, an approach that can rise above calamity and bloodshed is, in fact, highly prized in these positions.

Here are some nonprofits that work in the public safety, disaster, and relief segment.

The American Red Cross The American Red Cross, a humanitarian organization led by volunteers and guided by its congressional charter and the seven fundamental principles of the International Red Cross Movement, provides relief to victims of disasters and helps people prevent, prepare for, and respond to emergencies. The American Red Cross functions independently of the government but works closely with government agencies, such as the Federal Emergency Management Agency (FEMA), during times of major crises. The disaster with the highest death toll since the founding of the American Red Cross was the 1900 Galveston, Texas, hurricane in which an estimated 6,000 people were killed. Clara Barton herself, founder and then president of the American Red Cross, gathered a team and traveled by train from Washington, D.C., to Galveston as soon as she heard news of the disaster. The most expensive disaster was Hurricane Katrina, which necessitated the greatest mobilization of Red Cross workers for a single relief operation.

i-Safe, Inc. In this day and age, everyone knows students can explore the marvels of the world and travel to the most intelligent realms of our galaxy on the Internet. But many do not know that if students are not cautious, they can become entrapped in the most detestable realms of the human imagination. Concerned people realize that true online safety is not found in software filters but in education and community support. Founded in 1998 and endorsed by the U.S. Congress, i-SAFE is the leader in Internet safety education. Available in all 50 states, Washington, D.C., and Department of Defense schools located across the world, i-SAFE's mission is to educate and empower youth to make their Internet experiences safe and responsible. The goal is to educate students on how to avoid dangerous, inappropriate, or unlawful online behavior. i-SAFE accomplishes this through dynamic K–12 curriculum and community outreach programs involving parents, law enforcement, and community leaders. It is the only Internet safety foundation to combine these elements.

Recreation and Sports

Do you love the great outdoors but feel stuck inside all day at work? Are you a weekend warrior who counts the days until it's gloriously Saturday once again? Do you look back on your childhood days at camp as some of the most influential and meaningful experiences of your life? Why not combine your passion with your abilities and work in one of the many nonprofits focused on bringing recreation to the masses?

Recreation and Sports

The recreation and sports component of the nonprofit sector includes:

- *Camps*
- *Physical fitness and community recreation facilities.* Parks, playgrounds, and recreation centers
- *Sports associations and training facilities*
- *Recreational clubs*
- *Amateur sports.* Leagues of any sport you can imagine, from badminton to horse jumping
- *Amateur sports competitions.* The Olympics or Special Olympics

---

Camps, gyms, and recreation clubs exist in the for-profit sector and nonprofit sector alike. Running them is not hugely different in either sector, with the exception of those organizations that cater to specific populations. The nature of their business remains the same. People with consumer-oriented backgrounds and a deep love of activity may enjoy combining their business expertise with a recreational hobby or a cause dear to their heart.

NED EAMES   FOUNDER AND PRESIDENT, TENACITY, INC., BOSTON, MASSACHUSETTS

Ned was captain of the San Diego State men's tennis team and played professionally on the ATP satellite tour for three years. He worked for five years in sales and marketing, earned his MBA from Boston University, and then became a management consultant to *Fortune* 500 companies. Yet after six years of consulting to some of the largest corporations in the country, Ned was left feeling unfulfilled, constrained by the limited nature of the project-based relationships he had with his clients, and uninspired by the internal competition he found rampant among his colleagues. He began to ask himself some tough questions.

"I needed to do something that not only tapped my business skills and interests but also fed my soul," he says, "so I asked myself where I could be of the most service, given who I am today—not who I wanted to be or who I was supposed to be, but who I really am today." The answer that kept coming back to him, even though it was an answer he'd long fought against, was tennis. "I lived in the housing projects for five years as a child," he explains, "and the life lessons that I got from tennis about winning and losing, humility, discipline, motivations, and attitudes helped make me who I am today." Tennis teaching, however, was something that Ned had hoped to avoid when he left the professional circuit.

Ned founded Tenacity, a Boston-based nonprofit, which provides an intensive youth development program with a focus on literacy, character development, and tennis, enabling at-risk youth to achieve on the court, in the classroom, and in life. Tenacity was born out of a convergence of Ned's personal passion about the life-changing effects of tennis on at-risk youth, his desire to be a social entrepreneur, his professional training around large systems change and orga-nizational development, and renewed public attention on after-school programming policies. To date, Tenacity has raised more than $9 million since its inception in 1999 and has served more than 11,000 children.

Why did Ned choose to start his own nonprofit?

"I had always enjoyed my entrepreneurial man-agement classes in my MBA program," he says, "and knew secretly deep down that I always wanted to start something of my own, so I left my fancy consulting job and my suits behind and started working on my business plan." To start his nonprofit, Ned spent almost two years visiting others whom he considered role models, and he surrounded himself with people who had "good character, lots of contacts, and finan-cial resources…but mostly good character." He also picked up 20–30 hours a week of private tennis lessons to pay his rent and buy his grocer-ies until he opened Tenacity's doors.

Why has Tenacity been so successful?

Ned didn't surround himself with a board full of nonprofit types, nor did he take classes in nonprofit management. Tenacity was a perfect blend of his avocation with his vocation. "I lived the experience of growing up poor but also working with *Fortune* 500 CEOs," he says, "so I know what life is like on both sides." What he brought with him was a deep personal passion, personal credibility, and excellent management skills. Along the way, Ned has allowed his staff and their external partners to help him envision and build the program because, as he says, "In the nonprofit sector, like in the for-profit sector, people support what they help create."

Ned's Key Lessons Learned:

- "I refer to nonprofits as businesses. There are a lot of similarities. You've still got to bring the bucks in and that is a very competitive process oftentimes, and you have to provide a great service."

- "I felt that I knew a lot about how tennis could help a person grow, having had that life experience, and knew that when I started my program, I would have both legs underneath me in full force."

- "Work is a big part of your life, so you ought to find something that feeds your soul, something that you want to live every day."

Following are a couple of nonprofits with recreation or sports missions.

Outdoor Explorations Imagine that you have a disability, as do one in five Americans. Maybe you were born with it; maybe you acquired it as a result of an accident or illness. Either way, the result is the same. You are excluded from many of the things you'd like to do. Maybe people don't think that you can keep up, don't think they can afford the cost of the adaptations you would need, don't think others will be comfortable around you, or simply don't think about you at all. For nearly 15 years, Outdoor Explorations has been creating a world where those barriers do not exist, each year helping more than 700 people with all types of disabilities experience the outdoor freedom that others take for granted. Using adaptive equipment, a cooperative attitude, and a lot of good humor to create enjoyable, empowering adventures, Outdoor Exploration's programs create the kind of shared success in the outdoors that transforms people, where barriers are broken and new abilities emerge.

The Fresh Air Fund The Fresh Air Fund was created in 1877 with one simple mission—to allow children living in disadvantaged communities to get away from hot, noisy city streets and enjoy free summer vacations in the country. When The Fund began, New York City was overflowing with poor children living in crowded tenements. Many of these youngsters were hit by a tuberculosis epidemic, and "fresh air" was considered a cure for respiratory ailments. Over the past 125 years, The Fresh Air Fund has provided free summer vacations in the country to more than 1.7 million New York City children from disadvantaged communities. Each year, thousands of children visit volunteer host families in 13 states and Canada through the Friendly Town Program or attend Fresh Air Fund camps.

Youth Development

Are you a firm believer that children are the future? Do you take extra time to mentor a neighborhood youngster or guide one of your children's peers? Did a mentor, a teacher, or an extracurricular activity once have a life-changing effect on you, so much so that you want to share it with the next generation? If so, think about joining one of the many nonprofits which serve youth. They include those that promote and support scouting, mentoring, tutoring and scholarship, orphanages, prevention of abuse and neglect, juvenile delinquency, camps, extracurricular programming, and agricultural apprenticing.

Youth Development

The youth development segment of the nonprofit sector includes:

- *Youth centers and clubs*
- *Adult- and child-matching programs*
- *Scouting organizations*
- *Youth development programs.* These might focus on agricultural, business, citizenship, or religious leadership.

During the last 15 years, nonprofits facilitating youth service (i.e., youth performing dedicated and demonstrable volunteer work) have exploded in number. Some of the best are run by social entrepreneurs, those individuals who walk and talk like an MBA and care and share like a nonprofiteer. Opportunities abound in the youth service and development segment for those with a corporate background to make a real change in the future.

You know some of these organizations from your own childhood: the Girl Scouts, your local YMCA, Big Brothers, Big Sisters, Camp Fire, and 4-H Clubs. Let's take a look at some newer youth-oriented organizations.

City Year Calling itself an "action tank" for national service, City Year helped found the national and community service movement. It demonstrated, improved, and promoted the concept of national service as a means for building a stronger democracy in 17 cities nationwide and in South Africa. City Year's signature program, the City

Year youth service corps, part of the AmeriCorps movement, unites more than 1,000 young adults, ages 17–24, from diverse backgrounds for a demanding year of full-time community service, leadership development, and civic engagement. It seeks to be a catalyst, engaging people and institutions in the citizen service movement and leads innovative policy discussions around national service policies and initiatives. Since 1988, City Year has graduated 8,200 corps members, and a recent study found that alumni are more likely to vote and volunteer. City Year's vision is that one day, the most commonly asked question of a young person will be, "Where are you going to do your service year?"

Strong Women, Strong Girls Strong Women, Strong Girls is a small, start-up non-profit based in Boston, Massachusetts, that sees youth not just as clients but as active participants in shaping the program. Strong Women, Strong Girls forms "Strong Women Clubs" on college campuses in Boston and Pittsburgh and teaches them about contemporary and historic female role models, mentoring, and skill-building activities. These women, in turn, adopt a class of at-risk girls in grades 3–5. For a year, the women work with these girls to build positive self-esteem and skills for lifelong success through reading biographies of influential women and completing hands-on projects about them. Relatively cheap to run, this nonprofit has figured out how to bring community and corporate partners on board as investors in the program and its outcomes.

General Human Services

If you are coming to the nonprofit sector because you simply want to help people, but none of the human services causes seem holistic enough, you may be looking for a nonprofit that simply serves populations as a whole. Perhaps you want to help autistic children, teenage mothers, or disabled adults? Maybe you are interested in facilitating adoption or improving the life of those in foster care facilities? Perhaps you once got trapped in a cycle of debt and, having slowly crawled out, vowed you would assist others who found themselves in a similar predicament? If so, look no further than the many nonprofits who generically, but ably, serve our wonderful human race.

Human Services

The human services component of the nonprofit sector includes:

- *Human services.* The Urban League, Salvation Army, Volunteers of America, Young Men's and Young Women's associations, and neighborhood centers
- *Children and youth services.* Adoption, foster care, and child day care
- *Family services.* Single parent agencies, family violence shelters, in-home assistance, family services for adolescent parents, family counseling, and pregnancy centers
- *Personal social services.* Financial counseling and transportation assistance
- *Emergency assistance.* Traveler's aid and victims' services
- *Residential and adult day care programs.* Hospices, supportive housing for older adults, group homes, and adult day care centers
- *Centers to support the independence of specific populations.* Centers that work with seniors; developmentally disabled persons; immigrants; the blind or visually impaired; the deaf and hearing impaired; and lesbian, gay, bisexual, and transgendered individuals

Human services nonprofits are historically funded in large part by public sources, relying heavily on city, county, state, and federal dollars. Public funding means public scrutiny, and public scrutiny means the books have to be spotless. Corporate transitioners may well find abundant opportunities in finance, administration, and operations roles in these nonprofits.

Following are two examples of human services nonprofits.

Camp Starfish When most people think of summer camp, the images that come to mind are of canoeing and soccer, arts and crafts, nature hikes, and care packages filled with candied contraband. They also remember making friends, trying new experiences, and succeeding at things they never thought possible. Come to Camp Starfish, and you'll see the same things: the ubiquitous smiles, the contagious laughter, and the camaraderie that only summertime can bring. But look a little closer, and you'll start noticing that something is a little different. Camp Starfish, founded in 1998, serves at-risk children with emotional, behavioral, and learning problems. With its unique and remarkable one-to-one camper-to-staff ratio, Camp Starfish enables children not only to succeed but to learn that success is, in fact, an option available to them.

The Home for Little Wanderers The Home for Little Wanderers is a nationally renowned, private child and family service agency. It is the oldest organization of its kind in the nation and the largest in New England. Each year, The Home serves thousands of children and families through a system of residential and community-based prevention programs, direct care services, and advocacy. The mission of The Home is to ensure the healthy emotional, mental, and social development of children at risk, their families, and communities. With a nimble, adept management team, The Home has weathered significant changes in our nation and has adapted its services and practices to address the impact of those changes on the life of children and families. It does this by asking, "Are we helping?" and "How do we know?"

International, Foreign Affairs, and National Security

Did you ever dream about running off and joining the Peace Corps? Have you noticed that while the world has gotten a lot smaller, you feel we do not yet know or respect our neighbors enough? Are you fed up with feeling helpless about foreign atrocities? If so, the international, foreign affairs, and burgeoning national security segment of the nonprofit sector is for you.

International, Foreign Affairs, and National Security

The international, foreign affairs, and national security segment includes:

- *Promotion of international understanding.* Cultural exchanges, academic exchanges, and other international exchanges
- *International development.* Agricultural and economic development, international relief, and the development of democratic or civil societies
- *International peace and security.* Arms control, national security, and United Nations associations
- *International affairs, foreign policy, and globalization.* The development of international economic and trade policy
- *International human rights.* International migration and refugee issues

---

These days, businesses large and small operate in a global community. Transitioners who can bring a global focus and understanding to the nonprofit sector can thrive in one of the many international, foreign affairs, or national security nonprofits.

Let's take a closer look at several such organizations with an international focus.

Trickle Up Program

Trickle Up Program is a 26-year-old nonprofit global microenterprise development organization working in Asia, Africa, Latin America and the Caribbean, and the United States. Trickle Up provides opportunities for the very poorest people to improve their living standard by developing microenterprises via a combination of seed capital grants, training, and support services. Working with a network of partner agencies in 14 core countries, Trickle Up helped start or expand 8,673 businesses in 2005, improving the life of nearly 28,000 people around the world.

People to People International

With the notion that "peaceful relations between nations requires understanding and mutual respect between individuals," President Dwight D. Eisenhower founded People to People International (PTPI) in 1956. It was removed from the government and placed in the nonprofit sector in 1961. Since then, hundreds of thousands of people—from elementary students to senior citizens—have participated in PTPI Chapter activities, worldwide conferences, adult exchange programs, or student exchange programs. PTPI underwrites its activities through revenue-generating ventures such as cultural exchange trips, clothing sales, conferences, and holiday cards.

Center for State Homeland Security

The National Emergency Management Association, the Adjutants General Association of the United States, and Mitretek Systems (a nonprofit scientific research and engineering corporation) have teamed up to create the Center for State Homeland Security. This organization offers objectivity, technical depth, and support for homeland security planning, analysis, engineering, technology evaluation, and information-sharing needs across all states and their local jurisdictions. The Center assists state and local governments in implementing their homeland security missions by supporting strategic planning and facilitating widespread and timely access to the best available information, facilities, and tools. The Center facilitates state and local governments' access to resources to acquire needed equipment, develop and train personnel, and coordinate services.

Public and Societal Benefit

Do you find yourself defending those who cannot defend themselves? Are you constantly pushing the agenda of social justice within your corporation or community? Have you been able to build capacity in your local nonprofit by sharing your business skills as a board member of volunteer? If encouraging nonprofits to expand their reach through increased voluntarism, grant making, leadership development, or mutually beneficial relationships interests you, than consider a career in the public and societal benefit segment.

Civil Rights, Social Action, and Advocacy

Set up either to influence public or political opinion around a population of people for the long term—the AARP will never run out of subjects to tackle—or the short term to pass or defeat a certain piece of legislation on the ballot this November, advocacy organizations exist on every conceivable subject. They may focus broadly on getting out the vote, voter registration, or voter education; provide facilities or services to political campaign activities; or support, oppose, or rate political candidates. Or they may spotlight a specific issue, like gun control, abortion, government spending, separation of church and state, school vouchers, nuclear weapon disarmament, labor rights, zoning, capital punishment, ecology and conservation, consumer protection, peace, drug and alcohol abuse, welfare, urban renewal, or pornography.

Civil Rights, Social Action, and Advocacy

The civil rights, social action, and advocacy segment includes:

- *Civil rights.* Minority, disabled, women's, seniors', children's, and lesbian and gay rights
- *Intergroup and race relations*
- *Voter education and registration*
- *Civil liberties.* Reproductive rights, right to life, censorship and freedom of speech and press, and right to die/euthanasia

---

Those with legal backgrounds can find an abundance of opportunities in civil rights, social action, and advocacy nonprofits. With educational campaigns and lobbying being a huge piece of the advocacy puzzle, transitioners with public relations and advertising can also find a place.

We'll look at a couple of nonprofits in the civil rights, social action, and advocacy segment.

Electronic Frontier Foundation If you are enjoying free speech on the Internet, you have the Electronic Frontier Foundation (EFF) to thank for it. EFF is the first line of defense when freedoms in the networked world come under attack. EFF broke new ground when it was founded in 1990—well before the Internet was on most people's radar—and continues to defend free speech, privacy, innovation, and consumer rights today. Blending the expertise of lawyers, policy analysts, activists, and technologists, EFF achieves significant victories on behalf of consumers and the general public. EFF fights for freedom primarily in the courts, bringing and defending lawsuits, even when that means taking on the U.S. government or large corporations.

Kids Voting USA In 1988, three businesspeople from Arizona traveled to Costa Rica on a fishing trip. During their visit, they learned that the country's voter turn-out is typically around 90 percent. This high turnout was attributed to a tradition of children's accompanying their parents to the polls. The businesspeople were intrigued by the idea but also recognized a missing link to education. They launched a school-based pilot project in a Phoenix suburb that since has grown into the national Kids Voting USA organization. Students learn about democracy through a combination of classroom activities, family dialogue, and an authentic voting experience where students go to official polling sites to cast a Kids Voting ballot—right alongside the adults. With changes in adult voting procedures, Kids Voting affiliates are offering students many of the same options. Some Kids Voting students now vote by mail, vote early, and complete absentee ballots. In 2004, 1.5 million students turned out to vote for president and local and state candidates and to make their voices heard on important issues.

Community Improvement and Capacity Building

Do you regularly join local civic league or community service projects? Do you believe that change begins in your own backyard? Are you frustrated by the way nonprofits are managed and want to find ways to increase their knowledge, ability, and skills needed to fulfill their important missions? Do you enjoy teaching others the skills you have gained in the for-profit sector but want to do it in an environment where the end result is social change rather than just an increase in shareholder value? Are you a proponent of compulsory national and community service for high school graduation, or would you like to see voluntary community service as an option with benefits similar to the GI Bill? Take a look at the community improvement and capacity-building segment.

Community Improvement and Capacity Building

The community improvement and capacity-building segment includes:

- *Community and neighborhood development.* Community coalitions and neighborhood and block associations
- *Economic development.* Urban, community, and rural development
- *Business and industry.* Chambers of commerce, real estate associations, or boards of trade
- *Nonprofit management.* Nonprofit development and support
- *Community service clubs.* Rotary, Knights of Columbus, or 100 Black Men

---

Community involvement and capacity-building nonprofits are likely homes for people with a background in business. Partnerships have long been formed between nonprofits and the communities in which they work; their boards include for-profit community members, and they fundraise from local professionals. Nonprofits benefit from consultative support around a specific problem, like strategic planning, fund development, or an earned income business launch.

Let's look at a few community improvement and capacity-building nonprofits.

First Book National Book Bank The First Book National Book Bank provides new books to children from low-income families across the country using generous donations from children's book publishers, service donors, and volunteers. By making large-scale donations to the First Book National Book Bank, publishing companies save the cost of multiple book shipments to fulfill donation requests and can refer organizations requesting book donations to First Book. In addition, First Book integrates donations into cause-based marketing campaigns and creative, large-scale media and marketing efforts that serve the promotional goals of publishing companies. Thanks to generous donations of book surpluses from its publishing partners and assistance in distribution from the U.S. Coast Guard, the First Book National Book Bank reaches programs in every corner of the country, serving national and local nonprofit organizations and serving the broad spectrum of children in need.

Taproot Foundation As you well know, barriers exist between business and the nonprofit sector, and these barriers lead to a squandering of talent available to both sectors. The Taproot Foundation harnesses human capital by connecting millions of business professionals in the United States with nonprofits who need their talents and experience. Through these partnerships, the Taproot Foundation helps nonprofits develop critical infrastructure, redefines volunteering for businesspeople, and fosters an ethic of service across professional fields. To date, the Taproot Foundation has awarded more than $15 million in pro bono services to almost 400 nonprofits through the work of more than 5,000 business volunteers.

Georgia Center for Nonprofits Georgia Center for Nonprofits (GCN) is not a typical statewide association by any means. While the Center does offer standard services such as professional development, research, advocacy, and group insurance to its members, GCN is always looking for innovative ways to serve the sector beyond its geographic borders. By delivering national solutions such as OpportunityKnocks (a dedicated employment Web site that connects nonprofit organizations with the talent they need to run their organizations effectively) and Nonprofit Marketplace (a management solution that helps nonprofits spend less money on everyday purchases and put more dollars into their mission), GCN ensures that Georgia-based nonprofits benefit from the stronger nonprofit sector as a whole.

Philanthropy, Voluntarism, and Grant-Making Foundations

Do you often find yourself gathering friends and family members to volunteer at a local charity event? Do your children expect every weekend to bring a service project of some sort? Do you feel that it is everyone's social responsibility to help those in need? Do you still hear echoes of President John F. Kennedy's challenge to Americans: "Ask not what your country can do for you, but what you can do for your country"? If you enjoy galvanizing the energy and passion of those around you to change the world, then the philanthropy, voluntarism, and grant-making universe may be for you.

Philanthropy, Voluntarism, and Grant Making

The philanthropy, voluntarism, and grant-making foundations segment includes:

- *Private grant-making foundations.* Corporate, independent, and operating foundations
- *Public foundations.* Community foundations
- *Voluntarism promotion.* Nonprofits focused on increasing or leveraging volunteering
- *Philanthropy, charity, and voluntarism.* Nonprofits focused on increasing or leveraging philanthropy, charity, and volunteering
- *Federated giving program*
- *Named trusts*

While finding a job in a foundation is difficult, finding a position in a nonprofit that encourages philanthropy or voluntarism is not. Business minds that can leverage relationships and funds, take advantage of technological advances, and package products in new and exciting way will do well here. Some of the most innovative nonprofits today are working to galvanize new energy and resources in the sector.

VolunteerMatch What if, somewhere on the Internet, a community of people gathered who believed in the power of volunteering to enrich our life and the world around us? What if, somewhere on the Internet, millions of good people and good causes could come together to form relationships that serve us all? What if, somewhere on the Internet, technology were being used to advance the values and partnerships that strengthen our civil society? Well, that somewhere exists at *www.volunteermatch. org.* Since 1998, VolunteerMatch has been helping volunteers and businesses find local nonprofits by zip code, get involved based on skills and interests, and support a community network committed to civic engagement. Since its founding, Volunteer-Match has helped volunteers make more than 2 million matches to more than 42,000 nonprofits throughout the United States.

Let's look at two examples of nonprofits working to promote involvement and increase capacity in the sector.

Social Venture Partners Created in Seattle in 1997, Social Venture Partners builds philanthropic communities by using a model that parallels venture capital practices. The first half of the model is investment that builds the long-term capacity of organizations rather than short-term projects or programs. Investment might include cash grants, skilled volunteers, professional consultants, leadership development, and management-training opportunities. Partners make an annual contribution of at least $5,000 and make decisions about how to share their collective investment as well as provide volunteer support in areas such as marketing, finance, technology, strategic planning, and human resources management. The second half of the model is the mobilization of a community of lifelong, informed, and inspired philanthropists. Through engagement with its nonprofits, connections with other partners, and participation in education events, partners are inspired to reinvest and make new investments in more nonprofit organizations in the future. Currently, Social Venture Partners organizations are in 20 U.S. cities with investments from over 1,100 partner households across North America.

Science and Technology

Do you have fond memories of your early science classes, where your imagination was set afire and the universe was yours to discover? Has your intellectual curiosity been stymied by market whims and financial forces? Have you learned how to utilize technology in ways that have benefited your wallet and the wallet of others but want to do more? Consider taking your technical expertise to the nonprofit sector, either in an organization focused on science and technology or in the application of science and technology to another social mission.

Science and Technology

The science and technology segment includes:

- *General science.* Marine science and oceanography are two examples.
- *Physical and earth sciences.* Astronomy, chemistry, mathematics, and geology fall into this category.
- *Engineering and technology.* This includes computer science and engineering.
- *Biological and life sciences*

An easy crossover point for those in the technology arena, this segment is filled with people who crossed over the sector border repeatedly. Those with project management expertise, technical skills, and a deep belief in a social mission will enjoy the work they find here.

Following are a couple of nonprofits in the science and technology segment.

Benetech Founded in 2001, Benetech is a unique bridge that connects the social sector with business and technology leaders. Joining the heart of social mission with the mind of high-tech process and project management, Benetech leverages the vast technical skill base in Silicon Valley to serve humanity. Benetech operates much like a start-up company in a venture capital environment. It identifies needs and opportunities where technology could have a tremendous impact, improving the life of thousands, potentially millions, of people and applies research, analysis, and business planning to develop and implement it. Current projects are in the areas of disabilities, human rights, poverty, and education and literacy.

Science Service You may not have heard of Science Service, but you certainly remember the science fair. Since 1921, Science Service has been encouraging students, parents, teachers, and communities to explore, appreciate, and understand the vast world of science through publications and educational programs. Science Service publishes *Science News*, a weekly magazine, and operates Science for Kids, a popular Web site for middle school science students. Science Service also administers three of the premier science competitions in the county—the Intel Science Talent Search, America's oldest and most highly regarded science contest for high school seniors; the International Science and Engineering Fair, the only worldwide science competition for students in grades 9–12; and the Young Scientists Challenge, which enables middle school children to participate in a national competition that emphasizes the student's ability to communicate about science. Together, these science education programs reach over 3.5 million students worldwide.

General Public and Societal Benefit

Are you a proponent of privatizing public services? Do you think that the world would run more smoothly if only the government and private sector worked together better? Have you spent your career on one side of the private-public fence and have expertise and experience you could lend by hopping to the other side? If so, those organizations serving the public through partnerships or by developing the next generation of public sector leaders may be for you.

Public and Societal Benefit

The public and societal benefit segment includes:

- *Government and public administration*
- *Military and veterans' organizations*
- *Public transportation systems*
- *Telecommunications*
- *Financial institutions.* Credit unions are one example.
- *Leadership development*
- *Public utilities*
- *Consumer protection*

Many nonprofits that fuse public-private partnerships rely on the business relationships built by their formerly corporate staff. In addition, they emphasize developing current and new leaders, a mission that nicely complements the background of those in human resources, training, and development.

Let's take a look at a couple of public and societal benefit nonprofits.

The White House Project When women leaders bring their voices, vision, and leadership to the table alongside men, the debate is more robust and policies are more inclusive and sustainable. The White House Project is a national, nonpartisan, nonprofit organization that aims to advance women's leadership—and raise the level of debate—in all communities and sectors, right up to the U.S. presidency. By filling the leadership pipeline with a richly diverse critical mass of women, The White House Project looks to make American institutions, businesses, and government truly representative. To advance this mission, The White House Project strives to support women and the issues that allow women to lead in their own life and in the world by providing them with training, messages, and other important resources.

American Water Works Association Founded in 1881, the American Water Works Association (AWWA) is an international nonprofit scientific and educational society dedicated to the improvement of water quality and supply. AWWA is the largest organization of water supply professionals in the world with its more than 57,000 members representing the full spectrum of the water quality community: treatment plant operators and managers, scientists, environmentalists, manufacturers, academicians, regulators, and others. Membership includes more than 4,700 utilities that supply water to roughly 180 million people in North America.

Consumers Union

Consumers Union is the name you don't know. But you'll recognize its product, *Consumer Reports*, the magazine you buy whenever you are about to purchase a large appliance or vehicle. Since 1936, *Consumer Reports* has been the most trusted name in unbiased advice about products and services, personal finance, health and nutrition, and other consumer concerns. For 70 years it has tested products, informed the public, and protected consumers with income derived solely from the sale of *Consumer Reports* and other services, never from advertising or sponsorships.

Religious Nonprofits

You may already volunteer through your place of worship. But have you ever thought of making a career out of it? Religious nonprofits include the obvious—churches, synagogues, and mosques—but also organizations supporting missionary or evangelical work and publishing, gift shops, or other auxiliary activities.

Religion

The religion-related segment includes:

- *Religion-specific nonprofits.* Support of Christianity, Judaism, Islam, Buddhism, Hinduism, and other religions
- *Religious media and communications.* Film and video, television, printing and publishing, Internet, and radio
- *Interfaith coalitions.* These may aim at reconciliation and peace, dialogue, or mutual support.

Religious organizations fund their proselytizing and spiritual work through fund-raising efforts; membership fees; and sales of books, gifts, spiritual travel, or other profitable ventures. In other words, despite being thousands of years old, religion today is very much an entrepreneurial effort. Further, with the government placing more of the burden of human services on faith-based communities—as well as opening up new streams of funding for them—religious organizations have become a dominant force within the social sector. Just as there may be a place for religion in your business mind, there can be a place for a business mind in your religion.

Many religion-related nonprofits, such as your neighborhood places of worship, are instantly recognizable and need no further explanation. Instead, let's look at other ways people bring the love of their faith and their corporate expertise to the nonprofit sector.

American Friends Service Committee

The American Friends Service Committee (AFSC) carries out service, development, social justice, and peace programs throughout the world. Founded by Quakers in 1917 to provide conscientious objectors with an opportunity to aid civilian war victims, AFSC's work attracts the support and partnership of people of many races, religions, and cultures. AFSC's work is based on the Quaker belief in the worth of every person and faith in the power of love to overcome violence and injustice. The organization's mission and achievements won worldwide recognition in 1947, when it accepted the Nobel Peace Prize with the British Friends Service Council on behalf of all Quakers. The AFSC is directed by a Quaker board and staffed by Quakers and other people of faith who share the Friends's desire for peace and social justice.

The Interfaith Alliance

The Interfaith Alliance (TIA) was founded in 1994 to challenge the radical religious right, and it remains committed to promoting the positive and healing role of religion in public life by encouraging civic participation, facilitating community activism, and challenging religious political extremism. TIA strives to protect both the sanctity of religion and the integrity of government, using religion's power to unite rather than divide. Its members, totaling roughly 185,000, are people of faith, good will, and conscience drawn from more than 75 different religions and belief systems, including individuals who subscribe to a no-faith tradition. TIA's grassroots base now includes

75 local activist groups in communities across the country and an extensive online action network.

Mutual-Membership Benefit

Have you recently retired and begun collecting your pension? Ever wondered how that pension operates or how it was put together? Have you noticed that your regular Thursday nights at "the lodge" seem to be increasingly gray-haired? Want to get some fresh blood into the pipeline but don't have the time with your day job? Perhaps you could turn that hobby into a career in the mutual-membership benefit segment of the nonprofit sector.

Mutual-Membership Benefit

The mutual-membership benefit segment includes:

- *Insurance providers.* Workers' compensation associations, mutual insurance companies, and local benevolent life insurance associations
- *Pension and retirement funds.* Teacher retirement fund associations, employee-funded pension trusts, and multiemployer pension plans
- *Fraternal societies.* Orders, councils, societies, chapters and unions—secret and not—where members come together for a shared purpose
- *Cemeteries and burial services*

Typical transitioners are people with experience running company benefit programs, employee education programs, or local community partnerships. In addition, those with investing and financial sales and advisory expertise can find themselves either on the front lines or in the back office of one of the many benefits firms.

Following are a couple of nonprofits in the mutual-membership benefit segment.

Armed Services Mutual Benefit Association

The Armed Services Mutual Benefit Association (ASMBA) provides comprehensive, affordable life insurance coverage to military personnel and their families. ASMBA was established in 1963 by military personnel headed for Vietnam who wanted to provide for their families' security but couldn't get insurance coverage because they were going into a war zone. So they created ASMBA, a nonprofit fraternal military benefit association, which provides security and peace of mind for members of the armed services and their families. And because the value of a life is not determined by rank or branch of service, ASMBA's founders made life insurance plans available to all ranks of all services, during all times of peace or war, with no rank, duty, or geographical restrictions.

Teachers Insurance and Annuity Association, College Retirement Equities Fund

Better known by its acronym, TIAA-CREF, this nonprofit has been offering a wide range of investment products and services for employees in the academic, cultural, and research fields for more than 85 years. With a portfolio of $380 billion, their charge is clear: to serve those who serve others by providing them with financial expertise to plan for and live comfortably through retirement.

CONCLUSION

Changing your career requires a long, hard look inward. Are you running toward a new job or away from your current job? In reading this chapter, you likely have solidified the passions you already knew lay inside you, and you may have uncovered some you hadn't realized. Perhaps your imagination is afire with all of the wonderful things you might do in the nonprofit world, from practical plans to dramatic dreams. However, determining which cause you want to assist or which societal problem you want to solve is a big decision, but it is only one of three you will have to make.

Now, let's figure out the rest of your nonprofit equation.

CHAPTER 3

Nonprofit Trends and Job Profiles

As you have just read, today's nonprofit sector is a vast world of great innovation and variety. That means your new career in the nonprofit sector can encompass service to any number of causes you may wish to address. Yet some nonprofits make for easier transitions than others, and each gives you an opportunity to serve that special cause differently. Certain trends in the sector have made room for many new skill sets—such as yours from the private sector—to find a home. The nonprofits that have internalized these trends allow for smoother transitions than those that have not.

To some, picking a favorite cause is like picking a favorite child. It's a nearly impossible task. Many come to the sector just looking to give back in any way they can. Others have a particular cause in mind. Either way, determining your driving social concern is only one of the three decisions you will need to make. To expedite your transition into the nonprofit sector, you will also have to determine which tactical approach you would like to take in solving your pressing social concern and which nonprofit lifecycle stage best fits with your professional personality. Once you've done that, you will need to make your last major decision, which entails looking at your entire body of work, including both your paid and volunteer experiences, to determine where your skills can best be put to use. Each of these three decisions is equally important. While your gut has likely answered the first already, reading this chapter will help you answer the second and third.

Let's start with some of the trends in the nonprofit world.

TRENDS IN THE NONPROFIT SECTOR ARE CREATING OPPORTUNITIES FOR CAREER CHANGERS

The nonprofit sector is changing every day. As it changes, trends have begun to emerge. These trends point to increased opportunities for those with business skills.

Nonprofit Mergers

In the past decade, the number of nonprofits in the United States has increased by 64 percent.[1] Yet the rate of donations has not grown at the same pace. Because of repeated natural disasters, such as Hurricane Katrina and the Asian tsunami, and acts of terrorism like 9/11 and the war that followed, donors feel tapped out or simply exhausted. Receiving an increased number of solicitations from additional nonprofits being set up every day is not helping matters. As a result, a larger number of nonprofits find themselves competing for a relatively smaller pool of available funds.

The influx of business thinking has, in part, set off a wave of nonprofit mergers across the sector. Merged nonprofits find that they can consolidate staff, reduce competition, and minimize overhead costs. This trend is good news for corporate career changers, as merger and acquisition work is uncharted territory for many nonprofit staff.

Revenue-Generating Subsidiaries

As the competition for funding dollars increases, nonprofits are realizing that they will be more successful if they rely less on the whims of individual donors or government funding and more on themselves. Doing so means that they must come up with new ways to fund their programs. Youth service nonprofits might run fee-for-service summer programs; transitional houses and long-term shelters might teach their residents job skills; and fair trade advocacy groups might sell chocolate made from cocoa harvested by fairly paid workers rather than trafficked children.

An example of a successful revenue-generating subsidiary is the Greyston Bakery, a New York–based nonprofit that has become a leader in community development and a role model for other socially conscious businesses. Greyston sells award-winning cakes, tarts, and other baked goods, yet, as varied as its products might be, the main

---

1   Sasha Talcott, "Nonprofit Mergers Catch on in Region," *Boston Globe*, April 6, 2006, *www.boston.com/business/articles/2006/04/06/nonprofit_mergers_catch_in_region/* (accessed November 26, 2006).

KAPLAN

ingredient in each item is its dynamic social mission. Greyston's profits support the community development work of the Greyston Foundation, which includes housing, child care, health care, a computer learning center, and more. In addition, the bakery actively recruits and hires employees who have had difficulties finding employment in the past. Finally, Greyston partners with and serves a network of other businesses, such as Ben & Jerry's and Stonyfield Farms, that share its social concerns.

Public-Private Partnerships

Nonprofits have learned that it is not enough to work on their own, even if they do outstanding work. Some of the most exciting work in the nonprofit sector today is done in collaboration between the for-profit and nonprofit sectors. It seems so simple, but bureaucracy, misunderstandings, and stereotypes have long kept these sectors apart. More and more, nonprofits and for-profits are joining together, breaking down barriers of language and culture and creating new and innovative programs.

Venture Philanthropy

The new trends in philanthropy—led by dot-com millionaires and venture philanthropists—mean that foundations look at their role in the nonprofit sector entirely differently than they may have ten years ago. Many foundations still stick to the old way of heavy-handed, slow thinking, but more and more often, foundations are catching on that they can create the change they want to see in the world. Empowering their nonprofit partners to do what they have already done well even better, more broadly, and with better efficiency is a successful business model. The idea of the nonprofit as a partner, not just the recipient of a carefully constructed, tightly managed grant, is new, and this method of venture thinking (i.e., scalable, demonstrable, innovative, and creative) is most successful with agile and responsive nonprofits. Nonprofits that employ business minds, MBAs, and corporate types have an advantage because they speak the language of the for-profit sector, understand the business model, and have worked with others who share the same mentality and benchmarking for success.

Management Matters

With the increasing focus on the bottom line and with more and more competition for funding, nonprofits are getting wise that management techniques matter. Once considered taboo, nonprofits no longer feel shy about incorporating best practices from the private sector. It is not uncommon to hear a nonprofit executive director discussing some of the latest ideas from famed management gurus, from Jim Collins's ideas about getting the right people on the right seats on the bus, for example, or Peter Senge's thoughts on building learning organizations. Where once such comments would have been met with horror and shock, they now are met with heads nodding in agreement. However, great management in the nonprofit sector means nothing if it is not done compassionately. For-profit managers who can bring the mind of a businessperson coupled with the heart of a social worker will do very well in, and by, the nonprofits they serve.

Now let's find the right nonprofit for you.

DEFINE YOUR TACTICAL APPROACH

As we've discussed, nonprofit organizations are often broken down into the following groups: arts, culture, and humanities; education; environment and animals; health; human services; international and foreign affairs; public societal benefit; religion-related; mutual and membership benefit. In each of these groups, the water is a little muddy; for example, a historical museum may hold the world's largest collection of 16th-century Scottish armor but have as one of its central purposes the education of young children. In the end, organizations are defined by how they describe themselves in their applications for tax-exempt status.

Legally Defined Categories of Nonprofits

Most nonprofits fall into one of a few categories. They are public charities, advocacy-lobbying organizations, or membership associations.

Public Charities—501(c)(3)s

The more than 1.9 million public charities in the United States fall into a few distinct groups:

- *Social service organizations.* The driving principle of these public charities is simply the betterment of others through delivery of some sort of service or good. These organizations include Easter Seals, the American Red Cross, and your local food bank, library, or homeless shelter.

- *Foundations.* Foundations exist to fund specific types of activities of non-profits or individuals, as defined by their mission statements or charters. Social service organizations work to create hands-on change in these areas, while foundations fund their work. Foundations range from the largest, like the Ford Foundation or the Gates Foundation, to the smallest community foundation.
- *Support/capacity-building organizations.* As the nonprofit sector becomes more organized, a new level of nonprofits has arisen to support their work. Like the for-profit sector, which has legions of consultants and outside experts, the nonprofit sector now, too, benefits from management support organizations and board-training centers to accomplish their goals. You may know these organizations as the United Way, CompassPoint (formerly the Support Center for Nonprofit Management), or Board Source (formerly the National Center for Nonprofit Boards).

Advocacy or Lobbying Organizations—501(c)(4)s

Political in nature, these organizations exist to sway public or elected opinion to change existing public policy or upcoming legislation. Different from political action committees (PACs), 501(c)(4)s do not work specifically on behalf of or against a particular candidate for public office but may take a stand on one of them depending on whether they agree on the issues. Also, unlike political action committees, these 501(c)(4) organizations must file returns with the IRS. Nearly 140,000 of these organizations are registered with the Internal Revenue Service (IRS), including Greenpeace, the National Rifle Association, the American Teacher's Union, and NARAL.

Membership Associations—501(c)(6)s

These professional organizations represent members brought together because of a shared trade, skill, area of focus, or career path. These include individual membership and trade organizations like the National Association of Realtors or entities like the National Council of Nonprofit Associations, the latter itself an association of local and state nonprofit associations.

IRS Classifications for Nonprofits

To qualify for tax-exempt status, a nonprofit organization must operate in one of the following IRS classifications:

§ 501(c)(1): Corporations organized under an act of Congress (including federal credit unions)

§ 501(c)(2): Title-holding corporations for exempt organizations

§ 501(c)(3): Charitable organizations

§ 501(c)(4): Social welfare organizations

§ 501(c)(5): Labor, agricultural, and horticultural organizations

§ 501(c)(6): Business leagues

§ 501(c)(7): Social clubs

§ 501(c)(8): Fraternal benefit societies

§ 501(c)(9): Voluntary employees' beneficiary associations (VEBAs)

§ 501(c)(10): Fraternal lodge societies

§ 501(c)(11): Teachers' retirement fund associations

§ 501(c)(12): Benevolent life insurance associations, mutual ditch or irrigation companies, mutual or cooperative telephone companies, etc.

§ 501(c)(13): Cemetery companies

§ 501(c)(14): State-chartered credit unions, mutual reserve funds

§ 501(c)(15): Mutual insurance companies or associations

§ 501(c)(16): Cooperative organizations to finance crop operations

§ 501(c)(17): Supplemental unemployment benefit trusts

§ 501(c)(18): Employee-funded pension trusts (created before June 25, 1959)

§ 501(c)(19): Organizations of past or present members of the armed forces

§ 501(c)(20): Group legal service organizations

§ 501(c)(21): Black lung benefit trusts

§ 501(c)(22) and (24): Withdrawal liability payment funds (ERISA Trusts)

§ 501(c)(23): Armed forces organizations

§ 501(c)(25): Title-holding corporations or trusts with multiple parents

§ 501(c)(26): State-sponsored high-risk health coverage organizations

§ 501(c)(27): State-sponsored workers' compensation reinsurance organizations

§ 501(d): Religious and apostolic associations

§ 501(e): Cooperative hospital service organizations

§ 501(f): Cooperative service organizations of operating educational organizations

§ 501(j): Amateur sports organizations

§ 501(k): Child care organizations

§ 501(n): Charitable risk insurance pools

§ 521: Farmers' cooperative associations

§ 526: Shipowners' protection and indemnity associations

§ 527: Political organizations and political action committees

§ 528: Homeowners' associations

§ 529: Qualified state tuition programs

§ 530: Education individual retirement accounts

Minor but Major Differences

Advocacy organizations and trade associations will, of course, tell you that they are serving a social purpose, and they are. However, the line between them exists because of IRS rules about how donated money can be spent.

Money given to a 501(c)(3), such as the American Red Cross or the Girl Scouts, can be used to deliver goods and services to, but not advocate on behalf of, individuals or causes. Money given to a 501(c)(4), such as Handgun Control or the National Rifle Association, can be used for advocacy. Donations made to a 501(c)(3) are tax deductible, while donations made to a 501(c)(4) are not. Some 501(c)(3)s define their outreach work as "educational," but if the work gets close to a dangerous line—losing nonprofit status for violations is no laughing matter—some 501(c)(3) and 501(c)(6) nonprofits set up separate 501(c)(4) organizations to fundraise and spend entirely separately from their service delivery arms.

AARP is a well-known nonprofit that registers part of its organization as a 501(c)(3), part as a 501(c)(4), and yet another part as a 501(c)(6). Individuals can join AARP when they reach the ripe old age of 50 and begin receiving travel discounts, tax preparation help, driver safety courses, a monthly magazine, and all sorts of other benefits. They are given opportunities to donate their time in the many social service-driven AARP volunteer programs. AARP touts the voting power of its 36 million members in the halls of Congress. And so AARP and its foundation and membership subsidiaries exist as a public charity, a membership association, and an advocacy organization.

Another interesting example is Google.org, the foundation started by founders of the popular search engine, Google. With $1 billion in funding and a program direction aimed at global poverty reduction, energy, and the environment, it sounds like any other large foundation. Except for one thing: Google.org has organized itself as a for-profit entity, meaning that it pays taxes, but it can also raise and disburse money to nonprofits or for-profits and use its considerable muscle to lobby on behalf of the causes it funds.

KAPLAN

Philanthropy:

- Immediate cash gifts for first month's rent and security deposits on new apartments, enabling women to move themselves and their children away from an abusive partner

- For organizations, grants made to fund new programs, more first-line responders, or public affairs campaigns

Direct service:

- Twenty-four-hour hotlines, counseling services, and transitional housing, allowing victims to escape quickly and anonymously

- Interview training and professional clothing swaps for newly single mothers seeking first-time employment

Different Nonprofit Tactics

How can nonprofits work to end domestic violence?

Nearly one in three adult women experience at least one physical assault by a partner during adulthood. It's a problem of outrageous proportions, and no single approach can solve it. The tactics of different types of nonprofits can illustrate the importance of approach. Here are but a few examples.

Lobbying and advocacy:

- Public education campaigns about the effects of alcohol and drug abuse, economic downturns, or other factors linked to spikes in the incidence of domestic violence, or about the increase in domestic attacks on men

- Recent legislative action that makes marital rape a crime

Support and capacity building:

- Training of volunteers to become counselors to victims, in long-term relationships that provide stability and support

- Donations of, and training, on new computer systems or telephone systems that enable first-line responders to access historical data quickly on each relationship

Membership organizations:

- Pooled benefits for women previously trapped in abusive relationships because of the need for health insurance for sick children

- Support groups for victims and children

A Note about Foundation Jobs

Many career changers come to the nonprofit sector in search of a job in a foundation. Such positions seem, from the outside, to be the ultimate dream jobs. Foundations gave an estimated $31.8 billion in 2005 alone.[2] Who doesn't want to spend their days giving away someone else's money?

However, foundation jobs are notoriously difficult to get. Foundations have very little turnover. There are fewer foundations than other nonprofits—5.1 percent of the entire sector[3]—so there are fewer foundation jobs than there are other nonprofit jobs. In fact, foundations employ less than 0.5 percent of the workers in the nonprofit sector.[4] Corporate foundations tend to hire from within their own ranks, typically from retiring executives or marketing and public relations senior staff. Private foundations are often looking for people with deep field experience or a PhD, or sometimes both, in the field or fields that they fund. It is certainly worth pursuing a position at a foundation if that's what you truly desire, but keep in mind that your job search may take longer than you expect.

The grant-making world may also not be a good fit from the transitioner job seeker's point of view. Many foundations are slow and deliberative, often thinking and writing about subjects for years before determining funding priorities. Many are filled with academic types who are not sensitive to, or simply not interested in, the whims of the market. Staffs tend to be small, and individuals spend gobs of time alone in their offices reading proposals or other research-driven publications.

Corporate transitioners who insist on finding the holy grail of a foundation job would be well advised to look toward newer foundations, those founded by dot-com millionaires and venture capitalists like Bill Gates, Pierre Omidyar, and Jeff Skoll, which do not share the typical traits of older, more staid foundations. This new wave of young philanthropists are applying lessons from the private sector to address social needs. They see themselves not as ATMs for nonprofits but as partners, being hands-

---

2   The Foundation Center, *Highlights from the Foundation Yearbook,* (Washington, D.C.: The Foundation Center, 2006): 1.

3   Independent Sector, *National Almanac of Nonprofit Statistics in Brief,* (Washington, D.C.: Independent Sector, 1998): 5.

4   Independent Sector, *Nonprofit Almanac,* (Washington, D.C.: Independent Sector, 2001): 9.

on when they make grants, and as risk takers, venturing money on unproven but exciting ideas rather than the same old service delivery model.

The Washington, D.C.-based Venture Philanthropy Partners (VPP) is a perfect example of a philanthropic entity doing things in a new and innovative fashion. Raul Fernandez, Mark Warner, and Mario Morino founded VPP in 2000, then recruited 26 other technology and business leaders and several foundations to contribute more than $30 million to capitalize VPP's first investment fund. VPP works much like a venture capital fund, investing in high-potential nonprofits that are serving the core developmental, learning, and educational needs of children from low-income families in Washington, D.C. VPP does not fund program costs but, rather, focuses on funding growth strategies, talent searches, and other operational investments that have the greatest potential to improve the life of children and that can help VPP demonstrate its strategic, engaged, and highly leveraged approach.

Like VPP, the Case Foundation also invests more than money, partnering closely with a small number of organizations to advance large-scale social change. Founded in 1997 by Steve Case, AOL's cofounder, and his wife Jean Case, the Case Foundation looks for people and groups with the ability to scale and sustain their impact over the long term. The foundation's hands-on approach supports collaboration, entrepreneurship, and leadership. Less bureaucratic than its philanthropic peers, the Case Foundation leverages its relationships, experience, and staff expertise to help make its partners stronger and more effective.

JOB TITLES IN THE NONPROFIT SECTOR

Job titles in the nonprofit sector can be confusing. They don't correlate with those in the for-profit sector; for example, you are unlikely to find a total quality improvement specialist, a business analyst, or a loan support processing supervisor in most organizations. Similarly, you won't find an organic farmer, a community organizer, or a home detention caseworker in the for-profit sector. And just what is a program officer, anyway? Figure 3.1 shows two possible organizational charts, one for a larger nonprofit and one for a smaller nonprofit.

Job postings may have seemingly senior titles that don't, in reality, give the employee much authority. Many directors in the nonprofit sector are directors of their own work and precious little else. Make sure you research each job listing thoroughly to

Figure 3.1 Sample Organizational Charts

A larger nonprofit:

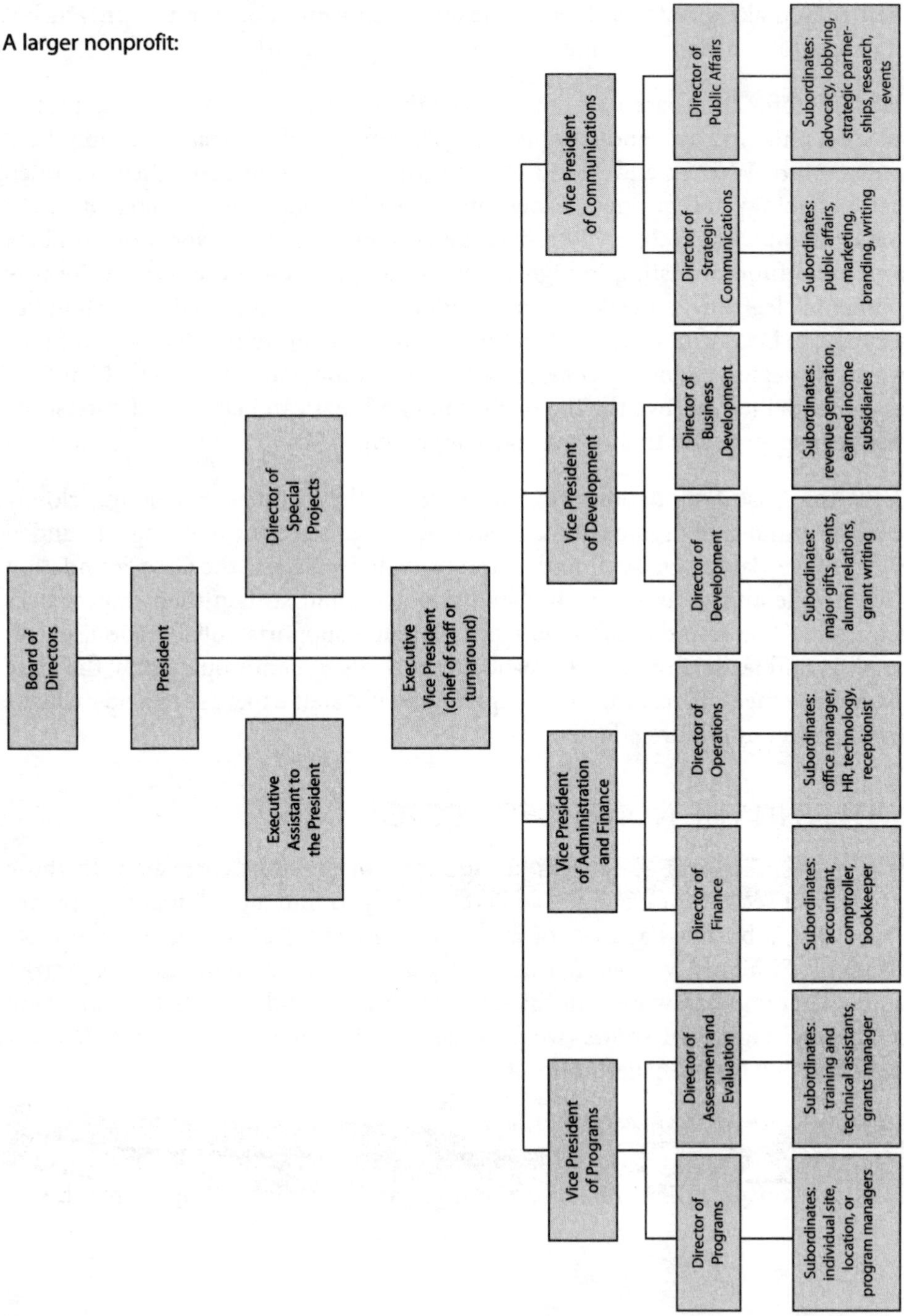

Figure 3.1 (continued) Sample Organizational Charts

A smaller nonprofit:

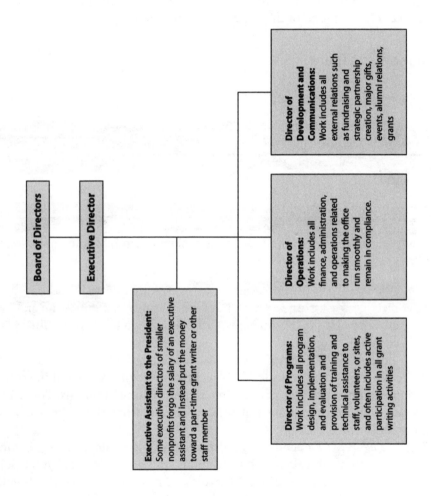

ensure that your experience is aligned with the substance of a job instead of applying for positions based on titles alone.

Generally, nonprofit titles can be grouped into several functional areas of work: management; programs; fundraising; communications; and administration, operations, and finance. Let's look at each of these areas in more detail.

The Management Team

Executive Director, President, or Chief Executive Officer

The executive director is often the chief professional officer of a nonprofit. Sometimes the executive director (ED) is called the president or the chief executive officer (CEO). A nonprofit that is more in touch with its business side is one that has a CEO rather than an ED.

The chief professional officer, whom we will call the executive director for the balance of this section, is hired by, and reports to, the board of directors (always a volunteer group in the nonprofit sector). The ED's job is broken down into four main areas of responsibility:

1. *Management.* The buck stops with the executive director. The ED has overall responsibility for hiring and firing, setting the organization's strategic direction, implementing its business plan, capitalizing on new opportunities, and overseeing the budget.
2. *Program oversight.* Nonprofits exist to serve a cause; that cause is reflected in the programs they provide. The executive director has a hand in creating, designing, implementing, prioritizing, and evaluating programs. The ED also decides when new programs will be launched and when the life span of an old program is over.
3. *Communications.* Depending on the nonprofit and its mission, communications might be called public relations, public affairs, lobbying, public education, or external relations. Regardless of its nomenclature, this function includes the responsibility of being chief spokesperson of the organization.
4. *Fundraising.* Last but certainly not least, the chief professional officer of any nonprofit spends a good deal of time every day raising money.

Deputy Director, Associate Director, Vice President, or Chief Operating Officer

Small nonprofits—those under $250,000 in budget—often rely solely on an executive director. Larger nonprofits—from $1,000,000 and above—have a more fleshed-out senior management team. Somewhere in the middle, nonprofits realize that they are big enough to warrant a deputy director or vice president. This usually happens as the executive directors of start-ups or growing nonprofits find that they are spending more time on developing the organization's vision and raising money and less time on the structures and procedures that nonprofits need to withstand change and flourish.

Deputy directors may take on the chief operations officer role or may be the chief program director, or they may be both. Each nonprofit defines these roles differently. Generally speaking, all oversight for executive, programming, fundraising, and operational functions usually reside with the executive director and the deputy director.

Some nonprofits take this a step further, anointing the board chair as president, or moving a founder into a president's role, while making the executive director the chief professional officer. In these cases, the structure follows the same internal-external division of duties between a president and a vice president that you find in the for-profit sector.

MALINDA ANDERSON VICE PRESIDENT OF ADMINISTRATION, SPECIAL OLYMPICS
COLORADO, DENVER, COLORADO

Having gone back to school after becoming a single parent, Malinda chose a practical major, accounting, through which she could support her family. She got a great job offer from one of the nation's largest accounting firms. "Two weeks into my auditing career," she says, "I realized that I'd made a huge vocational error." Despite being promoted repeatedly, Malinda felt that her work lacked meaning. When one of her clients, a restaurant group in Scottsdale, Arizona, offered her an in-house position, Malinda quickly made the move.

"I was working in their accounting department as a general ledger supervisor and auditor, and I was bored," she says. One day, Malinda approached the chief operations officer and asked what he thought about creating a regional marketing position and hiring her to do it in their Denver, Colorado, cluster market. "In order to be successful in my new job and to get to know the community," she says, "I started volunteering on the funds distribution committee for the United Way as soon as I got to Denver." One of the people she met through her volunteer work was a headhunter who told her about a position at a local but nationally renowned nonprofit Montessori early childhood education agency. "They hired me because I could bring business thinking to their nonprofit organization," she says.

How did Malinda find her current position at the Special Olympics of Colorado?

After 14 years with the Montessori school, Malinda was told by another headhunter about two positions in administration and finance for Special Olympics Colorado. "I'd donated to them for years," she says, "but I was afraid that neither of the positions by themselves would be challenging enough for me." Instead, Malinda approached them about the possibility of combining both positions into one senior-level position and leaving some room in the budget to hire a junior staff member for her team. "Nonprofits have got to keep up with the market," she says, "and so taking a more creative look at this position was the right thing for them to do."

What difficulties did Malinda encounter as she made her transition from "Big Accounting" to a small nonprofit?

Malinda was most surprised about the lack of procedures and the lack of administrative controls in the nonprofit sector. "There seemed to be a lack of expertise at the administrative level," she says, "because so many program administrators started off as great front-line program staff

and got promoted without the proper administrative training." Likewise, Malinda met many administrators without a program background who didn't understand how to approach problem solving in a way that would resonate with their coworkers. "People in the nonprofit sector aren't driven by the same motives as their for-profit counterparts," she says. "They understand that the bottom line is important, but it's only part of the equation. Learning how to talk about numbers in the context of services provided and lives changed is the key to success in the nonprofit sector."

Malinda's Key Lessons Learned:

■ "A good first step is to get involved with United Way or a community board."

■ "Many who wish to transition see marketing and development as logical first steps, and so there is a lot of competition for those jobs. Keep in mind the financial and accounting areas, too."

■ "If you want to succeed in solving problems, be prepared to soften your approach a bit and speak the language of the heart-driven people in the nonprofit sector."

The Senior Management Team

Rounding out the senior management team are, along with the executive director and the deputy director, the chiefs of all major areas of the organization. This normally includes—in nonprofits large enough to have all of these positions—the director of programs, the director of fundraising, the director of operations, the director of administration and finance, and the director of communications. Because nonprofits tend to collapse more functions into fewer positions, you may find that all of these positions are represented with fewer bodies. These functions are described in the sections that follow.

The Program Team

For-profits make money through the sale of products or services. Nonprofits spend money in the output of products or services. Those products or services are distributed through the programs of the nonprofit. This doesn't mean that the position of product manager or service manager in the for-profit sector corresponds directly to that of program officer or program manager of a nonprofit. It may sit in the same place on the organizational chart and carry out similar functions, but the knowledge required for the position is quite different. Most program staff hold a deep understanding of the subject matter of the nonprofit's programs, have worked in the community for years, and are deeply ingrained in the relevant issues. Because of this required knowledge base, program positions are some of the hardest for career changers to transition into, and even when secured, they often result in the least successful transitions.

The program team may be one person or one person per site, or it may consist of several individuals. The program staff of a nonprofit is responsible for the following:

- *Program design.* The architecture of a program is a major factor in its ultimate success or failure. Nonprofits are given awards and positive public attention for innovation in program design, leading to increased financial support.
- *Program implementation.* Efficiency in program implementation matters, despite what you may hear. The better the implementation, the better the results.
- *Program assessment and evaluation.* Like private sector investors, funders demand bang for their buck. Rather than seeing return on investment (ROI) in terms of dollars, funders see the return as numbers of immunizations delivered or houses built.

The Fundraising Team

The smaller the nonprofit, the more likely that the executive director is the entire fundraising team (also known as development team) for the organization. Given that the executive director is the chief spokesperson and champion for the cause, it makes sense that this position will play a key role in all major funder relationships. As nonprofits grow, most will bring on a fundraising associate, prospect research assistant, or grant writer before bringing on a development director.

The senior staff in a nonprofit wake up in the morning and go to bed at night thinking about how to raise more money. The fundraising team is responsible for bringing in the dollars by one method or another. It may be accountable for the following:

- *Event management.* Large nonprofits, and especially old nonprofits, tend to host a plethora of events designed as both fundraisers and "friendraisers." With the exception of the major galas you might read about in the *New York Times* Styles section, fundraising events tend not to bring in large amounts of money, but they do reinvigorate constituents and introduce new people to the organization.
- *Grant writing.* Most foundations award funds through a long, drawn-out grant application process. They put out requests for proposals (RFPs) and often ask applicants to jump through multiple hoops to apply. Grant writing is both a skill and an art, and career changers who learn about it will be well served.
- *Major gifts.* Major gifts are just what they sound like: major gifts from private individuals or corporations. This type of fundraising might come most naturally to a career changer in that it is similar to one-on-one sales pitches.
- *Direct mail.* Nonprofits also raise money through direct mail solicitations. These tend to be annual drives, often conducted in December to take advantage of donors looking for tax breaks.
- *Capital campaigns.* Capital campaigns are one-time, large fund drives focused on the purchase or improvement of a physical space, like a building or a playground.
- *Membership development.* Finally, people are needed to recruit and retain members. Because donations to a membership organization are not tax deductible, but the cost of membership might be, the membership development professional is tasked with bringing in the money to fund programs.

Fundraisers tend to move around a lot, and nonprofits are always looking for good ones. If you look on any nonprofit job board, you will find an overwhelming number of development jobs. Other than the executive director, the director of development is often the highest-paid individual on staff; in some cases they make even more than the executive director. Some nonprofits, to justify the high salaries demanded by fundraising professionals, combine fundraising and communications under one external affairs umbrella.

The Communications Team

Depending on the nonprofit and its mission, communications might be called public relations, public affairs, lobbying, public education, marketing, or external relations. Regardless of its nomenclature, communications includes the following functions:

- *Media relations*. In public advocacy nonprofits, great emphasis is put on issuing press releases and placing stories in print, television, radio, and Internet outlets.
- *Public education or lobbying*. If crossed, this tricky line could include a nonprofit's tax status. Therefore, nonprofits are careful to ensure that they are either informing the public about issues and leaving the action to them or directly lobbying for policy change at local, state, or national levels.
- *Public affairs*. Nonprofits use all sorts of methods to get the word out. This can span the spectrum from direct marketing to public education.
- *Membership services*. In associations, the membership services coordinator is the first line of interaction between members and the organization. Like the executive director, the membership staff act as public faces for the nonprofit.
- *Online functions*. These constitute a whole new set of roles for nonprofits, despite their existence in the corporate sector for years. These jobs most likely are bundled together to include Web site design, programming, blogs, donation databases, and more.

In most nonprofit organizations, the executive director and the director of development are both very public faces. Because of that, the emphasis on communications functions has lagged behind that in the for-profit sector. Even in nonprofits without a director of communications, there may be several of these other subfunctions. Where there is no director of communications, they may report to the director of development or a director of external relations.

The Administrative, Financial, and Operations Team

Given that nonprofits tend to lag far behind their for-profit counterparts in structures and systems, it probably won't surprise you to know that many nonprofits lump administrative, financial, and operations functions together in one or just a few individuals. This is where the attraction of the nonprofit sector to generalists is the strongest. While no one expects that the accountant will know how to disperse employee benefits, nonprofits simply may have one person overseeing the functions of several part-time staffers or consultants who fill these needs.

That all being said, larger nonprofits have begun investing more and more in their infrastructure, and the result has been a more professionalized view of the administrative, financial, and operations functions of their organizations. Career changers will find that, despite a few new compliance rules to learn, their most natural transition happens in the following functions:

- *Accounting and financial.* The CPA or bookkeeper on board—and yes, these jobs do sometimes fall into a bookkeeper's hands in a smaller nonprofit—might handle all grant disbursement, accounts payable and accounts receivable tasks, overall responsibility for profit and loss, and the annual audit.
- *Operations.* Those who oversee operations can be anything from office managers—ensuring that supplies are always in stock—to facilitators of strategic planning. When nonprofits look to relocate offices, implement organizational policies and procedures, and streamline functions, they turn to the operations people.
- *Legal/general counsel.* Few nonprofits are large enough to have an in-house lawyer. Those who do house them in the office of the general counsel.
- *Human resources/staffing.* Depending on the size of the nonprofit or the amount of hiring it does each year, nonprofits will outsource or bring in-house a human resources and/or recruiting function. Larger nonprofits with national offices and local affiliates tend to house human resources in central locations. More forward-thinking nonprofits place professional training and development in these functions as well. However, you'll be surprised at how many job postings list the executive director as the recipient of all résumés.
- *Executive assistance.* Anyone in the secretarial pool or working as an executive assistant may report directly to his or her manager or may be part of an overall customer service team. Because of the nature of nonprofits, even some of the most senior players may find themselves changing the toner on the copier from time to time.
- *Information technology.* Like online functions, nonprofits more and more are bringing IT experts in-house, an acknowledgment that their work is becoming increasingly data and technology driven. The crossover of skills in this area is clear, although corporate transitioners may be shocked at the rudimentary technology they discover on their nonprofit desk.

The Hierarchy of Nonprofit Jobs

Titles in the nonprofit sector differ from titles in the for-profit sector. Below, from most senior to least senior, is a sample hierarchy of titles:

- Executive director, president, chief executive officer (often interchangeable)
- Deputy director, associate director, vice president, chief professional officer (often interchangeable)
- Senior director or senior officer
- Director or officer
- Manager
- Coordinator
- Associate
- Assistant

Remember, in the nonprofit sector, raises and bonuses are harder to come by. As a result, nonprofits freely inflate titles. Beware the nonprofit where a director only needs three to five years of experience—unless, of course, you have four.

Consulting Services

Tens of thousands of people make their living consulting to the nonprofit sector, as a nonprofit or for-profit themselves, either individually or within a larger firm, in one or more of the capacities outlined above. In fact, many career changers find themselves consulting either as a volunteer or in a paid capacity during their job search; some find themselves so successful that they forget about the job search altogether and remain a consultant as long as the pipeline of work remains full.

As with anything, there are positives and negatives to being an independent consultant in the nonprofit sector. On the downside, consulting can be an isolating experience and, at times, a frustrating one. Consultants often complain that they not only miss the water cooler banter of the office environment but that they hardly ever get to see their work product implemented and, therefore, don't get to share in the celebration or reflection. On the other hand, individual consultants may set their own hours, choose their own clients, and offer only the services they enjoy providing.

Examples of For-Profit and Nonprofit Consulting Firms

Corporate transitioners looking to move into more traditional consulting within the nonprofit space should look at the various for-profit and nonprofit consulting firms springing up around the country. Here are some examples on the for-profit side, although certainly many assignments are done at cost, heavily discounted, or even pro bono:

- *McKinsey and Company's Nonprofit Practice.* Using consultants from across its industry practices, McKinsey's nonprofit clients experience the prototypical McKinsey approach but at reduced fees. McKinsey chooses its clients based on potential impact. It makes fee decisions based on ability to pay, yet it feels that paying something increases client commitment to the effort.
- *Isaacson, Miller.* A national executive search firm, Isaacson, Miller undertakes searches for a wide variety of organizations, including leading universities, research institutes, academic medical centers, foundations, cultural institutions, economic development organizations, human services agencies, national advocacy groups, and socially responsible businesses.
- *Accounting Management Solutions.* Based in New England, this outsourcing, recruiting, and interim financial management company brings businesslike practices to the nonprofit sector with industry-trained, experienced, short- or long-term accounting personnel who implement current best practices.

And following are some examples on the nonprofit side:

- *New Profit, Inc.* New Profit provides performance-based funding coupled with strategic resources to maximize the social impact and sustainability of other nonprofit organizations.
- *Commongood Careers.* This search firm connects highly skilled, passionate individuals to organizations that are dedicated to creating positive social change.
- *The Bridgespan Group.* Created by Bain and Company, this consulting group applies leading-edge management strategies, tools, and talent to help other nonprofits and foundations achieve greater social impact.

Typical Services Offered by Nonprofit Consultants

Administrative, financial, and operations:

- Accounting, bookkeeping, or other back-office services
- Insurance and risk management
- Online functions
- Software and Web development
- Information systems management
- Fund management
- Endowment management
- Financial management
- Operations management

Executive-level support:

- Coaching and mentoring
- Peer learning
- Executive transition
- Change management
- Temporary staffing (e.g., interim directors)

Fundraising:

- Annual campaigns
- Event planning
- Grant writing
- Fund development
- Strategic development planning

(continued next page)

Communications:

- Communications, branding, or graphic design
- Publications
- Writing and editing
- Public relations and marketing

Board development and support:

- Retreat planning and facilitation
- Board and volunteer placement
- Board development

Organizational development:

- Cross-cultural awareness and diversity training
- Capacity building
- Executive search
- Training, workshops, and seminars
- Group facilitation
- Mediation
- Organizational development and assessment

Program support:

- Survey research
- Research
- Evaluation and assessment

Becoming a Consultant to the Nonprofit Sector

Consulting positions within the nonprofit sector, either through a for-profit or nonprofit business model, are attractive to former consultants, project managers, or strategists in the for-profit sector. Experience with a nonprofit as a board member or through a previous client relationship is a must, because coming to the sector cold with only business expertise provides a limited perspective. That said, many for-profit consultants have had at least some exposure to the nonprofit sector through their firm's pro bono work.

DAVID ORLINOFF   SELF-EMPLOYED CONSULTANT, CONCORD FINANCIAL ORGANIZATION, CONCORD, MASSACHUSETTS

"I quit my job as the chief financial officer of a $50 million business at 6:00 P.M. on a Friday night," explains David, "and, according to my wife, it was the first time in three months that I came home standing up straight." Having spent ten years in senior corporate financial positions, David suddenly found himself without work. "As I started thinking about what to do next, I came upon the idea of becoming a 'CFO for hire,' or as one of my friends called it, an RFO, a roving financial officer." With a background in technology, software, and manufacturing, David sought out only corporate clients.

In the spring of 1990, after three years of consulting, David's biggest client hired a permanent financial officer, and for the first time in two years, David opened up the help-wanted section of the newspaper looking for potential consulting opportunities. He saw an ad for Combined Jewish Philanthropies (CJP) and set out to sell himself as a consultant. On meeting CJP's president, he learned that only a full-time job was available, and he decided to accept it when it was offered.

"I had been there less than a month when I realized that the nonprofit world is where I belong," explains David. "There was an understanding of values that went beyond financial incentives." When David found himself at the top of his profession in terms of status and compensation, he headed back into consulting. "In 1996, I hung out my shingle again as a consultant, but this time saying, 'I am an expert in nonprofit management, having worked at one.' Luckily, this strategy worked."

As a consultant, how does David remain connected to the missions of his clients?

"There is a cliché in business that everybody is in sales," explains David, "but in nonprofits, everyone is in fundraising." Regardless of their connection or particular professional specialty, David believes that everyone must act as a representative of the mission of their nonprofit. Further, David understands that a nonprofit's program and fundraising can succeed only if they are intimately intertwined with smart financial management. "The finance staff needs to approach the program and fundraising staff as their customers," he explains. "Internal customer service is essential: it's not that the customer is always right, but the customer at least deserves an explanation."

Why did David go into consulting, and how did he build his practice?

"Consulting gives me the best opportunity to combine my experience and interest in finding new challenges for the benefit of mission-driven organizations." His three dozen clients over the past ten years have ranged from very small community development organizations to larger nonprofits like Oxfam America and the Boston Ballet. Referrals come from business contacts such as lawyers, bankers, and accountants and from satisfied clients. Often David arrives at a nonprofit on short notice to replace a CFO who has left, whether voluntarily or not. "Usually I'm not competing for an engagement directly with another potential consultant," David explains, "Rather, I'm competing with the possibility that the organization will do nothing until it hires a permanent new CFO."

What has made David successful as a consultant?

David combines financial management acumen with the sensibilities of community, mission, and values. "I have learned that nonprofit managers and directors seem to respond to my ability to explain to them in their own vocabulary what they need to know about my area of expertise," he explains. Further, he has truly internalized the structural differences that go beyond the legal form of organization or the bottom line of the organization. "In a nonprofit, since we know that no one owns it, you have to really be sensitive to all of the stakeholders."

David's Key Lessons Learned:

■ "People looking to transition from industry to nonprofit often act as though their experience automatically qualifies them to work for any nonprofit of their choice. I tell them, 'If you are looking for a job in the nonprofit world, don't start off by saying you want to give something back. If you are looking to give something back, write a check. Instead, approach your target nonprofit by telling them why they need you, not why you need them.'"

■ "It is almost always harder to manage in the nonprofit sector because of limitations on resources and the multiple accountabilities. But if you have a tolerance for ambiguity— which a lot of financial people don't have— you'll find managing in the nonprofit sector much more gratifying than managing in the for-profit sector."

■ "If you want to go into consulting, you really need to believe in it. Otherwise, you are just a person in between jobs, and you and the world will see you that way. For me, the watershed, psychologically validating event was the first time I had two clients at the same time."

Many training programs are available for those interested in impacting the nonprofit sector through a consulting approach. The Institute for Nonprofit Consulting, run by CompassPoint for the past eight years, is a three-day training program. It is designed specifically to help nonprofit consultants establish a framework and strengthen their skills in an approach called client-centered consulting. Third Sector New England presents its annual Nonprofit Workout conference, complete with training sessions for nonprofit consultants. In addition, most state nonprofit associations provide training calendars for both nonprofit managers and consultants alike; attending these trainings enables you to register in their database as a consultant available for hire.

Opening Your Consulting Practice Doors

Once you've established yourself as a consultant to the nonprofit sector, you can register your practice at these sites, to name but a few:

- Idealist.org (*www.idealist.org*)
- Management Consulting Services (*www.managementconsultingservices.org*)
- Executive Service Corps Affiliate Network (*www.escus.org*)
- CharityChannel (*www.charitychannel.com*)

WHICH NONPROFIT IS RIGHT FOR YOU?

Now that you have given some thought to what type of approach you would like your nonprofit work to take—direct service, advocacy, or support—and the type of cause to which you would like to dedicate your work, let's add one more layer to the decision-making process. In addition to choosing the direction of the work and the mission that interests you, consider the environment in which you want to work. For most career changers, the environment and kind of work are as important, if not more so, in guiding eventual success or failure than passion for the nonprofit's particular mission.

Like the corporate world, the nonprofit sector is made up of many different types of nonprofits. Like your corporate job, the personality of your employer or workplace supported your successes or created challenges. The nonprofit sector will be the same. Your job search will be shorter, and your tenure on the job will be more enjoyable, if you determine early on which type of nonprofit is the right match for you.

Nonprofits have personalities all their own. Choosing the right kind of nonprofit matters. Depending on your corporate experience, you may be more comfortable in a large organization with built-in practices and administrative support rather than a small, grassroots nonprofit where each employee is chief, cook, and bottle washer. Or if your experience has been in smaller environments where each person manages his or her own portfolio and reaps the rewards of his or her own success, you may enjoy the scrappiness of a bootstrapping, community-based, grassroots nonprofit, where existence is hand to mouth but big changes seem up-close and personal. Nonprofit start-ups are a whole other animal, resembling the gambles of the for-profit sector start-up but with an entirely different payoff.

Your Nonprofit Personality Match

If you need an environment that gives support and stability, you may wish to choose a nonprofit that has been around for many years. If you thrive on chaos and change, you might like an organization that is just getting started, where funding is uncertain and impact is untested, or one that follows a political calendar, with a rebirth each new campaign season. You may be more contemplative and thoughtful, so an academic or foundation environment might suit you best. But if pondering ideas endlessly might make you crazy, a more nimble, fast-acting organization might be the one for you.

Finally, if you are making this transition to be closer to the action, and that action might be described as the hands-on helping of people, then you should choose a grass-roots-based nonprofit. If you want to get into the big meetings with decision makers, you might be better served by looking for a job in a smaller, flatter organization.

Refer to Table 3.1 to get a better grasp of the type of nonprofit for which you are suited. An *x* signifies that you are likely to find a given characteristic in the type of organization listed above.

The Nonprofit Organization's Life Cycle

As in business, nonprofit organizations have a life cycle. They can either just be starting out (which may or may not be founder driven), transitioning to their mezzanine level, experiencing radical growth, have set a steady and stable course, or be in their decline. Each of these phases brings a different challenge.

Nonprofits enter and exit each of these phases more often because of crises than from planning. Most nonprofits are so focused on fulfilling their mission and helping their constituents that they pay precious little attention to their own governance and structure. Making matters more complicated is the abundance of managers and leaders in the sector who either don't value or don't understand the importance of internal systems building. Then there's the pesky problem of getting funders to pay for things

Table 3.1 Characteristics of Nonprofits

	Founder-driven	Start-up	In Transition	Growth-oriented	Strong and Stable	Grassroots
Decision-making Style						
I enjoy contemplative environments where ideas are vetted thoroughly before decisions are made.			x	x	x	x
I prefer decisions to be made quickly, sometimes with gut-level reactions.		x	x	x		
I like to make decisions on my own.	x	x	x	x		
I seek input from large groups of people before making a final choice.	x			x	x	x
I do not enjoy making decisions and am happiest following others' leads.	x				x	
Pace of the Workplace						
I enjoy an office environment where people stop to chat.	x		x		x	x
I would rather get my work done quickly than stand around and waste time.	x	x	x	x		
Support Network						
I enjoy multitasking, taking on multiple projects, and working autonomously.		x	x			x
I need the support of others around me to operate at the highest level.	x			x	x	
Structure						
I work best in a structured environment where the decision-making methods are clear.				x	x	x
I enjoy a more free-form atmosphere where decisions are made by whomever is in the room at the time.	x	x	x			x

like long-range strategic planning, even when the nonprofits know it makes sense. All of that being said, many nonprofits get it, do it, and thrive because of it. As you might imagine, these nonprofits will likely be more inviting to those with business résumés.

Start-Up

Most nonprofit start-ups are just that: nonprofits that are just starting up. But don't be fooled into thinking that only young nonprofits are in start-up mode. Nonprofits are forced to reinvent themselves every so often, either in response to world affairs, donor whims, market forces, or major personnel changes. At these times and, of course, when they are just starting out, they may find themselves taking on the characteristics of a nonprofit in start-up mode.

Start-up nonprofits look similar to start-up for-profits. Money is uncertain, the vision is ambitious, and failure is not an option. Donors must be placated about the probability of success, often without a track record as evidence of potential accomplishment. The board may or may not be a rubber-stamping board, gathered together quickly to submit IRS paperwork. Staff have to work in an "all hands on deck" capacity, often leading to a mismatch of resources and energies.

Still, start-ups happen every day and often produce some of the most exciting and innovative work going on in the nonprofit sector. The Charles Schwab Foundation provides social entrepreneur awards, as does *Fast Company Magazine*, in partnership with the Monitor Group, to some of these innovators. Those with corporate backgrounds are well suited to these start-ups, because the pace is normally quicker than entrenched organizations and the opportunity to create systems and structure from the group up exists in spades.

In Transition

At a certain point in every nonprofit start-up, the staff, board, and other stakeholders realize that explosive start-up growth can only be managed for so long. Pairing continued growth with the continued execution of high-quality service is difficult at best. Nonprofits in transition are no longer adding new locations, for example, and are instead starting to serve more people in a specified area or provide better quality or additional services to existing numbers.

Nonprofits in transition often find themselves with a leadership change, whether voluntary or forced. The dynamism and charisma of a founder or of a founding executive director is not necessarily part of the skill set needed to establish the organization in known territory. Few founders relish spending their time examining systems and structures to make sure that their organization can withstand any looming difficulties. Most would rather spend their time acting as an ambassador for their great idea, an advocate on behalf of the cause they serve, or as a champion raising money on its behalf. In truth, such activities are the highest and best use of their time, so having them stick around as an executive director while their organization is in transition is detrimental to everything they have built.

Nonprofits in transition tend to be three to seven years past their start-up mode. They are often on their second or even third executive director, and they have begun adding senior staff positions, like operations, finance, or administration directors. They may likely also be adding development as a full-time role for the first time, because the outgoing founder did all that personally. Great opportunities exist for corporate career changers in these organizations, as long as you don't try to transition the organization too quickly.

Growth-Oriented

Growth-oriented nonprofits are either looking to add more cities, deepen their impact, or improve their quality. They are being pushed by their funders or by their business plan, if they have one, to grow larger. They have likely gotten a larger grant to do more or similar work in a new location or have identified a hole in the services provided to their targeted population and are seeking to fill it.

Often, nonprofits moving from start-up through transition into growth mode do not have the systems and structure in place to support them at this larger level. In some cases, the existing systems and structures simply can't handle larger demands. Change can and should be made in these nonprofits, but even in growth mode, culture shift takes time.

Growth-oriented nonprofits must be careful about "mission drift," which ails nonprofits that seek to shift their work ever so slightly, at first, to satisfy donors or market whims. Mission drift is akin to moving away from your core business to satisfy a customer. Doing it once might be permissible, but with each additional shift, the nonprofit risks losing itself in the process.

Nonprofits experiencing new growth, site expansion, or service extension are likely good places for corporate career changers. Opportunities exist for entrepreneurial sorts to start up a new nonprofit in a new city, thus combining the start-up energy of a new site with the established playbook of the national office. Further, growth opportunities enable nonprofits to look at how they accomplish their business, allowing for the insertion of best practices from the corporate world where appropriate.

Steady and Stable

Many nonprofits are in a steady and stable mode and remain there for years. Just as nonprofits with histories spanning a hundred years may suddenly find themselves in start-up or transition mode, young nonprofits may, too, find themselves charting a steady and stable course. Steady and stable nonprofits know what they do, and they do it well. They are more interested in perfecting their work and, possibly, sharing best practices among the field or influencing policy than in pursuing explosive growth. Nonprofits like these have experienced start-up and sometimes transition phases and have mastered their work in one or two cities. Then, 10 to 15 years later, they might suddenly find themselves expanding to 10 or 15 cities at once.

Steady and stable nonprofits spend time perfecting their external work but also looking at internal systems and procedures. The lack of crisis-mode thinking gives them an opportunity to sit back and reflect. Some nonprofits take advantage of this; many do not.

Corporate career changers would be wise to ask hard questions in the interviews and in their networking about how serious the nonprofit is about "fixing what some on staff might think isn't broken." They might also be forewarned that the pace of these organizations will likely be the slowest in the nonprofit sector, and the culture might be the hardest into which a new approach, person, or business background can integrate itself.

In Decline

Nonprofits in decline have either been steady and stable too long, while the market has passed them by, or they got the market wrong and their startup or growth was a colossal failure. It's not hard to spot a nonprofit in decline. They may have board members who have been around for more than ten years; after five or six, most board members are tapped out of fundraising contacts and intellectual contributions and should move on. They may have a stagnant, nondiversified funding base or, worse yet, a shrinking one. As with any business, reliance on one or two big customers— in the nonprofit sector, donors—is dangerous. For example, an organization may be relying on government funding when a change in the state legislature can easily cut funding by three quarters.

Nonprofits in decline don't necessarily fail. Some get revitalized and enter into start-up or growth mode again. Others must go through a founder transition or a leadership change. Some get a random act of media, the much coveted notice by Oprah or a feature on the local news, that sparks new interest and new funding. As you would size up the prospects of any company for whom you would work, do the same with the nonprofits that interest you. Ask to see a budget. Read the annual report. Determine if there is new thinking, new blood, and new energy or if the nonprofit will be relying chiefly on you to bring those qualities to the table.

A Note on Founder-Run Organizations

Founder-run organizations are an animal all to themselves. Before we get too far, let's make one thing clear: founders are the people who start an organization but they may also be the ones who get it through a major opportunity, crisis, or collapse. They did not necessarily give birth to the organization, just the organization as you know it today. In response to their energy, the organization becomes a cult of personality, where the staff and board are all working to please the leader regardless of whether directives fall in line with the business plan. (For the rest of this section, we will refer to these leaders as "founders.")

Founders have specific character traits. They are charismatic and dynamic; they can talk almost anyone into doing or giving almost anything. They are singularly focused on the mission at hand but wear blinders against anything that might get in their way. Through sheer willpower alone, they often seem to trample roadblocks. They may surround themselves with sycophantic true believers unlikely to play devil's advocate or point out landmines. They are energetic and exuberant, and no one will work harder for a cause than they will.

Founders can be enormously exciting to work for, especially when they are in their element. Founders in start-ups or growth-oriented nonprofits can leap light years ahead of where a more staid manager might take an organization. However, founder types in nonprofits in transition, at a steady and stable point, or in decline can be phenomenally destructive. As in the for-profit sector, the nonprofit sector recognizes "founder's syndrome," even if the founder doesn't. No founder wants to stay past their prime, but most simply don't see that it has passed. In fact, staff and board are often complicit in founder's syndrome, continuing to remain supportive in public even if they have begun snickering in private.

Beware the founder who is still "hiring" board members or participating in all staffing decisions, prizes loyalty above skills, personally holds all close donor relationships, or who seems dismissive of opportunities to change. Make sure to ask about a founder's exit strategy; most won't have one. Any founder who does is worth entertaining as your next boss.

When founders retire or leave, many organizations go into a tailspin. A personality crisis arises, and a leadership vacuum emerges. Corporate career changers can get caught in this middle of a confused board and a staff fighting to retain their core nonprofit values. Corporate transitioners looking to work for a founder should look to organizations with business savvy and a history of hiring those with for-profit experience. Doing so will ensure that they aren't left holding the bag when the executive office empties out.

Nonprofit Language Clues

Which words does a nonprofit use to describe itself? Its language may give you insight into its life cycle stage.

Start-up:

- Entrepreneurial
- Adept and agile
- Angel investors

Growth-oriented:

- Scalable program model
- Strategic partnerships
- National model

In transition:

- Reexamination in progress
- Internal assessment and evaluation
- Rebuilding and renewing

Steady and stable:

- Proven program model
- Continuing excellence

In decline:

- Increased turnover
- Homogenous funding base

Founder-run:

- Singular vision
- Driving force
- Staff-driven

The life cycle stage of a nonprofit is one of the most obvious indicators of success for a sector switcher. It is also one aspect of your job search that you can easily control. Forecast your success by discerning the nonprofit's life cycle stage before it assigns you a desk and prints your business cards. Pay careful attention to the clues found in the job description, the annual report, grant applications, or the interviewing style of your future coworkers. If they are saying one thing but acting otherwise, you may have found an organization not quite ready for change. Conversely, if all signs point to progress, proceed knowing that this nonprofit has likely accepted and embraced its future.

AN ALTERNATIVE: SOCIALLY RESPONSIBLE BUSINESSES

For some, transition is motivated by an overwhelming urge to do good but does not necessarily come with a temperament or skill set that works well in the nonprofit sector. Rest assured that there are still plenty of ways to create social impact, even without compromising your personal economic value or your operating environment comfort level. Consider the socially responsible business as a promising alternative.

Socially responsible businesses give substantial consideration not just to their economic value but to their social value as well. This category does not include corporations that invest large chunks of profits into nonprofits bearing their name; while a noble and much-needed endeavor, the Ronald McDonald House does not alone make McDonald's into a socially responsible business. Rather, the "double bottom line," doing what is right even if it means shaving off some profits, makes for corporate social responsibility.

Often, the social value provides great public relations fodder for the business, thus raising the economic value in turn. In addition to the public relations benefit, companies with socially responsible charters also find that they are better able to retain staff, align management and board with shareholders, and create brand loyalty for reasons above and beyond product quality. Some socially responsible businesses were founded on social value principles, while others have recently internalized corporate social responsibility as part of their mission and vision. Prospective sector switchers should see socially responsibly companies as a haven for corporate minds with conscientious hearts.

Socially Responsible Businesses

There are many socially responsible businesses. Here are just a few examples.

Consumer goods:

- Eileen Fisher
- Procter & Gamble
- The Body Shop

Food:

- Ben & Jerry's
- Newman's Own
- Stonyfield Farms

Personal investing:

- The Calvert Group
- Northstar Asset Management
- Putnam Investments

Service-providing:

- Bright Horizons Family Solutions
- United Parcel Service
- Working Assets

For more companies like these, check out Business for Social Responsibility (*www.bsr.org*) and Social Venture Network (*www.svn.org*).

CONCLUSION

For every corporate transitioner, there is a job in the nonprofit sector. Finding it demands a careful review of your priorities and passions, the approach you'd like to take in advancing your chosen cause, and the skills and experience you bring to bear. These past two chapters have taken you through the factors that go into these decisions. Once you have determined where in the sector you want to be, it is important to educate yourself about the special considerations that will face you in your transition. Let's get to those now.

CHAPTER 4

Special Considerations for Career Changers

The nonprofit sector of today is home to a great variety of organizations; running the gamut from social workers to social entrepreneurs, there is a place in the nonprofit sector for everyone. But what about you, the corporate transitioner? Where do you belong? What about the myths you've heard as you've told friends about your job search? What do you need to know, and how can you combat the stereotypes you will face? And, finally, the $64,000 question: what will it mean, financially, for you to make this move?

This chapter will discuss and dismiss ten widely held myths about the nonprofit sector. While one of those myths—that nonprofit employees are paid starvation wages—is blatantly false, there is a significant compensation gap. This chapter will help you consider the financial implications of your new career. We'll also discuss the common stereotypes that may be assigned to you, your career path, and your personal motivations and ways you can dispel them. Last, we'll review different personalities of nonprofits to determine which type is right for you and your corporate background, pointing out those types of nonprofits that make for an easier career change.

TEN MYTHS ABOUT WORKING IN THE NONPROFIT SECTOR

Myths about nonprofits abound. You may have heard a few from your friends and colleagues as you've told them about your nonprofit search:

- "You've turned into a do-gooder."
- "You've gone soft."
- "You will decimate your savings account."
- "If you want to work less, you should just retire."

In fact, none of these statements could be further from the truth. Every day, people come to work in the nonprofit sector because they have decided to do something bigger than themselves, to set in motion events that will solve a problem plaguing society, or to answer a call that they have felt inside for some time. Others come to the sector because they are looking for a more flexible schedule, because they have made their money and want to give back, or because they are looking for an entirely new challenge. Table 4.1 lays out the advantages—and disadvantages—of transitioning to the nonprofit sector.

Like the variety of people looking to join the nonprofit sector, the sector itself is full of differences. Yet some myths persist about the sector as a whole.

Myth #1: You Have to Starve to Work in the Nonprofit Sector

The fattest line on most nonprofits' budgets is payroll and benefits, yet nonprofit organizations remain infamous for underpaying talent. There is no disputing the fact that nonprofits generally pay far less than their for-profit counterparts for the same level of talent. This is not something nonprofits choose to do; it is something they are forced to do. Often, their funders demand it, expecting that the vast majority of any donation will address service needs in the field, not overhead at the home office.

The most difficult funding a nonprofit can secure is funding for general operating costs, including salaries. Funders want to say that their money went to hepatitis vaccinations for 600 infants, books for 100 students, or meals delivered to 50 elderly shut-ins. No one wants to boast to their friends or their board of directors that they gave $50,000 to the Boys and Girls Clubs of Atlanta to pay half the salary of one-third of the IT department. It's not sexy, although without that half salary for a third of the IT department, not one child in Atlanta would get the mentoring services that those "sexier" donations fund. At the end of the day, dollars are dollars to a nonprofit regardless of how they are earmarked; the earmarking just makes for harder accounting, which, ironically, costs the nonprofits more general operating dollars in the end.

Table 4.1 Advantages and Disadvantages for Transitioners

Advantages	Disadvantages
Your work will be rewarding. You will become rich in spirit, feeling purposeful in every action, and able to point to change made as a result.	You may not be rewarded as highly for your work. You are unlikely to become rich in dollars. While the nonprofit sector has become more competitive, salaries still lag behind those offered in the for-profit sector.
You will be asked to take on responsibility for a broad portfolio of work and will amaze yourself while doing what you thought you could never accomplish.	You will be asked to do more with less training and fewer resources and will have to learn along the way.
You will be able to advance your career easily, because nonprofits often have opportunities to capture or leadership vacuums to fill.	Your career advancement may not come in a strategic, linear fashion, nor will it come with training for the next level of work.
Opportunities to move within the sector abound, and increases in responsibility, pay, and authority can come quickly.	Smaller nonprofits often have opportunity ceilings when long-standing leadership has no plans to move on. Advancement often comes by moving into larger organizations.
The work environment will be positive, filled with people who share with you a higher calling around a specific mission area.	A singular focus on a mission area can sometimes hamper progress toward a goal.
Greater acceptance of and flexibility around lifestyle changes allow those with nontraditional availability to contribute meaningfully.	Bending too far to accommodate some staff can overextend others, leading to frustration and burnout.
Everyone gets a vote. By listening to opinions from a large and diverse group of stakeholders, nonprofits often make unexpected and wiser choices.	Everyone gets a vote. Meetings can sometimes be endless, opinions may be valued disproportionately to their merit, and staff can get disheartened.

However, while it is true that most nonprofits are looking for $300,000 of talent for only $100,000 a year, nonprofit salaries are becoming more and more competitive. Funders have become more sophisticated, and some have begun to use a venture philanthropy approach, rewarding high-functioning nonprofits with general (i.e., unrestricted) funds for purposes such as attracting great talent. Such funding has allowed nonprofits to pay more competitive wages for staff with a broader set of skills, like you and your fellow corporate career changers.

In addition, some nonprofits pay better than others. Organizations fighting for civil rights, human rights, women's rights, or animal rights tend to pay toward the lower end of the spectrum. In fact, it's not uncommon to find nonprofits that fight against poverty wages paying their own employees impossibly low salaries. Smaller organizations that have been run by the same person for long periods of time are less likely to have faced a competitive analysis of their wages. As such, they may not be paying current market value for their people. Conversely, nonprofits with high staff turnover have spent a great deal of time and effort negotiating job offers and better understand the wages they need to pay. Research institutions, colleges and universities, and foundations, for example, tend to pay toward the top of the nonprofit sector and also have more comprehensive benefits packages.

Myth #2: Working in the Nonprofit Sector Will Deplete Your Retirement

Years ago, nonprofits were lucky to be able to pay the wages of their employees. Nowadays, nonprofits know that to hire and retain excellent staff, they must offer competitive benefits packages as well. Nonprofit employees have come to expect retirement contributions, relocation reimbursement, flexible work schedules, health and dental insurance, life and disability insurance, and generous vacation plans. Some nonprofits even extend these benefits to same-sex or other domestic partners.

Nonprofits have—from both necessity and desire—become more creative in the benefits they offer. Instead of offering high salaries, some nonprofits offer inflated titles. You can't discount the feelings of a 30-year-old who is becoming senior vice president of operations after five long years as an anonymous staff associate in a large corporation. Some nonprofits have gone further, offering additional vacation time or a laptop to take home, knowing that employees are there because they care deeply about the work and are, frankly, not likely to take the additional vacation or are likely to put in time on nights and weekends. Finally, some nonprofits have become quite inventive, allowing their staffs to bring their pets to work or using some of their in-kind donations, like theatre tickets, restaurant gift certificates, or gym memberships, as performance rewards for high-achieving staff.

Finally, nonprofit work is steeped in nonmonetary benefits as well. Studies have shown that nonprofit workers have the healthiest morale compared to those in the government or private sectors. They have the easiest time connecting their day-to-day tasks with the overall mission of the organization and, thus, their specific contribution to society. Further, they feel that they have a greater opportunity to learn new skills, take on larger levels of responsibility, and be respected by society at large for their contributions to the world.

Nonprofit Salaries

In 2005, the leadership of some of the nation's largest nonprofits made salaries that, while likely far below what they would have made in the for-profit sector, were still quite attractive. According to the *Chronicle of Philanthropy's* annual salary survey, following are the annual salaries for 2005:

President	John F. Kennedy Center for Performing Arts	Washington, D.C.	$1,029,691
President	J. Paul Getty Trust	Los Angeles, California	$962,526
Surgeon-in-chief, pediatric surgery	Children's Hospital Medical Center	Cincinnati, Ohio	$823,675
President	Yale University	New Haven, Connecticut	$618,822
Executive director, global health	Bill and Melinda Gates Foundation	Seattle, Washington	$488,717
President	United Negro College Fund	Fairfax, Virginia	$375,288
Chief operating officer	Public Broadcasting System	Alexandria, Virginia	$367,715
Executive vice president	Ducks Unlimited	Memphis, Tennessee	$326,908
Chief legal officer	Special Olympics	Washington, D.C.	$225,000

Myth #3: Money Is Evil

If nonprofits pay living wages and decent benefits, then surely nonprofit employees must feel some guilt about earning money, right? Wrong! Money is not considered an evil in the nonprofit sector. In fact, nonprofits love money just like for-profits; it's just that they get the money as a reward for different achievements and from different sources. Long gone are the times when people in nonprofits apologized for coming from money, making money, or enjoying the spoils of having money. Still, a connection to the mission of a nonprofit is more important than a connection to money. In other words, you will be judged by your nonprofit peers more closely by what is in your heart than what is in your wallet.

Nonprofits are becoming increasingly sophisticated about their approach toward money. Not only do nonprofits embrace those with money as donors—not much has changed on that front—but they now embrace those who have money as employees as well. Nonprofits are increasingly adding revenue-generating projects to their portfolio of activities and expecting higher rates of return on investment of time, energy, money, and other resources. Doing so means that those from the for-profit sector are more and more attractive to nonprofits going forward.

Myth #4: All Nonprofit Employees Are Saints

One of the biggest fallacies spun by those in the for-profit sector about people in the nonprofit sector is that everyone in the sector is a good-doing do-gooder. Just because people work for good doesn't always make them good people. The same ladder climbing, social scheming, and personal selfishness exists in the sector of forgiveness and grace as it does everywhere else in the world. Foibles and quirks are endemic to human nature, regardless of the sector. While a nonprofit might hold its weekly staff meeting seated in a circle, you are unlikely to find a campfire in the center or hand-holding revelers breaking out in choruses of "Kumbayah."

Overgeneralizing the nonprofit sector into a place where idealists earn poverty wages to fight injustices for every member of society, changing the world one hot lunch at a time, or protecting every living creature no matter the cost is simply that, an overgeneralization. Certainly those people exist, and in much larger numbers in the nonprofit sector than anywhere else, but they aren't the dominant force. Nonprofit sector employees are just like you: focused on working toward a particular goal with both career advancement and competitive salaries in mind. It's just that the goal is different: instead of trying to get themselves a bigger slice of the pie, they are trying to make the pie bigger for all.

Myth #5: Nonprofits Are Lucky to Employ Whomever They Can Find

Many for-profit career changers believe that the passion they hold for the nonprofit's cause is enough to make them an attractive candidate for employment. The truth is that passion helps, but it isn't the whole picture. Consider that nonprofits have limited amounts of money for hiring and retaining staff, and remember that poor hiring choices cost the nonprofit more money than hiring no one at all. Knowing this, nonprofits can and will be picky about whom they choose to employ.

Nonprofits will not hire you if you don't hold the requisite skills and experience for you to hit the ball out of the park as you walk in the door. That being said, you'll also need the passion for the cause or a track record of volunteering for some mission-driven organization. Even if you haven't volunteered for a particular cause, a history of volunteering anywhere shows a side of you that is attractive to nonprofits.

YUTAKA TAMURA FOUNDER AND EXECUTIVE DIRECTOR, EXCEL ACADEMY CHARTER SCHOOL, BOSTON, MASSACHUSETTS

Yutaka was on the traditional consulting track. He had completed a corporate internship during his undergraduate years and, upon graduating, had landed a job at a prestigious firm in Boston. Yet after fighting to achieve his quantitative bearings and then being promoted twice in two years for his exceptional work, he found himself unhappy. "I finally achieved the level of basic technical skills needed to no longer be the person slaving away at the computer over data analysis," he says, "but I didn't feel personally connected to the work."

The education sector was always an interest of Yutaka's, so he began looking into positions in education both in the nonprofit and the for-profit sectors. "Nonprofit or for-profit, it didn't matter to me," he says, "Good practice is good practice wherever you are." Yutaka took a couple of positions with growing for-profit companies that provided educational services to youth, always with the plan to go to business school. His ultimate goal was to build an educational organization of his own. With his business school acceptance in hand and his deposit paid for Harvard for the fall of 2000, Yutaka's road took another turn.

Why did Yutaka turn down Harvard Business School twice?

Throughout his various jobs, Yutaka was able to interact with the founders of some of the nation's leading education nonprofits and corporations. He learned from them that he needed

something he couldn't get in business school. "It was a turning point for me," he says, "to have met these entrepreneurs who were doing what I wanted to do, and finding out that either they were happy to have had operational experience or that they wished they had."

Having been accepted to Harvard Business School (HBS), Yutaka applied at the last minute to a suburban private school and was offered a job as a teacher, so he declined admission to Harvard. Soon after beginning his teaching career, he applied and was accepted again to HBS, and he also applied to the Harvard Graduate School of Education. However, when the dean of students at his private school took a sabbatical, Yutaka accepted the interim dean position and declined his Harvard acceptances once more.

When he realized that private suburban education wasn't his passion, he once again applied to HBS, but this time he didn't get in.

How did Yutaka start his charter school?

A former colleague of his, who was attending HBS at the time, told Yutaka about Building Excellent Schools, a nonprofit that was coming to campus to recruit HBS grads to join a fellowship program and start charter schools. Four years later, as a graduate of the second class of the Building Excellent Schools Fellowship Program, Yutaka now runs one of the most successful schools in Massachusetts.

How did Yutaka prepare for the financial implications of his transition into the nonprofit sector?

Yutaka had saved some money, and he moved somewhere with a lower cost of living. "My rent when I was teaching was $100 less than what I paid for my parking spot in Manhattan," he says. Psychologically, though, Yutaka was following his real passion: education. "Ultimately, we are in a capital society," he says. "If this charter school was a $2 million Internet company that was at the top of its peer group, as we are today, I would be in a position to earn great sums of money. Yet I have worked for four years, never taken a week's vacation, and stand to gain very little financially from this endeavor. On the other hand, I have the opportunity to work on behalf of low-income, urban students who otherwise might not have the ability to get a college-preparatory education and put them squarely on the path to college, enabling them to ultimately change their socioeconomic status." Clearly, intrinsic rewards outweighed extrinsic costs for Yutaka.

Yutaka's Key Lessons Learned:

- "Go study the people who are the best at doing what you want to do. Learn from their lessons."

- "If you are motivated and if you do good work, most reasonable organizations will recognize that and promote you quickly. It may be a losing proposition over the short horizon, but if you look at it through the lens of your entire lifestyle, you will find yourself much richer in the end."

- "The hard skills that you have developed in the for-profit sector are not only 110 percent transferable to the nonprofit sector, they will be critical to your success."

Myth #6: Working in Nonprofits Is Not Challenging

Ask anyone in a nonprofit if their work is easy, and they will likely laugh at you—and for good reason. Not only is the work difficult, many would argue that it is much more difficult than working in the for-profit sector. Employees in nonprofit organizations are often asked to do more with less in shorter periods of time, while considering more opinions and keeping more people happy than do their for-profit counterparts. The results of this hard work are often intangible; it's harder to measure how much closer to a cure for breast cancer one got today than, say, how many miles of PVC pipe you sold. Similarly, the goals are often unattainable; it's difficult to get up every day and end world hunger or clean the planet's oceans. Simply put, the need never ends, so the job never ends.

If you are looking to do a little good work, take a little time to relax and feel as though you are making a contribution to society; make your next vacation an "alternate vacation," one that you spend contributing your time in service to a cause about which you care deeply. Volunteer. Make a donation. Find someone and help him or her. If you are looking to create systemic change in a full-time capacity, know that the work will be hard but likely the most rewarding work you have ever done. That old Peace

Corps slogan is brilliant: working in the nonprofit sector will be "the toughest job you'll ever love."

Myth #7: Nonprofits Are All Flat, Nonhierarchical Places

Culture shock for sector switchers comes in many forms, from salary discrepancies to the lack of updated technology. The biggest culture shock, however, comes for those expecting the direct line of authority they found in the for-profit sector. Many small nonprofits are flat organizations, where the intern has as much opportunity to voice opinions and affect change as the senior vice president. In some of the older, more staid nonprofits, this can be maddening. It impedes progress, slows decision making, and reduces a nonprofit's ability to affect change. It's a heck of a good strategy for increasing staff morale at the lowest levels, though, where staff are paid next to nothing and the work can be tedious.

However, there is no one organizational chart for all nonprofits. Some are more hierarchical than others. In today's nonprofit world, it is easier to find nonprofits that have adopted the latest in management techniques. In fact, as more and more *Fortune* 500 executives are leaving the for-profit sector for new, fulfilling careers in the nonprofit sector, they are taking their expertise with them and molding their management practices to drive success in the nonprofit sector. Career changers who choose the right nonprofits can find not only fulfilling work environments with familiar structures but also opportunities to create real change in issues close to their heart.

Myth #8: Nonprofit Jobs Are Secure

Some nonprofits—the United Way, Kiwanis International, and the Girl Scouts, just to name a few—have been around for ages. These community stalwarts are driven by volunteers and have likely been run by just a handful of leaders during their long existence. Most jobs in the nonprofit sector, though, can be insecure and depend highly on the whim of a funder or two. Remember that just because the issue is well funded now doesn't mean it will always be.

Take, for example, nonprofits that focus on issues related to AIDS/HIV. It was all the rage to fund AIDS research in the 1980s and 1990s; everyone was looking for a cure. However, once scientists came up with drug cocktails that extended the lives of those living with HIV and AIDS, the river of funding slowed to a trickle. AIDS nonprofits found that the demand was not for a cure, despite the fact that one has yet to be found, but for services that would increase the life expectancy and quality of those living with the disease. Cure-focused nonprofits were forced to shut down or change their missions to align with the desires of funders.

Myth #9: Nonprofit Managers Know How to Manage

Nonprofits can't offer the same professional development as their for-profit competitors. This isn't to say that nonprofits don't care about their people. They do, in fact, care deeply about their people; they just have odd ways of showing it. It's not typical in the nonprofit sector for there to be any purposeful focus placed on internal management development, successor grooming, or skills training. It is much more haphazard or sporadic than in the for-profit sector. There are two reasons for this.

First, many founding executive directors are in those roles because they were exceptionally good at the frontline, direct service work of the nonprofit sector. Someone noticed and gave them some money to expand and do more, and the next thing they knew, they were sitting on top of a ten-site, multimillion-dollar change agent that was a management catastrophe on the inside. These founders have the best of intentions but still a singular vision for the communities they serve. At the same time, they have gotten to where they are because of this vision. They are unlikely to have stopped along the way for management training or reflective thinking about building staff or grooming successors. Because of this, while they may deeply desire a well-oiled management team that employs sound business practices and effective staff development, they simply may not know how to make it a reality.

Second, resources of nonprofits are constrained. If faced with the choice of spending money on the guaranteed, quick return of more services to the field or on the uncertainty of training for a staff member who may or may not blossom and may or may not remain with the organization for the long-term, most managers would choose the former rather than the latter. Most nonprofits aren't large enough to offer a specific career path and an obvious "next step" internally, so with many staff members looking outside for their next opportunity, allocating resources to training becomes less attractive.

Nonprofit employees must take an active role in their professional development, seeking out mentors and training opportunities on their own and building a case to their management about why funds should be expended for training. The odds are that a good case will go far.

Myth #10: A Nonprofit Is a Nonprofit Is a Nonprofit

Nonprofits organizations are as different from one another as for-profit companies. Just as you would never compare Xerox to your local neighborhood copy shop, you shouldn't assume that the Girl Scouts of America is the same as Girls Scouts of Poughkeepsie or any other girls-mentoring organization. Beyond the obvious differences of mission and focus, key differences in nonprofits include size, age, outlook, business model, and bylaws.

Volunteering for a nonprofit will give you a good sense of the style of that particular organization. Volunteering for two organizations will allow you to start comparing differences. Each is like a piece of a patchwork quilt. Only once you've started to see the vast array of nonprofits can you begin to understand the beauty and complexity of the quilt as a whole.

DEALING WITH THE FINANCIAL IMPLICATIONS OF A NONPROFIT SALARY

If you are considering a move into the nonprofit sector, you have likely already accepted the fact that you will make less—perhaps a lot less—than you are currently making in your for-profit career. There is a reason they call it "for-profit" after all. Your nonprofit salary might be as little as 40 percent of your for-profit equivalent, but it doesn't have to be. Still, let's consider some ways to deal with the financial implications of your nonprofit salary.

Determine Your Readiness Factor

Are you an empty nester with the house paid off and the children out of school? Are you a single professional with only a cat to concern you? Or is college tuition for three kids looming? Has your for-profit gone public, yielding a return greater than expected? Determining your personal financial situation will allow you to decide whether you can afford to consider the nonprofit sector.

All of that being said, many for-profit employees find themselves in nonprofit job interviews because they simply cannot afford *not* to make this change. Something has happened to them, or to the world in general, that has set off a series of events leading them to feel that things must change and that they must be the one to make this change happen. For these individuals, money isn't a question.

Learn to Value the Intangibles

Nonprofit jobs come with many nonmonetary rewards. There is simply no direct correlation, as in the for-profit sector, between the salary you earn and the value you deliver to society. Don't focus on the paycheck—look around at the rest of the picture. You have saved the spotted owls. You have taught a child to read. You have reduced hunger.

Adding up the intangible benefits of working in a nonprofit will make you feel, in the words of Lou Gehrig, like "the luckiest [wo]man on the face of the Earth." This can sometimes be a difficult task, given that needs always outweigh resources, regardless of the nonprofit.

Change Your Lifestyle

If you are ready to make the move to the nonprofit sector but are not in a financial position to do so, consider scaling down your expenses and lifestyle. Perhaps the cause you hold dear is more important than those extra nights out at fancy restaurants or another designer handbag. Consider holding back any extra expenses for a few months to determine whether the sacrifice both gets you to where you need to be financially and is palatable for you in the long term. If not, you will come to resent your nonprofit's cause and its staff, souring you on the opportunity to transition later in your career, when you may have saved up enough money or emptied your nest.

Don't Settle for Less

Try to find a job that pays toward the upper end of the nonprofit spectrum. Don't settle for less money than you could comfortably afford to make. Consider the new social venture movement in the nonprofit sector or for-profit ventures of nonprofits that fund their work. Or look into socially responsible businesses as a way to make the move into the nonprofit sector in stages. Socially responsible businesses are for-profit businesses that demonstrate respect for ethical values, people, communities, and the environment. And since these businesses are for-profit entities, you might temporarily soothe your need to do better by the world while not doing too poorly by your bank account.

Rethink Your Value

An unfortunate byproduct of a market-driven economy is that we live in a society where self-value is often derived from what someone else thinks we should earn. Salary equals worthiness, right? Not so in the nonprofit sector. You need to separate your own self-value from the amount of zeroes printed on your paycheck. Agonizing over the difference in for-profit valuation and nonprofit valuation will get you nowhere. Instead, look at what you are earning compared to others performing similar tasks in the nonprofit sector. With all the talent and skills you are bringing along, you may find that you are, in fact, "paid" pretty well.

Think Ahead

Start thinking now about your cash-flow situation. When will your financial situation allow you to make this move? What do you really need to earn? What do you really want to earn? How much do you need to put away each month now to accept a lower salary later? Answering these questions will enable you to plan your nonprofit career change with increased comfort.

Remember that you still have options if your non-profit dream job comes with a less than dreamy, but still potentially palatable, salary. To make this move a reality, try to negotiate the total package, not just the annual compensation.

The Commission Fallacy

It is taboo for development professionals to earn a certain percentage of the money they raise. A better benchmark of success would be an increase in the organization's overall budget, numbers of new donors, or scale of services rendered. Ask for scheduled reviews of performance that link pay raises to specific goals met.

Tie Salary Increases to Achievements

When interviewing, ask if the job has a growth track. If it does, you may be able to accept a lower salary for six months while working toward the achievement of very specific benchmarks of success. Ask your hiring manager to write into your offer letter that you will sit down with your future boss after you have been on the job for six weeks to determine what you expect to achieve by the 6-, 12-, 18-, and 24-month anniversaries of your hire. Enlist a partnership with the nonprofit such that your earnings will rise as the nonprofit grows. Tying your salary to its overall growth shouldn't be hard for the nonprofit to imagine.

Just Say No

If you will be spending your work hours worrying about how to pay your bills, you won't be much use to a nonprofit. When a job offer is made that is too low for you to accept, call your interviewer and talk to him or her openly about how much you would love to accept the job if only it were just a little more financially viable for you. The person may be able to pull some strings internally or bend a few rules to increase a benefits package. Even if not, you have made a valuable connection when, later, you go back to this or another nonprofit organization. Saying no to an unattractive job offer puts you both in a better financial position in the long run and makes you more attractive to the nonprofit should you decide later that you can afford the reduced salary. In the meantime, you can cement your relationship with the nonprofit and prove your value by showing your stuff as a volunteer.

HEATHER ROCKER PRODUCT MANAGER, GEORGIA CENTER FOR NONPROFITS, ATLANTA, GEORGIA

Heather spent almost two years considering the move into the nonprofit sector from a position as a management consultant in an engineering firm. Prior to and during that time, Heather served as a board member for her local junior league, the America's Junior Miss Council, and the local chapter of her college alumni club. Heather read books about nonprofit jobs and conducted informational interviews with those already in the sector to determine whether she would need to go back to school for a nonprofit management degree or if her skills could translate without another degree. "After seven years in the world of consulting and through an extensive history of volunteer work," she explains, "I realized that I could effectively translate my technical and consulting experience to the nonprofit sector. And to be perfectly honest," she continues, "turning 30 does wonders for your life perspective and planning. It became a 'now or never' decision for me, and I'm thrilled that I took the leap."

To find her nonprofit job, Heather put the word out among her friends and colleagues whom she knew both through her business life and her nonprofit experience. Her main sources of job announcements were online job-posting sites, and she found the best luck in searching those sites that were specifically targeted at nonprofit jobseekers. In hindsight, Heather would have gotten involved with local nonprofit organizations (such as Atlanta Nonprofit Professionals) during her job search to network effectively and learn more about working at nonprofits.

What challenges surprised Heather most in her job search?

"The challenge that I never saw coming," explains Heather, "was the one of convincing potential employers that I would actually accept a large pay decrease (counterintuitive to the job-hunting process)." In several searches, Heather would make it to the end of the process and then get turned down for fear that she would not stick with a job at a smaller salary in the long run. "There is definitely a pervasive theory in the nonprofit sector that those getting burned out in their current field turn to the nonprofits for a 'break,'" says Heather, who was called a "corporate refugee" on more than one occasion. She was shocked to find herself having to assure hiring managers that she understood and accepted the financial implications of this career transition and that this wasn't a sudden and purely "feel-good" decision.

In what ways did Heather prepare for the financial implications of this move?

"To be perfectly honest," says Heather, "the first task was to revisit the monthly household budget, realizing that raises would likely be more conservative and performance-based bonuses were a thing of the past." Heather researched average salaries for the job types she was pursuing and had a realistic idea of what salary would be offered. "I had to establish the bare minimum at which my husband and I could continue life as we knew it (but with a few more coupons in tow)."

Heather's Key Lessons Learned:

■ "Don't assume that your job in the nonprofit sector will be without stress and pressures. One of the largest misconceptions about the nonprofit workplace is that the employees don't work as hard and everything is easier when, in fact, the opposite is true."

■ "Know your ultimate goal in the sector and make sure your job is aligned accordingly. It is important to realize that keeping the books at the Boys and Girls Club headquarters is not at all the same as volunteering directly with the children."

■ "Don't assume the nonprofit sector will be thrilled that someone from the for-profit sector wants to transition to the nonprofit field. Anyone making the switch had better hone their answer to, 'Tell me why you want to come to the nonprofit sector?' and mean it!"

COMMON STEREOTYPES ABOUT FOR-PROFIT JOB CANDIDATES

There is no doubt the hiring manager or headhunter looking at your résumé has seen many corporate applicants in the past. There is also no doubt, unfortunately, the manager has had bad experiences with some of them, just as he certainly had with nonprofit candidates. Most corporate career changers come to the nonprofit sector with any one of a number of expectations, and because of this, your application may be stereotyped.

Some of the most common stereotypes include the following:

■ "You are used to getting things done by delegating work to the many support staff you have had at your disposal."
■ "You expect that you will be rewarded handsomely for your work and will have plenty of resources to get the job done."

- "The impact of your work on the bottom line is the only appropriate gauge of success."
- "You think that because you have raised investment money, you will easily be able to raise nonprofit funds."
- "You are looking to step out of the rat race, slow down, and work less hard."
- "You think that nonprofits would run better if only they ran just like for-profits."
- "You are going to change the culture of the nonprofit by imprinting your corporate stamp everywhere."
- "You value money more than people and make only rational, not emotional, decisions."
- "You are not succeeding in your for-profit work and think the nonprofit sector will be easier."
- "If you really cared so deeply about the mission, you wouldn't have sold out to the for-profit sector so many years ago."

Now, before you gnash your teeth in anger, remember that the for-profit sector holds plenty of mistaken opinions about the nonprofit sector—including the ten myths we discussed earlier in this chapter—as well. Be prepared for your interviewer to hold one, more, or even all of these stereotypes. You can correct them. For example, the cover letter is a great place to discuss how you have sent your children to college and are more financially able to make the sacrifices necessary to give back to your community. Or use your résumé to list the volunteer work you've done throughout the years to allay concerns that you don't care about people. Networking is another chance for you to learn about and discuss how work in the nonprofit sector is different, proving that your expectations are aligned with reality. Let's look at these stereotypes one by one, examining them and developing strategic responses.

"You are used to getting things done by delegating work to the many support staff you have had at your disposal."

Expect to be asked about support staff in your interviews or, better yet, beat your interviewer to the punch and tell stories about how you single-handedly swept in and saved the day, especially if it was a task that an underling might have normally done. Avoid stories that involve your assistant making all the arrangements for a meeting, even if that has happened. Remind your interviewer about how your for-profit had to manage with less than expected at times and about the role you played in still achieving success.

"You expect that you will be rewarded handsomely for your work and will have plenty of resources to get the job done."

Avoid asking questions about expense accounts and budgets for less than urgent needs. Assume that there is no such money, but be prepared to make a case for what you need once on board. Tell stories about how you strategically reassigned resources or people to get the job done, and done right. Finally, use your cover letter to communicate that you understand that pay in the nonprofit sector differs considerably from that of the for-profit sector, and that salary, while important, isn't critical. Indicate that you are open to discussions, and do your homework before you begin any discussion.

"The impact of your work on the bottom line is the only appropriate gauge of success."

Nonprofits use all sorts of indicators to determine success, only a few of which are the numbers at the bottom of the budget. Yet it is hard for some career changers to wrap their minds around these softer benchmarks. Nothing is better here than telling a story about how you chose to do the nonprofitable, unpopular thing and how the company benefited and learned from it in the end. This proves you to be a change agent unafraid of making waves when doing the right thing is at stake. Nonprofits adore people like this.

"You think that because you have raised investment money, you will easily be able to raise nonprofit funds."

Raising money in either the for-profit or the nonprofit sector is both an art and a science. Many candidates come to a nonprofit development job assuming that raising money is raising money, regardless of the sector. It isn't. Your nonprofit donors are not going to see the for-profit equivalent of a return on investment, unless their bank cashes in good karma for groceries and rent. That being said, people donate to nonprofits for a variety of reasons: tax incentives, business development, community connection, and that good old karma, to name but a few. Having raised significant money in the for-profit sector may not guarantee that you'll be successful raising money in the nonprofit sector, but it may mean that you have some of the requisite arrows in your quiver to get started. Take care to point out what skills you have used in the for-profit sector and how they might help you do the same in the nonprofit sector. Just be careful not to assume for your interviewer that all those skills will equal success anywhere. If you lay out the argument well enough, they will get there on their own.

"You are looking to step out of the rat race, slow down, and work less hard."

If your motivation for transitioning to the nonprofit sector is unclear, your interviewer may be concerned that you are switching sectors merely as a way of slowing down. If you are a sector switcher late in your career, you may be viewed as someone looking for an off-ramp from the career highway. Counterbalance this view by presenting an active résumé that highlights tangible results and a cover letter describing what about this nonprofit at this time excites you. Convince the nonprofit that you are energized and excited by a career shift.

"You think that nonprofits would run better if only they ran just like for-profits."

Want to really tick off a nonprofit professional? Insist that running their nonprofit like a for-profit would solve all their woes. For some, this may be the truth. For others, it's the farthest thing from it. More likely, nonprofits and for-profits could each learn something from the other. Propose your solutions judiciously, biting off a little at a time, until you know more.

"You are going to change the culture of the nonprofit by imprinting your corporate stamp everywhere."

One of the biggest fears held by nonprofits it that the for-profit job seeker won't assimilate to the nonprofit but expect the nonprofit to assimilate to the job seeker. Highlight your flexibility and willingness to adapt. Come armed with stories about how, in your for-profit life, you changed your approach in light of new people, new information, or new opportunities. Don't be afraid to show your softer side.

"You value money more than people and make only rational, not emotional, decisions."

Nonprofits are filled with quirky people, most of whom are more tied to the mission of the organization than to their paycheck. Because of this, battles sometimes erupt over illogical things. Being able to diffuse tension while holding high the morale of the team is a key skill. Find ways to weave a track record of this into the stories you tell, but be careful not to malign any of the players, lest you seem callous and uncaring. Nonprofits believe that everyone has value; the more you actively appreciate that fact, the more likely it is that you will be seen as being an effective nonprofit manager.

"You are not succeeding in your for-profit work and think the nonprofit sector will be easier."

A common mistake made by nonprofit managers is thinking that the only reason people would enter the nonprofit sector in midcareer is because their for-profit career isn't going as planned. Life-altering crises, world events, or personal developments are easily identified entrance points for some candidates, but others just wake up one day and realize that they should be somewhere else doing something else. Use your résumé and cover letter to detail professional success as well as your reasons for making the move at this time.

"If you really cared so deeply about the mission, you wouldn't have sold out to the for-profit sector so many years ago."

We all are forced to live with economic reality. Sadly, the mortgage company won't give us back any points for helping the homeless, nor will the supermarket comp us groceries for feeding the poor. Working for the private sector is not and was not a sin, and you should be proud of the work that you did there. It has prepared you for the nonprofit sector in ways that will benefit the nonprofit for which you ultimately work. Yet a nonprofit hiring manager may not see it that way and might need some additional stroking. Take care to craft your story, your "Aha!" moment, when you discovered that you were unfulfilled by the pursuit of money, as it were, and wanted to chase this cause. Nonprofits love to hear about corporate denizens who wake up one day and realize that they want to do more meaningful work. If you wear your heart on your sleeve, you'll always get compliments about your fashion sense from your nonprofit coworkers.

FINDING A NONPROFIT THAT IS RIGHT FOR YOU

Combating these myths and dealing with the financial implications of transition can be complicated. Yet these complications can be alleviated by choosing the right non-profit through which to advance your career. Given that your first nonprofit job will likely not be your last, remember that your second job in the nonprofit sector will be easier to come by once you've had an initial success. Therefore, in thinking about your first nonprofit, consider one that is friendly to those seeking a career change and allows you the greatest chance of a smooth transition and, ultimately, a better nonprofit career trajectory.

"Friendly" Nonprofits for Career Changers

For-profit job seekers tend to be most successful in nonprofits that have already adopted business practices into their daily work. These nonprofits use words like *entrepreneurial* and *cutting edge* to describe themselves, and they use best practices from the for-profit sector to impact their missions. They actively recruit change agents for whom failure to achieve goals is not an option. In the funding hunt, these nonprofits look at traditional types of funding such as government and foundation grants, individual donors, and special events, but they also seek out new and inventive models of revenue generation, such as for-profit subsidiaries or fee-for-service work to underwrite nonprofit operations.

For-profit job seekers can also be successful in organizations that are standing on the precipice of great change. Nonprofits find themselves ready to, or forced to, change at key moments, such as when the interests of funders shift, an unexpected opportunity arises, or a crisis occurs. Whether demanded by their funders, their constituents, or their internal staff, these nonprofits often take this opportunity to examine what they have been doing—and with what kinds of talent—and make adjustments to the way they fulfill their mission. This moment strikes all nonprofits eventually, and when it does, these organizations open themselves to new ways of thinking, creative solutions, and previously untapped skill sets.

Nonprofits Career Changers Should Avoid

Beware the organization that wants to be an entrepreneurial, cutting-edge, business practice–utilizing nonprofit of the future if it isn't already one now. It is very much in vogue today—as demanded by the changing landscape of philanthropy—to want to apply the best practices of business to nonprofits. But it doesn't always work, sometimes because the people involved are incapable or not truly sold on the idea or, more often, business practices simply cannot be applied successfully to the nonprofit in question. Many sector switchers fail because they believe the words of the staff and board that change is afoot, but when push comes to shove, leadership gets cold feet and backs out. It is all well and good to try to tackle this challenge as your second nonprofit job, but make sure that your first is a slam dunk before getting more adventurous, lest the blame for the nonprofit's failure be laid at your feet, labeling you as incapable of making the transition out of corporate work.

For-profit job seekers are least likely to be successful when moving into a small, grassroots, hands-on, direct service position, regardless of the approach or overall business model of the nonprofit. Most former for-profit employees tend to be frustrated with the slower pace of change when faced with individual nonprofit constituents and find themselves much more satisfied when they can effect change with larger levels of impact. For this reason, most sector switchers tend to look for roles in senior management rather than in frontline service delivery.

CONCLUSION

Like most myths, the ones about the nonprofit sector are based more on prejudice than fact. The nonprofit sector of today hardly resembles the nonprofit sector of 5, 10, or 15 years ago. In fact, it barely resembles the nonprofit sector of last year. With each day, the sector becomes more savvy and more competitive, and this trend benefits you as a nonprofit job seeker.

Come to the nonprofit sector fully aware of the advantages and disadvantages of what working in it will mean for you personally, professionally, and financially. Like your job in the for-profit sector, there will be trade-offs, but with the proper choice of nonprofit and role, the fulfillment you feel at the end of each day will outweigh whatever burdens this career change may bring.

Choose the right type of nonprofit for your corporate background. The more experience the nonprofit has had with business practices or businesspeople, the more likely you will succeed right away and the more enjoyable your work will be. Now that you're acquainted with the nonprofit sector and the types of nonprofits for which you would like to work, let's get ready to start your job search.

Key Words to Look for in Nonprofit Descriptions

How does the nonprofit describe itself? The words it chooses may tell you a great deal about the type of nonprofit it is and what it will be like as a work environment. Here are some verbal cues to listen for:

- *Start-up mode.* Nonprofits in start-up mode operate similarly to for-profits in start-up mode. When they are just getting going, they have little definition in their culture and processes, and few expectations exist about the personalities or employees who can fulfill their mission.

- *Entrepreneurial approach.* The nonprofit sees itself as opportunistic, and its leadership is interested in surrounding itself with others of a similar stripe.

- *Crisis point.* The nonprofit is at a crisis point because of funding, politics, or leadership. When nonprofits are faced with an urgent problem, they look to people unlike those currently on staff.

- *Turnaround situation.* The nonprofit is in need of a turnaround. What has worked in the past no longer works, and without change, the organization will die.

- *Social venture, fee-for-service, or revenue generation.* The nonprofit includes a social venture component or other for-profit venture within its business model, which is used to fund its nonprofit operations.

- *Opportunity for change.* The nonprofit is standing on the precipice of major growth because of a large and unexpected grant, uninvited media attention, or other life-altering event. To go to scale, the nonprofit must look to those in the private sector who have done this in the past.

PART TWO

Ready, Set, Search!

CHAPTER 5

Job Search 101

Now that you have a greater understanding of the breadth, depth, and promise of the nonprofit sector, it's time to start looking for your perfect job. You want a new job, and you want it to be in the nonprofit sector. So you're ready to start sending out your résumé, right? Not so fast.

Most job seekers make the mistake of thinking that they are ready to apply for a job simply because they need or want a new one. Yet nothing is more frustrating to a hiring manager than an unprepared candidate, and nothing will more quickly sink your chances of making the sector switch than a poorly executed job search. You've likely done a lot of thinking about, or are interested in exploring deeper, what a career in the nonprofit sector might mean for you. The first thing you need to do is to make sure that your candidacy reflects that.

Hiring managers expect that you, as the job seeker, are doing everything in your power to present your best self during your job search. Any misstep makes them worry, "If this is you at your best and I'm questioning your ability, what will you be like when you've been on the job for a year, or if you've got a personal crisis at home distracting you, or if I don't keep you motivated, or if you are asked to work a bit too hard during a crunch time?" You can and should avoid this reaction by being polished and prepared, knowing yourself and your experience, understanding deeply the nonprofit sector and the challenges you will face, and being the best candidate you can be. This chapter will help you do just that.

For better or for worse, as a candidate coming from the for-profit world, you will have to jump over a higher hurdle than traditional nonprofit candidates to make your transition seem possible. There are stereotypes to correct, knowledge to gain, and a whole new language to master. Coming to the interview chair prepared to address these issues will make all the difference between a successful job search and one that lands you right back where you started.

SKILLS, EXPERIENCE, EDUCATION, AND INTERESTS ASSESSMENT

Let's begin by determining what kind of job you want. Before you start your job search, make sure you know what you *want* to do and what you are *qualified* to do. The answers to these two questions are often completely different. But don't be afraid of that divergence.

The nonprofit sector is filled with people who come from nontraditional, nonlinear careers. Dropping out of a Wall Street lifestyle to move to Africa to help save endangered animals won't make you an anomaly in the nonprofit sector. Don't shy away from something that might seem far out. Instead, keep an open mind, think broadly, and adapt your job search accordingly.

Nine Questions to Guide Your Job Search

Knowing you want to work in the nonprofit sector is easy. It's often been described by career changers as something they couldn't *not* do. It's a fire in the pit of your stomach, a yearning for more, a decision that life is more than a paycheck. Yet figuring out just where you fit into this vast and wide-ranging sector is not so easy. The following questions will help you begin to determine where and what you can do.

What skills are in your toolbox?

Knowing what you can do and what you have done is important, but don't get trapped by your current title or your current job. After all, it's the job you're looking to leave, likely for good reason. Simply replicating your for-profit job in the nonprofit sector gets you no more than a smaller paycheck. Think more deeply about what you do now and what you have done in other jobs so that your career change choices reflect the whole you, not just the most recent version.

On your résumé, remember to include work you may have done as a member of an ad hoc office committee, regardless of whether it involved your official line duties or not. Examine your projects and highlight any and all skills you have developed by completing each of the tasks involved. Regardless of how relevant these skills and tasks seem to your current job, they may matter greatly in your next one.

Where did you collect the experiences you will bring to your next job?

Not all experiences are gained through paid employment. Rather, much of the most fulfilling, most educational, and most relevant experience for the nonprofit job you seek may have come from volunteer work. Meaningful work is meaningful work, whether or not you got paid.

Looking at the larger collection of skills is particularly relevant for those just coming back into the workplace after getting an advanced degree or caring for a family member, or who have held the same job for a lengthy period of time. A certain amount of amnesia sets in, and a malaise about qualifications is not uncommon. Dusting off the old résumé and tacking on your most recent job does a disservice to you and your job hunt. Add all of your experiences, paid or volunteer, to the equation when determining the full scope of skills you bring to bear. They may add up to more than you think.

What would you do if you could do anything at all?

As you have learned in the first section of this book, the nonprofit sector is enormous and varied. You can do virtually anything you want to do in a nonprofit that exists and, if not, start one of your own. Consider this famous question: "If you won the lottery, what would you do tomorrow?"

Allow yourself to dream, and dream big. After all, if you are moving into the nonprofit sector to fulfill that certain something inside of you, why not go all the way? The time is now, and the price is right. Besides, the nonprofit sector is filled with dreamers just like you. You can always scale back or get creative when faced with unexpected realities that crop up during your job search. But until that happens, allow yourself to be carried away by the fantasy of making real change in the issue area or community of your choice. You will find that your enthusiasm is infectious and will excite those around you to help you more.

Which of your skills will transfer into the nonprofit sector?

Some skills transfer more easily than others. Most duties that fall under the operations, administration, and finance functions are easily transferable, even if there are some new rules or technology to learn. Some, like community building and fund development, can transfer well after a bit of tweaking. Other skills, those heavily reliant on subject matter expertise, are much more difficult to fit into your new nonprofit job, unless the nonprofit focuses in that area. For example, a marketing director focused on selling to educational outfits may be able to bring a quiver filled with both functional and subject matter arrows to a job raising money for a charter school association. On the other hand, an eye doctor will bring a deep understanding of the medical community and its support of blind children, but a lifetime of clinical expertise will not apply when budgeting, dealing with funders, or signing off on press releases. Those skills must come from elsewhere.

Many skills you have gathered are likely transferable to the nonprofit sector. However, before starting to write your résumé, make sure that the skills you think will transfer are in line with the requirements of the new position or the level of position you seek. The eye doctor just discussed, for example, might point to a track record running a successful, 200-patient practice, developing community support around an eye care program in local schools, and lobbying the state to earmark funds to an "Eye Care for the Elderly" program.

Determine Your Functional Areas Expertise: Where Do Your Capabilities Lie?

Your functional areas of expertise are those things that you can do well, either because of experience or study. These determine the type of role you might fill in a nonprofit organization.

- ☒ Accounting and finance
- ☒ Activism and organizing
- ☒ Administration
- ☒ Advertising
- ☒ Architecture
- ☒ Clerical and data entry
- ☒ Computers and technology
- ☒ Construction
- ☒ Counseling
- ☒ Customer service
- ☒ Database management

- ☒ Direct social services
- ☒ Driving
- ☒ Editing and writing
- ☒ Education and training
- ☒ Employment and human services
- ☒ Engineering
- ☒ Event planning
- ☒ Food service
- ☒ Fundraising and development
- ☒ Gardening
- ☒ Grants administration
- ☒ Graphic design

- ☒ Health and medical
- ☒ Legal
- ☒ Library sciences
- ☒ Maintenance and janitorial
- ☒ Management
- ☒ Marketing
- ☒ Photography
- ☒ Project management
- ☒ Public relations
- ☒ Research
- ☒ Sales
- ☒ Telemarketing

What traits have brought you success?

In most cases, subject matter expertise is only part of what has enabled you to succeed in your career thus far. Your personality, the way you go about doing your work or managing the work of others, and your general demeanor in the office complete the picture. You may be the type of person who operates well under pressure and in turnaround situations, or you may be better in a more stable environment where crises rarely pop up. You may be able to get the best from legions of young, idealistic, energetic upstarts, or you may be more skilled at managing a smaller cadre of seasoned professionals. You may enjoy a highly charged political atmosphere, or you may thrive, instead, in an environment where agendas are more transparent.

Each nonprofit has its own personality. Some of these personalities reflect the organization's issue arena. For example, human rights organizations tend to be more in-your-face with younger, idealistic staffers, while institutions of higher education tend to be more staid and steady. Yet in each of these categories, there are always exceptions. Discerning what environment brings out your best traits and allows you to flourish and finding a nonprofit that offers such an environment will allow you to enjoy your nonprofit work more.

Questions to Determine Your Best Work Environment

The nonprofit sector is broad enough to include organizations with all different personalities. Determine what kind of work environment you need and where your skills and traits might blossom by considering the following questions. Remember: there are no right or wrong answers.

Yes	No	
☒	☒	Do you like to know what you will face each morning when you walk into the office?
☒	☒	Do you enjoy the thrill of a new and possibly unknown challenge each day?
☒	☒	Do you prefer to work in a hands-on capacity, creating and seeing change up close and personal in the life of one individual at a time?
☒	☒	Would you rather make change from a distance, at a more strategic level, guiding larger programs that effect change in broader populations that you might not necessarily see every day?
☒	☒	Do you function better in environments where the goals are straightforward and the results are measurable?
☒	☒	Are you comfortable in a more amorphous role, where the goalposts are constantly changing and the field is ever in flux?

Yes	No	
☒	☒	Would you rather fill a position that has been held in the past by another, where the expectations are clear?
☒	☒	Do you enjoy creating your own path, blazing a new trail, and introducing functions into an organization?
☒	☒	Would you be able to perform a serious job in an organization where the majority of staff wear T-shirts and flip-flops to the office?
☒	☒	Do you wear a tie even on casual Friday, preferring a serious, staid atmosphere?
☒	☒	Are you an individual decision maker who can quickly determine the correct solution without much input from others?
☒	☒	Do you prefer to get the opinions of all around you, weighing pros and cons and talking until consensus is reached?

Many different types of personality and traits tests are available that can help you determine what your "organizational personality" might be. From Myers-Briggs to the Enneagram to Jung's theory on personality types, the Internet is a vast and wonderful world of self-help right at your fingertips. Try a few of these personality tests on for size. You might be surprised at what you find, but you'll also be better prepared to find the nonprofit that is right for you.

What type of formal education do you have?

Without a great deal of work experience, formal education determines what, substantively speaking, you are qualified to do. This is the whole of your subject matter expertise. For those just coming out of school, or with only one job under their belt, education is of paramount importance and will be weighted heavily by the hiring manager. What you know matters, and what you know has mainly come from schooling at this point.

For those who have been in the working world a bit longer, education is only one part of the equation. In some cases, like medicine or the law, a formal degree is a state requirement. Also, social workers and teachers must be licensed, and stock traders and accountants must pass certain exams. In other cases, like fundraising or association management, a degree or certificate is not a requirement but provides a leg up against other candidates. Determine what your formal education qualifies you to do and what degrees or certificates you might need to grab the job of your dreams.

Some managers, especially those in the foundation world, find that a deep, substantive knowledge of the work funded or being done by their grantees is vital to a candidate's success once on board. This is often borne out by a long career in the field or, for foundations, more likely a PhD in the subject area. In some cases, however, attaining more education is unrealistic. You are unlikely to enter medical school when you are 45, although certainly it has been done, and you are probably not going to get a PhD in oceanography to work at the Jacques Cousteau Foundation (however fun that may seem).

In other cases, degrees that teach skills and not subject matter expertise, such as programs on nonprofit management, fundraising, accounting, and operations, are easily attainable and make sense strategically. This type of education provides you with a current nonprofit peer group, access to a career center, and a mind filled with the best nonprofit thinking of the day. The second half of this chapter discusses additional educational resources in more detail.

What kinds of on-the-job training have you received?

Many job seekers have received enough on-the-job training to write a PhD thesis on the work that they do. In most cases, however, they just don't realize how much they've learned along the way. Figuring this out demands critical thinking about where you came from, your initial expectations of your career's trajectory, and where you have ended up.

What did you hope to get from your career? Are you there? What changed along the way? What do you do now that you never imagined you would be doing? What more do you know now than when you started this job, or the last job, or the job before that? And, again, don't forget about the community service, nonprofit volunteering, or board work that you have done. Each of your days has brought a lesson, and each lesson is valuable to your job search in some way. What have been your lessons?

What motivates you to make this move?

If you are switching sectors, you may find yourself applying for jobs that seem completely unconnected to where you have been and what you are currently doing. However, a unique, often life-altering experience as a volunteer, an illness in the family, or a major world catastrophe are often exactly the right, and perfectly plausible, times to make such a dramatic change. If properly framed, your underlying motivation will make sense to the person judging your candidacy.

Consider those people looking for the nonprofit sector lifestyle: that idyllic world where people don't work that hard and go home early on Fridays, where accountability is scant and responsibility is shared, where everyone is kind and sweet and no one ever fights. That world is about as realistic as the mirage of an oasis in the desert. Times have changed, the nonprofit sector has changed, and the jobs within it have changed, too. Expect to work harder than you ever have but for a cause you deeply love.

Think about your underlying motivation to make this move. Is your motivation just a passing fancy that will flame out when met with rough times, frustration, and defeats? Or is it from deep within your core that will enable you to face down the difficulties inherent to the nonprofit sector and make an organization's dream a reality for all? Ask yourself tough questions about how you really feel about this major career change and keep asking until you feel you have an honest answer. This is what will drive your job search, your enthusiasm, and your ability to make change a reality.

Figure Out Your Issue Area:
What Interests You, What Excites You, What Must You Impact?

Determine the difference between what interests you and what drives you. Knowing that your job search may not be linear and that you may have to expand your options to move to your perfect job in stages, divide this list into the following categories:

- No, work in this issue area doesn't excite me (N).
- I might find work in this issue area interesting (M).
- I yearn to be part of the change in this issue area (Y).

___ Advocacy

___ AIDS/HIV

___ Arts and culture

___ Associations

___ Children and youth

___ Community-building and renewal

___ Community service

___ Computers and the Internet

___ Consumer protection

___ Corporate social responsibility

___ Crime and safety

___ Disability

___ Disaster relief

___ Diversity

___ Economic development

___ Education (preschool)

___ Education (K–12)

___ Education (college and university)

___ Energy conservation

___ Environment

___ Family and parenting

___ Farming and agriculture

___ Foundations and philanthropy

___ Gay, lesbian, bisexual, and transgender

___ Government and politics

___ Government oversight and reform

___ Health policy

___ Health services

___ Housing and homelessness

___ Human rights and civil liberties

___ Human services

___ immigration

___ International issues

___ Job training and workplace issues

___ Labor movement

___ Legal assistance

___ Library and resource centers

___ Media and publishing

___ Men and boys

___ Mental health

___ Multiservice community agency

- __ Network of nonprofit organizations
- __ Nutrition/hunger
- __ Peace and conflict resolution
- __ Personal finance
- __ Philanthropy
- __ Poverty
- __ Prison reform
- __ Public authority
- __ Public policy
- __ Public relations/ communications

- __ Public-private partnerships
- __ Race and ethnicity
- __ Recovery, addiction, and abuse
- __ Recreation, sports, and leisure
- __ Religion and faith-based organizations
- __ Rural issues
- __ Security/defense
- __ Seniors and retirement

- __ Social justice
- __ Social services
- __ Spiritual and meta-physical issues
- __ Technology
- __ Transportation
- __ Veterans
- __ Voting and enfranchisement
- __ Wildlife and animal welfare
- __ Women's issues

Why is this the right time for you to move into this new type of work?

Your children may have left the nest, you may have a sick relative, you may be unable to stomach one more day of corporate profiteering, or you may have benefited greatly from your career and can now write your own rules. Everyone has his or her reasons, and all of them are real and valid. However, only some of them should influence your job search. The timing must have everything to do with how a particular job, including the lifestyle and financial considerations that come with it, play into your present life.

Perhaps your company is downsizing, and this is a move you have always desired. Perhaps you are a board member for a nonprofit whose chief executive just announced plans for retirement. Perhaps you are just coming back to work after raising your children, and because of that life-transforming experience, realize that you cannot go back to the job you held before. Realizing why this is the right time for you, for your family, and for your bank account is key to deciding which kind of job to seek.

Determine Which Job Is Right for You

As you may have noticed, these questions fall into different categories: professional experience, education, individual skills, and personal interests. None of these categories is mutually exclusive of another. For example, don't be fooled into thinking that just because you were educated as a lawyer means you have to practice law in the nonprofit sector. The education gained to become a lawyer is substantive and puts you in good standing to practice in your particular field of the law. However, the professional experience you may have gained as a lawyer and the individual attributes that have made you successful allow you to do so much more. Lawyers learn to negotiate, mediate, research, and apply critical thinking in one area to another, to give but a few examples. Some have managed law practices with significant budgets and staff and have had to rid themselves of any shyness about asking for money. Most have had to market themselves and their abilities and have learned a great deal about public presentation, inside a courtroom and in the world at large. A good lawyer will have developed personal attributes such as the ability to talk to lay audiences and peers, patience with bureaucratic systems, and the perseverance to continue an argument when it looks as though all hope is lost. Combine that with the desire to change a community, state, or country, and you have yourself a pretty powerful nonprofit leader. Breaking down your career and the jobs you have held will yield a fruitful dossier for your nonprofit job search.

Don't Expect a Linear Path

Your move from the for-profit sector to the nonprofit sector may take a few twists and turns before you find your dream job. In fact, you may have to make your move in stages, first for function, then for issue area, until you have amassed the right experience in your targeted area. For example, it is unlikely that you will go from a role as a senior financial analyst for General Electric to become the vice president for operations and finance for the Minnesota Human Services Coalition without a couple of jobs in between. You'd need to get experience regarding nonprofit operations, get a basic level of understanding about human services, learn more about nonprofit financial accounting, get a sense of Minnesota politics, and have a more senior perspective about nonprofits. The nine questions you just answered are designed to make you more strategic in choosing your next job, thereby minimizing the steps needed to get from here to there.

BRUCE TRACHTENBERG EXECUTIVE DIRECTOR, THE COMMUNICATIONS NETWORK, NAPERVILLE, ILLINOIS

Bruce was serving as the public relations director for the Reader's Digest Association in the early 1990s. The company had just gone public, resulting in a windfall for the two private grant-making foundations created by the founders of Reader's Digest—DeWitt and Lila Wallace—who until then had held a majority of the stock in the company. Over the next couple of years, Bruce watched—and occasionally was asked to help out with some communications needs—as the DeWitt Wallace-Reader's Digest Fund and Lila Wallace-Reader's Digest Fund began to grow and establish themselves as major national grant-making organizations. "I'd been at Reader's Digest for more than ten years," Bruce explains, "and felt like my time at the company was nearing an end. I was ready for a move."

Around this time, the president of the two Wallace Foundations called Bruce and told him that the board had just approved plans for a major staff expansion to accommodate the growing assets of the foundation. One of the positions was for a communications director who would be responsible for starting an in-house operation; when the president asked Bruce is he knew of any good candidates, Bruce hesitated, hung up the phone, and after a few minutes of thought called back and said, "I know just the person for you. Me."

How did Bruce prepare himself to move into his nonprofit job?

"I didn't have a lot of time to prepare," says Bruce. So once he announced his intention to leave, he didn't waste time. Instead, Bruce did most of his learning on the job. "I spent lots of time in conversation with my colleagues, learning what they do and how I could help them," he explains. He also began making connections with as many people as he could who were outside the foundation but involved in philanthropy. One very helpful organization was called, back then, Communicators Network in Philanthropy. It was a volunteer group made up of people who held communications jobs at foundations whose primary reason for coming together was to network, exchange ideas, share best practices, explore common problems, and be available to lend a hand. Some 15 years later, that organization has evolved into The Communications Network, a stand-alone nonprofit that Bruce now leads as executive director.

How did Bruce go about finding his nonprofit jobs?

"The Wallace-Reader's Digest Funds job fell into my lap," says Bruce, "but I eventually left the foundation in 2000, drawn by the siren song of the dot-com sector and Worth.com." When the company started to teeter nine months later, Bruce began putting out feelers. A friend told him that the Edna McConnell Clark Foundation—a foundation he had long admired and whose past communications director he had respected—was looking for a communications director. Bruce dashed off a quick letter and a résumé, only to be told that the search was virtually closed—the foundation was only looking at candidates in case their finalist fell through. Still, he persevered, and it paid off. The finalist fell through, and Bruce, having impressed the recruiting firm and the search committee, was given the job.

- "Be prepared that things move more slowly in the nonprofit sector. Patience is a virtue."

- "The quality of a person's character and integrity matter as much as the person's skills and work experience."

- "After working in the nonprofit sector, 'settling' for a corporate position would have felt like a step backward."

NETWORKING: IT'S ALL ABOUT WHOM YOU KNOW

In the for-profit sector, the vast majority of jobs are filled through word of mouth. In the nonprofit sector, it is even more extreme. Advertising for an unexpected vacancy requires an unexpected allocation of money, and money, especially when it's needed unexpectedly, is in limited supply in the nonprofit sector. If a nonprofit can fill a job through the people in its network before spending a dollar on advertising, it will do so every time.

The Importance of Networking

Networking is important. Underline that sentence three times. There is simply no substitute in a job search, whether in the for-profit or nonprofit sector. In fact, it is so vital to a successful job search that it bears repeating: *networking is important.*

A good rule of thumb is to spend 75 percent of your time networking—very little of which should be spent pursuing executive search firms directly—and only about 25 percent of your time answering advertisements found online or in the paper. You will find out about more opportunities that are currently available and soon to be available that way, and your candidacy will be taken more seriously. Consider this: If someone submitted a résumé to you because a mutual connection put you in touch, wouldn't you take that applicant more seriously than the one who responded, along with a hundred others, to the advertisement in the local newspaper? Of course you would—doing so is simple human nature, and you can easily use it to your advantage.

Before you get nervous that you are a corporate person with no ties to the nonprofit sector, think again. Everyone you know has some connection to a nonprofit. They may be involved with or members of the following:

- An alumni association
- A parent-teacher organization

- A neighborhood coalition
- A church, synagogue, or mosque
- A political campaign
- The Boy Scouts or Girl Scouts
- A citywide cleanup effort
- A local chorale or chamber music ensemble
- The Junior League
- Countless others

Each of these people knows scores of others who are involved with them, and each of them, in turn, knows scores more, and so on and so on. Suddenly, you have access to hundreds of potential connectors. By tapping into your existing network, you may find yourself surprisingly close to key decision makers in nonprofits of interest to you. Telling everyone you encounter about your search, then, will greatly increase the likelihood that you will be successful.

Similarly, each day you encounter many valuable resources that should be tapped for your job search. In addition to the individuals you know or meet, these resources may include networking associations, community organizations, or alumni groups, all of which may provide precious links to otherwise unknown opportunities. Figure out where you want to be and work backwards, creating a relational map to someone in that organization. Draw lines between connectors until you have found the person who makes the hiring decision. Then start taking advantage of these relationships and resources. You will be amazed at whom you know and whom they know.

Tips for Successful Networking

Networking can seem like an unpleasant assignment. You may feel as though you are bothering people or taking up their time with matters they do not care about or even understand. Truth be told, they have been there, too. Each of them once looked for a job, and each of them used some form of networking, large or small, in his or her job search. Furthermore, remember that you share a common interest: working in the nonprofit sector or issue area in general and perhaps that nonprofit organization specifically. Your enthusiasm for its work will carry the conversation.

Whether you relish the idea of networking or not, having some tools in your pocket will make it more fun.

Become Active in Your Issue Area of Choice

Hundreds of networking associations exist in every city on almost every imaginable topic, from women executives, to grant writers, to outdoors enthusiasts, to left-handed unicyclists. Getting involved in one or more of these affinity groups is a surefire way to multiply your network in a targeted, quick, and efficient manner. Most of these groups have regular gatherings, job postings, and other valuable networking opportunities. Join every club you can and begin to accept any and all invitations that come your way.

In addition to providing a directly relevant group of contacts, involvement in your issue area of choice will teach you the appropriate lingo, keep you up to date on current trends and challenges, provide invitations to speaker forums or other events where leaders will be presenting, and introduce you to the movers and shakers in the field. The knowledge you gain will make you both more successful in your job search and more likely to hit the ground running once you are hired. Finally, this activity will begin to form a history on your résumé of real involvement, showing that you are serious about making a move.

DEBORAH DINKELACKER   FORMER EXECUTIVE DIRECTOR, VOLUNTEERMATCH, SAN FRANCISCO, CALIFORNIA

Deborah had a successful traditional corporate career. She studied political science at Yale University and got her MBA in finance at New York University. She worked in consumer packaged goods and then in consumer finance at PepsiCo and Colgate Palmolive. Deborah shifted into marketing at American Express in New York City, where she stayed for ten years and ultimately rose to be vice president for marketing of the consumer card group.

Deborah greatly enjoyed her time at American Express and, in fact, looks back on it with great fondness and deep appreciation. "My for-profit experience helped shaped the leader and manager I have become," she explains. Yet Deborah recognized toward the end of her tenure that, while her financial satisfaction was quite high,

her personal satisfaction was not. "I felt a remoteness from results," she says, "and at the same time, I began to develop an intellectual interest in, although not a personal passion for, mission-driven organizations."

What started out as intellectual curiosity developed into much, much more. "I began to feel a sense of injustice that nonprofits were somehow considered less worthy of excellent talent or the best new business thinking," she says. "While I knew that nonprofits had large numbers of excellent leaders, I felt that they still weren't getting their fair share of the talent and brain trust when forced to compete with for-profits for employees." When it came time for her partner to take a job on the West Coast, Deborah moved too, shifting both her home and her career.

Deborah took her first nonprofit position as the national director of marketing for membership services and donor development for the Sierra Club, but after a mediocre experience there, briefly went back to the for-profit sector. When the opportunity arose at VolunteerMatch, she jumped at the chance to be its second president, following in the footsteps of a founder.

What made Deborah's first nonprofit experience harder than she expected?

Deborah didn't seek out enough advice before she made her move. "What I have since come to understand," she explains, "is that there is a tremendous amount of cultural diversity in the nonprofit world, and choosing the right nonprofit culture is essential to an employee's success, no matter where you were before." In looking for her second nonprofit, Deborah chose one more in line with her work personality. VolunteerMatch is a more analytical and information-oriented culture, and it exercises greater structure and discipline around decision making. Still, Deborah notes, "I had a lot to learn."

What was different the second time around for Deborah?

Sierra Club helped Deborah to understand what she needed to do: "Establish trust and establish credibility right away." Deborah's predecessor in her role at the Sierra Club had not been incred-

ibly successful, and, as a consequence, Deborah was greeted with skepticism. "I had never been hired into a position before where failure was expected by some, and I didn't take proactive measures to combat this self-fulfilling prophecy." When she got to VolunteerMatch, Deborah spent an enormous amount of time actively listening to her board members and staff, reflecting on how she was going to adapt her work style, and taking more time to explain her thought processes and secure consensus around decisions, even minor ones, because as she learned, "Few decisions in the nonprofit sector are minor."

Deborah's Key Lessons Learned:

- "Striking the right balance between the 'discussion' culture of the nonprofit sector and the 'action' culture of the corporate world can be hard. Action implies having to say yes to one option but no to several others, and turning down the option to help is difficult for most nonprofits to do."

- "You are not a savior. You have as much to learn from this nonprofit as it has to learn from you. Make sure you listen so that you don't miss it."

- "Instead of jumping right into a nonprofit job when the impulse strikes, spend a year volunteering, either in a frontline, direct service role or as a board member, to get a better understanding of the cultural diversity present in the nonprofit sector."

Find a Buddy

Even in the best of circumstances, job searches are long, arduous, and often lonely processes. In fact, searching for the perfect job can take six months to a year, depending on what you are looking to do next and how well your past has prepared you. The added difficulty of moving from the for-profit to the nonprofit sector will certainly add time as well.

It is easy to get discouraged and give up, especially if you are doing it alone. Setting up a regular session with a friend, coach, or job search counselor can renew your energy, rebuild your self-esteem, and keep you focused on the end game. Many professional networking associations have job-seeker subgroups, which can prove to be both professionally and personally rewarding; undoubtedly, you will also find some job seekers in the personal affinity groups as well. Don't be shy about asking them to get together; they will be thrilled for the company.

Set Benchmarks of Success

Another great way to keep focused on your search is to give yourself homework. Try to set some benchmarks: Make 20 calls per week, have coffee or lunch with someone every day, never let anyone off the phone without their giving you at least three more names and follow up within one week. Successful job searches thrive on momentum, and benchmarks like these will assure that you have it.

The first step is to create a list of names. Try to get as many as you can on paper, but don't let yourself off the hook until you've jotted down at least a few dozen. Write down the name of anyone with whom you currently work; worked with in previous jobs; sit with on a community committee; see in the car pool pickup line; or encounter where you worship, play sports, or ballroom dance. These are your first points of contact and the place to begin your networking. You can always remove names later—if, for example, you are unable to tell people at your current job just yet—but having these names written down now means you will be able to be more strategic when you begin to go public with your job search.

Walk in the Footsteps of Others

In your networking, keep an alert eye out for others who have already made the move from the for-profit to the nonprofit sector. Finding a former corporate denizen happily ensconced in a nonprofit benefits you in many ways. First, you are more likely to get in the door, because the person behind it knows what you are going through. They may have been helped by someone along the way and want to pass along the good karma or perhaps not helped at all and want to make life easier for those who are coming up behind him or her. Second, they will already understand where you are coming from, so you might not have to sell them quite as hard on why the nonprofit sector is the right place for someone with a business background. As successful career changers, they can then, in turn, be credible advocates on your behalf. Third, you will be able to ask questions about breaking into the nonprofit sector, their particular nonprofit, and challenges that they faced in their own sector switch. The answers you get will contain acceptable language to use in your own answers when you ultimately get asked these same questions in interviews.

Don't Discount Your Corporate Contacts

According to the Bureau of Labor Statistics, in a report compiled by the Corporation for National Service, 65.1 million people volunteered in the United States during 2005. This means that the person in the next cubicle, despite having a career in the for-profit sector, may spend time on the weekends volunteering at a local soup kitchen or serve on the board of the local zoo. Volunteering is hip, and it helps even corporate ladder climbers get ahead. You, too, can use this to your advantage by hitting up your corporate contacts for their nonprofit connections.

Keep Detailed Notes

If you are truly networking as much as you should be, you will get confused about where people are working, what they are doing, to whom they have referred you, and the purpose of their organization. Remember that most people work at a particular nonprofit to serve its mission. It is more than a bit insulting—and will come across as patronizing from someone in the corporate sector—to mix up one nonprofit's mission with another's.

Buy a notebook into which you staple business cards. Set up a database on your computer. Create index cards. Draw giant maps on your walls connecting contacts to each other and, ultimately, to your dream job. Do whatever you need to do to keep your networking straight. Your airtight organization will be seen as a laser-like passion for the mission and a deep respect for those who work to fulfill it.

Be Clear and Concise

Arm your networking contacts with the ability to help you by giving them clear and concise directions on what, specifically, they can do for you. One of the biggest mistakes a job seeker can make is to ask for general help and hope, expect, or assume that their contacts will do the math for them. That doesn't happen.

If you aren't concise and clear with your needs, you will still get promises of help but, in reality, will be leaving your contacts with little or no tools to follow through. Your contacts have limited enough time so that burdening them with extra work—for example, figuring out what your skills and experiences add up to—will generate frustration and failure. No matter how much they want to help, they will be unable to do so.

Be clear. Be concise. Above all, give your contacts specific requests to which they can respond.

Opportunities: Lost and Gained

- *Lost opportunity.* "I'd like to move into the nonprofit sector and think I could do good for lots of different kinds of organizations. Do you know anyone who is hiring?"

- *Gained opportunity.* "After ten years of honing my skills in brand management in Corporate America, I've decided that I'd like to dedicate myself to what has always been a passion of mine: leadership training for girls, preferably in the junior high school years. I know that you have been active in the Girl Scouts, and I think my experience would transfer well into their organizationwide efforts to create more chapters. Whom do you think I should call to begin networking into the right circles? Where is the most innovative thinking in the sector right now? Do you know of any organizations that have these types of jobs, whether filled or vacant, where I can connect to like-minded individuals?"

Be careful not to treat a networking opportunity like an informational interview. Informational interviews, discussed later in this chapter, are wonderful opportunities to delve more deeply into how your contact sees your skills and expertise, how they think you might be able to transition into the sector, and what they feel is missing from your résumé at present. Informational interviews should include the usual networking questions, of course, but networking should never include informational interview questions. If you trap someone expecting a quick networking encounter in a long conversation—especially at an event where the person has his or her own networking expectations and agenda—yours won't be a welcome phone call later on. Keep it light, keep it quick, and always ask if you can call the individual to follow up with an informational interview later.

The Sector Switcher's Elevator Speech

Imagine that you've just stepped into an elevator only to find, unguarded by her brick wall of an assistant, the woman with whom you've been trying unsuccessfully for months to land an interview, a telephone conversation, or even just a returned phone call. You have no more than maybe 11 floors, or 15 to 30 seconds, to make your case. What are you going to say to her? Hence, the so-called "elevator speech." Thankfully, most networking elevator speeches are delivered under far less pressure, but being prepared, no matter what life throws at you, will enable you to deliver this information in a casual but impressive manner.

The typical elevator speech includes a little about you and a little about what you want to do next. Yours must have more. The sector switcher's elevator speech includes answers to four key questions:

1. Who are you?
2. What do you do currently?
3. What makes you an interesting and likely successful sector switcher (e.g., your volunteer work, additional education, board responsibilities, or passions)?
4. What do you want to do now and why?

Remember to include more than just the "what" in your speech but the "why" as well. It is the burning question on the mind of anyone interested in hiring you and can and should be answered in both of its forms: "Why this mission?" and "Why now?" Gauge your level of sentimentality for your particular audience; some may be amazed that you harbor this secret love for their mission, but some may find your emotions too personal and too revealing all at once.

Example #1: With a Potential Employer "Hi, my name is Ellen Torres. I'm currently the chief of investor relations for State Street Capital, Ltd. While my day job has honed my ability to craft excellent communications for corporate investors, my volunteering has shown me that my real passion lies in caring for our aging population. I'm currently looking for a position where I can combine my expert public relations knowledge with my passion for our nation's greatest living treasure, the elderly. I saw your announcement for a director of communications and would love to set up a time where we can meet to discuss what I can do for you. What is the best way to contact you?"

Example #2: At a Career Fair "Hello, my name is Max Vonhaven. I've been working for the past five years as a computer engineer for a regional supermarket chain. I helped design and implement a data management system for multisite operations across four different states. On the side, I've gotten involved in our corporate volunteering effort with Habitat for Humanity. I see that you are looking for someone to build your technology capacity as you expand your house-building efforts regionally, and I know that I can bring the right skills to help you do that. Here is my résumé. Can we set up a time when I can tell you more about how I can help you get to where you'd like to be?"

Example #3: Over Dinner with Friends, Family, or Acquaintances "I've decided that I am going to make the leap to the nonprofit sector, and I'd like to enlist your help. As you know, this is a natural progression of my career, because I have been performing many of the tasks associated with the jobs that I want for the past 25 years. I am focusing my job search at the executive director level in organizations that focus on one of my three areas of passion: getting young people involved in politics, leadership programs for women and girls, and community service. Whom do you think I should call to further explore this dream of mine?"

Practice, practice, practice your speech. In fact, remove the "speech" from the speech. Make it a conversation opener, not a monologue. It should roll off your tongue and be natural, not memorized or stilted. Say it to your friends, your neighbors, your parakeet. This is the first time people are imagining you in this different role, and your ability to seem natural in its presentation will affect their interest in helping you get there.

Be Thankful

Unfortunately, some for-profit job seekers see their decision to work for less money as a favor they are bestowing upon the nonprofit sector. The nonprofit sector doesn't see it that way. A few bad apples have left a bad taste in the mouths of many nonprofit hiring managers. Be sure to be thankful along the way to avoid being tagged as an ungrateful job seeker.

Collect business cards from, or make notes of, the people with whom you interact during a job search. Send thank-you notes to each and every one of them, even if they were not all that helpful. They probably think they were, and telling them so will make them willing to try harder next time. Saying thank you will allow you to call them up repeatedly for advice, counsel, and new ideas without fear of reproach or dismissal.

Use your thank-you notes as strategic opportunities to share more information, make your case again, or simply say something you may have forgotten in a rushed encounter. A thank-you note is a perfect and, sadly, unexpected opportunity to thank an interviewer (even for an informational interview) for spending time with you and to remind the person of your strengths. Tell the interviewer about your search and, specifically, what you would like him or her to do for you. If appropriate, enclose an additional or updated copy of your résumé.

Never forget about thanking your networking contacts or those who have agreed to be references for you in your job search. Thank-you notes to them are not only surprising but keep you and your job search fresh in their mind for longer. Remember, even if your contacts want deep in their heart to assist you, you are not their first priority, and they will tend to forget. Don't be shy about reminding them gently how they can fulfill their wishes to help. Even if they were unable to come through for you on this job search, there will be others, and thanking them profusely, even for doing nothing, puts you in good standing for next time.

Informational Interviews

Throughout your networking, you should be asking both for additional connections and informational interviews. Informational interviews enable you to accomplish several things at once. They allow you to do the following:

- Introduce yourself to someone who may have a job opening in the future
- Learn more about the people who work at this nonprofit
- Receive direction and guidance from someone who was once in your shoes
- Learn a name to drop in your networking and personal connections you can use
- Gain valuable insights from an insider about trends in the sector in general, this nonprofit specifically, and the language to use to describe both
- Hear about some concerns, assumptions, or stereotypes that might be affecting your sector switch and how you might combat them
- Audition some preliminary answers to obvious interview questions when a particular job isn't on the line

Informational interviews can be a great boon to your job search if done well. If done poorly, however, they can only hinder your transition. Beware of the following "major don'ts" as you embark on your informational interviews.

Major Don't #1: Asking for a Job

One thing you are not seeking from an informational interview, ironically enough, is a job. You are there to get information. You will talk about your skills and experience and why you think you could be right for the nonprofit sector, and, of course, you will leave your résumé. But this isn't a job interview. You are the interviewer, not the interviewee. Bring some directed questions, but mostly listen to what your interviewee has to say. If you seem right for the organization, and there is an opening, rest assured that your interviewee will put two and two together and move your résumé along to the right person.

That being said, come prepared for an informational interview as if it were an interview where you might land a real job. You never know if it might turn into one. Most jobs are not advertised, and many employers do not even realize they have a need until they meet a person who might fill it. Be ready with great answers, extra copies of your résumé, and an open mind so that you can pivot quickly to the interview chair if the opportunity arises.

Major Don't #2: Disrespecting Interviewee's Time

Never ask to meet for coffee or lunch—even if it's your treat—unless the time is offered to you. It is a bigger time commitment than the person might want or be able to make, and likely they value that time more than the $6.95 sandwich he or she would get out of the deal. Instead, offer to come to their office for a 15-minute conversation. Everyone has 15 minutes, and the easier you make the interview for the interviewee, the more likely he or she is to give it to you.

To keep your contacts motivated to help you, never give the impression that your time is more important than their time. Be ever conscious of how much time you are taking. Disrespecting the 15 minutes you were granted by asking question upon question will turn a friend into a foe or, at the very least, a complacent contact. Complacent contacts don't open up and hand over names of their friends and colleagues lest you commit the same time-sucking crime with them, too.

Major Don't #3: Being Unprepared

A huge mistake many informational interviewers (that's you) make is to assume that this is a chance to get basic information about an organization. Don't waste your time or the interviewee's time by asking basic things that you could have found out by conducting even the most limited research. Interviewees won't feel as though you value the opportunity to speak with them and will feel undervalued, even insulted, as a result.

Arriving at an informational interview with more than basic knowledge about the person or the organization is more then just impressive; it's essential. It makes you ask smarter questions. Be creative, be ingenious, and put information you've learned about the person and the organization together with other information you've gathered elsewhere. You will look more intelligent and more like someone interviewees might take a chance on introducing around, either at their own office or to friends who might have job openings.

Major Don't #4: Talking Too Much

You come to an interview to learn from the person on the other side of the desk, not vice versa. Avoid the temptation to jump into the conversation as soon as you see an opportunity to talk about your skills and how great a job you would do in the nonprofit sector. Remember, studies show that people who talk more in conversations think that those conversations went very well. Why not give your interviewee a chance to be a "great conversationalist," leaving a positive impression about you while at the same time getting valuable data about the organization and the nonprofit sector?

Bring specific questions and allow your interviewees to answer them. Be prepared to be asked questions, too. You'll want to be able to pinpoint what you'd like to do and where you'd like to do it, but make sure you are using most of the time to learn more from them than they from you. There will always be another time for them to interview you if they are impressed from your first conversation.

Major Don't #5: Not Listening

You are getting this time as a gift; use it wisely. Don't ask the obvious, and avoid asking the same question over again. If you've run out of questions, say thank you and leave. It's that simple. You can always call back later if you think of more questions. However, if you seem as though you are fishing around to fill time because you are unprepared or because you were unfocused for the first few minutes, your follow-up calls will likely go unreturned.

Pay exceptional amounts of attention to what the interviewee is telling you, but treating this opportunity like a college lecture with a quiz coming tomorrow will come across as strange and stilted. Take notes as needed but not so much that you fail to converse normally.

Ten Smart Questions to Ask at an Informational Interview

You are unlikely to get all of your questions answered in an informational interview, so be direct about your most important ones. The smarter the questions, the smarter the questioner looks.

1. What brought you to this nonprofit and this mission area? In what ways has it lived up to your expectations? In what ways have you been disappointed?

2. I read with great interest about how your organization is expanding programs into four new states. This is particularly interesting to me as an entrepreneur. Can you tell me about the funding challenges that poses and how, given current philanthropic trends, you are planning to handle them?

3. Whom do you consider to be your competition for funding, for media, for members, etc.?

4. What is the working atmosphere like here? Is this typical for the nonprofit sector in your experience? What do you enjoy, and what do you dislike?

5. I notice that many of the staff here, like you, have business backgrounds. What difficulties did that pose to you when you came into the nonprofit sector? In what ways did it make things easier? (Or, conversely, I notice that few of the staff have business backgrounds and wonder how you feel about the ability of people to switch sectors?)

6. Which skills, experiences, backgrounds, or personality types have you found to be most successful in your role? Which have not?

7. How has this organization and your role changed since you've been here? In response to what? How does it need to continue to change?

8. How would you assess my background, and where would you think I ought to focus my professional development to be successful in the type of position I seek?

9. Do you have any words of wisdom, advice, or warning based on your experiences? What do you wish you knew when you started that you know now? Who else might have valuable insights and a good network of friends and colleagues?

10. May I follow up with you as my job search evolves to keep you posted and get additional advice along the way?

JOB-HUNTING RESOURCES

Many new resources are available for job hunters, thanks to technology and to the enormous growth of the nonprofit sector. There are resources to help you get connected, get headhunted, get active, and get smart. In fact, from face-to-face conversations to Internet research to virtual networks, a good job seeker has more tools than time to use them.

Before you start using these resources, however, make sure that you have some tools of your own already set up. Strip your answering machine of any music, children's voices, or silly outgoing messages. Invest in faster computer access or learn the hours of local libraries, Wi-Fi-enabled coffee shops, or public access technology centers. Find a fax number, like one at a local copy shop, so that you can give it out if asked. Set up an e-mail account with a serious outgoing address that you use for this and only this purpose. Treat your job search as if it is your job, and you will find yourself being taken more seriously.

Getting Connected: The Internet Is Your Playground

There is no better resource for today's job seeker than the Internet. With the thousands of job announcements, networking groups, membership lists, and Web sites spoon feeding you all the data you need for a successful job search, it is nearly impossible to go wrong. Yet the Internet can be overwhelming if you fail to use it in a constructive and strategic manner.

Online Job Boards

The Internet has been overrun with recruiters and human resource managers trawling for the best candidate catch. Their bait is placed on Web pages large and small, nonprofit and for-profit, exclusive to the nonprofit world and not. But you can't bite until you find their hooks, and that's not always easy.

Literally hundreds of sites on the Internet list jobs. There are the big ones, like Monster.com, CareerBuilder.com, and HotJobs.com, and there are small ones that list jobs in specific fields or only in certain geographic areas. You should spend limited time trolling around the big sites and pay more attention to the smaller, more directed ones. This may seem counterintuitive, but let's consider the facts.

CareerXRoads, a highly respected publication that ranks job boards by popularity, produced an alarming study in 2003 that showed that hiring rates from these sites were, in fact, quite low. Of the companies interviewed, only 3.6 percent made a hire through Monster.com, only 1.5 percent made a hire through CareerBuilder.com, and a miniscule 0.5 percent hired anyone through HotJobs.com. That's less than 6 percent of all hires through these big boards.

On the other hand, entrepreneurs seeking profit and/or social change have invaded the nonprofit job search universe with dynamic, directed, cost-effective job boards. Ranging from sites that list the full range of available jobs across the nonprofit spectrum to sites that list jobs only in certain mission areas or functional expertise—like social work, education, or accounting and finance—there are job boards in this sector that make sense for your search.

You can use most good job boards in two effective ways: actively or passively. Either way should provide you with ease of use, clear directions, and, most important, security and privacy.

Active Engagement You can visit job boards as often as you'd like, entering your mission interests, functional expertise, and geographic desires, and be presented with a listing of current jobs being advertised by employers. Some job boards add details about the organization and what it does. Others link directly to the organizations.

Another way to engage good job boards actively is to enter your résumé in an easy-to-read fashion. Such boards offer the employer paying to post the job the option of searching their résumé databases to find candidates. Some boards allow you to withhold identification information, and others allow you to approve who gets to see your résumé before the hiring manager is granted access.

Passive Engagement One of the most useful features of good online job boards is getting a personalized e-mail delivered to your inbox on a daily or weekly basis. Once you have entered your requirements for your next job into their online forms, their systems identify posted jobs that meet your interests, then send an e-mail directly to you. Surprisingly, for all the new advertising and outreach technology out there, some boards do this better than others.

Don't let the proliferation of Web-based job searching make finding a job harder rather than easier. If you find that you are overrun with jobs for which you hold no interest or are completely unqualified to fill, unsubscribe yourself from the e-mail service and go back to doing things the old-fashioned way by manually searching the Web site each week. Further, if you find yourself getting lazy in your networking and relying on these e-mails as your only source of information about new jobs, unsubscribe at once and force yourself to work a little harder.

Nonprofit Job Boards

Here are some major nonprofit job boards that will act as great launching points for your job search journey.

- *www.idealist.org.* A project of Action Without Borders, Idealist is the granddaddy of nonprofit job boards. At $50 a posting for employers, it's considered a "can't miss" by most nonprofits. There are job postings from upwards of 45,000 non-profit organizations in 180 countries in addition to volunteer and internship opportunities, events, resources, and programs.

- *www.philanthropy.com.* The *Chronicle of Philanthropy* is the newspaper of the nonprofit world. It is the number-one news source, in print and online, for charity leaders, fundraisers, grant makers, and others involved in the philanthropic enterprise. Each week, the *Chronicle* sends more than 168,000 e-mail messages to more than 15,000 users of this service.

- *www.execsearches.com.* Since its launch in 1999, ExecSearches.com has been a leader in mid- to senior-level job announcements with up to 400,000 visits per month from professionals seeking employment in nonprofits, the public sector, education, health, and the government.

- *www.nptimes.com. The NonProfit Times* covers the business of the nonprofit sector. Published in print 24 times a year, it is read by over 78,000 full-time non-profit executive managers around the country.

- *www.associationjobs.com.* CEO Update posts jobs for free, but the salary to be paid must be at least $50,000 a year. CEO Update also publishes a 28-page print list of jobs and sells subscriptions for its national registry of CEO-level jobs.

A thorough list of other exceptional general job boards and boards broken down by geographic region, issues area, or functional expertise can be found in Part 3 of this book.

Online Networking Forums

The Internet has revolutionized job searching. Rather than dragging yourself to a monthly job networking meeting in a damp church basement, virtual networks have sprung up all over the world to provide quick and efficient methods of introductions, information transfers, and assistance requests. Sure, these groups still meet face-to-face at times, but now in a more targeted fashion, allowing you better to utilize your limited time.

Young Nonprofit Professionals Networks YNPN promotes an efficient, viable, and inclusive nonprofit sector that supports the growth, learning, and development of young professionals. With 5,000 members nationwide, YNPN engages and supports future nonprofit and community leaders through professional development, networking, and social opportunities designed for young people involved in the nonprofit community. There are currently chapters in Austin, Boston, Chicago, Denver, Milwaukee, New York City, Orlando, San Francisco, southern California, and Washington, D.C., with more chapters on the way.

LinkedIn LinkedIn is an online network of more than 6 million experienced professionals from around the world, representing 130 industries. Signing up, which is free, allows you to set up a profile, complete résumé, and begin using the contacts of your friends and colleagues to meet their contacts of friends and colleagues. Simply by reaching out to contacts and asking them to introduce you by e-mail to a contact they have, you can multiply your network quite rapidly.

Net Impact Net Impact's mission is to improve the world by growing and strengthening a network of new leaders who are using the power of business to make a positive social, environmental, and economic impact. Alumni from MBA programs, these individuals are looking to use their business education for good. There are more than 120 chapters worldwide, a central office in San Francisco, and a flourishing online community.

Craigslist A virtual version of the giant community bulletin board in your local supermarket, Craigslist.org now operates sites in most major cities worldwide, listing more than 400,000 new jobs each month and many more issue-related service and networking opportunities. It is a no-frills site, and its price tag reflects that: it is free to read and mostly free to post.

Various Local Listservs Listservs exist on every imaginable topic, and nonprofits are no exception. Doing just a little research, you can find listservs oriented toward, for example, Jewish philanthropy, gay fundraising professionals, or women in community development. There are also many listservs for nonprofits based on city, state, or region. These listservs include messages on current regulations, funding availability, lobbying activities, networking events, training and technical assistance, and job announcements. Even just lurking (i.e., reading, not posting) near these listservs can serve as a Nonprofits in Your Neighborhood 101 course. A more detailed listing of some of the larger listservs can be found in Part 3 of this book.

Getting Headhunted: A Note about Nonprofit Executive Search Firms

Larger organizations that can afford to retain a nonprofit executive search firm to assist them often do so. A typical search firm will charge one-third of the successful applicant's first-year's cash compensation to perform this work. Some have minimum fees of anywhere from $25,000 to $40,000. While they seek nonprofit executives, the search firms themselves are mostly for-profit endeavors.

A search firm is only as good as the searches it has in-house at any given moment. As such, it does not pay to spend a great deal of time trying to get a headhunter to call you back. That said, many retained nonprofit executive search firms, just like their counterparts in the for-profit sector, specialize in particular fields—from higher education, to health care, to advocacy—or functional areas of expertise, such as development, finance, or operations. If a firm doesn't have a search that is right for you presently, they may get something appropriate next month.

A great way to crack executive search firms is to find a way to help them in a search where you are not a potential candidate. For example, if a search firm is representing a nonprofit with a job in finance, but you work in operations, call the headhunter and tell him or her about the people you know who might be appropriate or interested, or about the issue-related networking group you have joined where you could distribute the job announcement. Of course, once you have helped the headhunter, take a minute or two to mention your own job search. Note that you will send, along with the contact information of the individuals or groups you are recommending, your own résumé for their file. Because you have just helped them, they may be more open to hearing about your own search. Then, when you need to call a firm about the job you actually want, you can say that you "are Joe Smith, and as you'll recall, we talked about a search you did last month for…." Headhunters see hundreds of résumés each week. They are unlikely to search for your résumé when they get retained to fill your dream job, but they will remember that you talked and that you were helpful. With additional reminding, you'll be able to have your first directed conversation about your own skills and qualifications.

Many search firms are organized internally as individual profit centers. Recruiters may work together or operate their own individual business under the larger firm's umbrella, sharing overhead, staff support, and databases. Never assume, then, that if you know one headhunter at a firm, you know all of them or, more important, that they know you. Use your networking assistance accordingly. For example, you "are Joe Smith, and you talked last month with their colleague, Nancy Jones, about a job that was too finance related for you, but now you're excited to learn about the operations job they have just been retained to fill." Suddenly, you seem like a known quantity, someone who has already cracked the firm's armor. If you're in, you must have been approved by someone, right? Therefore, the headhunter may be predisposed to talk with you.

Unlike the for-profit sector, there are no nonprofit executive search firms that represent job seekers as their agents. Some, though, like the (shameless plug coming...) Nonprofit Professionals Advisory Group (*www.nonprofitprofessionals.com*) are staffed with experienced headhunters who provide fee-based services to job seekers, like résumé consultation, interview training, or job search strategy development. Using these services is a good way to make sure that your for-profit background is resonating with a recruiter in the nonprofit sector and that you are going about your search in the best possible way. A list of many nonprofit executive search firms can be found in Part 3 of this book.

Getting Efficient: Career Fairs

Career fairs are a great opportunity for those with ten or fewer years of experience to approach a large group of nonprofit employers at once. Used well, these fairs can provide you with a quantum leap in your networking because they give you direct, in-person, focused access to the right people at the right organizations.

These career fairs will, in some ways, resemble the career fairs you went to as you were seeking your first job out of college. There will be the same tables of employers with videos, brochures, job listings, and banners, and there will be the same overeager job seekers battling for their attention, except at nonprofit job fairs, at some tables either or both the employer and/or the job seeker may be wearing a T-shirt and Birkenstocks instead of a three-piece suit.

By far the biggest and most wide-ranging nonprofit career fairs are held by Idealist, a project of Action Without Borders. They include the typical tables of employers but also attract organizations looking for volunteers or interns. In addition, Idealist now includes panels of experts providing valuable information on job searching or working in the nonprofit sector. Roughly a dozen or so have been held each year since the spring of 2001. Sixty fairs in 25 cities across the United States have attracted over 3,000 organizations and 30,000 job seekers. The fairs are free for job seekers—though at any price, they would be worth a day spent networking.

What to Wear

Dress accordingly. Don't wear your blue pinstripe suit and leather wingtips. Normally, khakis and a button-down shirt will suffice for men and a skirt or pants and a sweater or blouse is fine for women. As with anything else, however, consider your audience. If you are looking for a job in a highly entrepreneurial nonprofit already friendly to MBAs, a suit may be better. If you are looking to move into a conservation group, that alligator-skin briefcase your grandmother gave you when you graduated from college might be a real turnoff.

What to Bring

You may be asked to set up an appointment for an interview, or quite likely you will be interviewed on the spot. Be prepared for either with your calendar, your résumé, and your compelling story about why you want to move into the nonprofit sector at this time in your life and career. Keep business cards handy, either from your current job or some that you have printed on your own from one of the many free outlets found online.

What to Do

Most career fairs advertise a list of nonprofits who have confirmed attendance as a way to attract job seekers and more nonprofits. This list is normally available ahead of time, with an updated list available at the door. Before charging up to the first table, review this list very carefully. Know who is there and whom you want to impress and create a plan of attack.

Do not approach a nonprofit and ask it to "tell me about yourself." Technically the nonprofit is there to market the organization, but it is also there to fill specific positions. The staffers behind the table have been delivering their marketing pitch all day, and they may well be frustrated and tired. Research the nonprofit in question before you get to its table and ask directed, strategic questions that go beyond a basic understanding of who they are and what they do. They will be delighted to delve more deeply with an educated, informed conversationalist. This approach will not only set you apart from other job seekers, but will show that you are taking this move into the nonprofit sector—and your desire to work for their nonprofit specifically—more seriously than your résumé alone might communicate.

Gaining Experience: Putting More Than Just Your Foot in the Door

One of the best ways to immerse yourself immediately in a nonprofit network is to start working or volunteering for one. This can be as a one-time volunteer, a long-term volunteer, a consultant (paid or pro bono), a board member, an intern, or a temporary employee. We will cover, in more detail, volunteering and board memberships as a way to improve your résumé and increase your knowledge in Chapter 6. However, should you have time to begin working full-time or part-time in the nonprofit sector, there are avenues of assistance.

Internships, Temporary, and Temporary-to-Permanent Positions

For those just getting started, internships are an ideal way to get your foot in the door. Some are paid; some are not. Either way, you should design your internship to be like a real job, where expectations are clear on both sides. Tell your employer that you are looking to perform a very specific scope of work to learn or further hone a set of skills. In exchange, you would like assistance in networking in the nonprofit sector and a recommendation, if the employer feels comfortable, about the work you have performed.

Remember that many temporary jobs turn into permanent jobs. Others lead to permanent jobs with different responsibilities within the same nonprofit. While you are doing your assigned work, keep an eye out for other assignments that could showcase your broader skill set. Just because you were hired to answer the phones doesn't mean you can't do other things, too. Treating your temporary position as if it were your dream job—answer every single call quickly and with gusto—will serve those less fortunate for whom the nonprofit exists, and it will be a shot in the arm for your job search. And, if you do it well, the nonprofit will be happy to give you more assignments.

Temporary Staffing Agencies

Temporary staffing agencies that expressly serve nonprofits have begun to spring up across the country. Like search firms, these agencies tend to be for-profit ventures. Most cover a functional area of expertise or a geographic area. Some examples include:

- *Professionals for Nonprofits.* Working in New York City and the greater Washington, D.C., area, Professionals for Nonprofits provides temporary, permanent, and consulting staff to nonprofits. See *www.nonprofitstaffing.com*.

- *Nonprofit Staffing Solutions.* Based in Washington, D.C., Nonprofit Staffing Solutions offers the opportunity to "Temp with a Purpose" to job seekers, while fulfilling the executive search, temporary, contract, and direct hire staffing needs of local nonprofit organizations. See *www.nonprofittemps.com*.

- *Accounting Management Solutions.* With both for-profit and nonprofit placement arms, Boston-based Accounting Management Solutions offers temporary, permanent, and temp-to-perm opportunities for all types of financial positions, and this agency understands well how candidates can move between sectors. See *www.amsolutions.net*.

Second Careers for Baby Boomers and Early Retirees

There are 78 million baby boomers in the United States, and many of them are realizing that a retirement of nothing but golf and travel may sound like a dream come true at first, but only sustains them emotionally, mentally, and financially for so long. This is the generation that lived through Vietnam, the civil rights movement, the Peace Corps, and the assassinations of John F. Kennedy, Robert F. Kennedy, and Martin Luther King Jr. They are the fastest-growing talent pool in the nonprofit sector and have a lifetime of righteousness, angst, and social justice stored deep inside, perfect for fueling their second career in the nonprofit sector.

The nonprofit sector is standing up and taking notice of the baby boomers. In fact, many nonprofits have been created to help ease these energetic, active, and interested professionals into a second career in the nonprofit sector. Civic Ventures, a nonprofit based in San Francisco, is leading the charge. Its recent research has shown that Americans in the second half of life—regardless of income, educational level, or race—want to explore options for the next stage of life; retool skills, obtain new training, or pursue educational interests; use their skills and experience in flexible work or service opportunities; and make meaningful connections with their peers and their community.

The Next Chapter, an initiative of Civic Ventures, was created to provide expertise and assistance to community groups across the country that help people in the second half of life set a course, connect with peers, and find pathways to significant service. Local Next Chapter projects and related programs exist in dozens of communities nationwide and are growing every day.

In addition, other nonprofits, like Experience Corps and Senior Corps, have been founded with the express intent of providing significant volunteer experience with demonstrable results. Programs that provide long-term, direct service or where you can volunteer in central office administrative work are a good way of testing your mettle for this type of work, your dedication to the mission, and the level at which you'd like to do it.

Turning Networking into Consulting Assignments

Nonprofits often need high levels of support around major, organizationwide changes. These can include, but are certainly not limited to, executive searches, reorganization, training, or event management. At these times, nonprofits turn to consultants, individuals who can provide expertise without placing a heavy burden on the salary line of the budget. As nonprofits become more sophisticated, they are looking for consultants who can bring business expertise to their nonprofit world, and that is where you might come in.

Corporate career changers increasingly find themselves offered small consulting gigs to work on a specific project for a nonprofit while they complete their job search. Wonderful opportunities, these assignments allow career changers to get to know the nonprofit world from the inside out while getting paid a little something for their trouble. For example, a nonprofit needing assistance with creating a growth plan may want someone with the expertise to benchmark their competition's strategic decisions and how those decisions impacted their success. Or they may need someone to create accounting and bookkeeping systems as they set up a social enterprise venture in-house. The possibilities are endless, and job seekers who are creative can turn them into fruitful opportunities.

Getting Smart: Where to Learn More

Due to the legal and accounting requirements to retain nonprofit status, and because their donors demand it, the organizations you are targeting in your search are forced to be much more transparent than if you were looking for a job in the corporate sector. Getting information about nonprofits is relatively easy, and having it at your fingertips will impress your interviewers. Further information about specific non-profits is available through a number of different avenues.

IRS Form 990

GuideStar's Web site includes a searchable database of more than 640,000 nonprofit organizations in the United States and is the easiest place to find a nonprofit's tax return and audited financial statements. The "990," as it's simply known in the sector's lingo, lists the annual budget of the organization, it's mission, address, revenue sources, highest-paid consultants, equity, and expenses of the nonprofit, and can provide valuable insight to its financial sustainability. Nonprofits with revenue over $25,000 must file, although religious organizations and government entities are exempt.

Give.org

The Better Business Bureau's Wise Giving Alliance (*www.give.org*) provides charity evaluation reports as well as a National Charity Seal of Approval for charities that solicit contributions nationwide.

Annual Reports

Most nonprofits publish annual reports in some form or another. Larger nonprofits produce multicolor, multipage books and distribute them to thousands of stakehold-ers, donors, friends, and volunteers. Smaller nonprofits may have a two- or three-page version in a PDF file on their Web site. Regardless of their format, annual reports exist to tell donors how their money was spent in the prior year, what programs were run, who was served, and any exciting news about expansion of work over the past year or in years to come. They are both a description of the past and a road map for the future, and reading them before you interview will allow you to talk about how your strengths fit into this particular nonprofit and its needs, using its own language and focus.

The Nonprofit's Web Site

It may seem obvious, but many candidates never take the time to read the organization's Web site thoroughly. Not doing so is like writing a book report after renting the movie version. In fact, it is about the same as writing the report after dozing off during the movie's trailer. Reviewing the nonprofit's Web site is an essential part of developing your knowledge about the nonprofit, its programs, its people, and even its competition, as well as its technological savvy and the resources it has to put toward public relations and communications. Some Web sites even go so far as to list the biographies of the people you will be meeting; you can't get better prepared than knowing if you have something important, like an alma mater, in common with your interviewer.

Conferences and Seminars

Invest in attending conferences and seminars held by the leading lights in the nonprofit sector, whether they are on substantive topics, such as the latest trends in environmental programming, or procedural points, like board training. Doing so will put you in a room with like-minded people who already are doing the jobs you would like to do. Plus, you will learn volumes of interesting, salient data to bring up in your networking and interviewing. These conferences vary widely, from the tactical to the ethereal; a good rule of thumb is that if you start rolling your eyes in the first 15 minutes, you are in the wrong place. Regroup, reregister, and try another conference.

Third-Party News Stories

Make sure to visit the Web sites of the sector's main newspapers and journals, such as the *Chronicle of Philanthropy*, the *Chronicle of Higher Education*, the *Nonprofit Times*, and the *Nonprofit Quarterly*. Do a Web search to see if any newsworthy items have been published recently about the organization. You may learn about scandals or crises, or about major grants and new projects. Either way, you will be more knowledgeable in your networking if you know the organization's public history.

Libraries

Often overlooked in this day and age of easily accessible Internet connections, the library is a terrific, free resource that should be utilized by all. Librarians know where to get any piece of information you can imagine, can put their fingers on databases and membership lists that are not accessible to the general public, and can point you in directions that will save you valuable time and resources. And, of course, libraries have Internet access too.

Nonprofit FAQs

Finally, one of the best resources out there is Putnam Barber's overwhelmingly comprehensive Nonprofit FAQs. Hosted by Idealist (*www.idealist .org/if/idealist/en/faq/nonprofit/home/default*) and begun in the early 1990s, this Web site acts as a veritable road map of the nonprofit sector's inner workings. Got a question about tax requirements? It's in here. Want to know what political activities are allowed by nonprofits? That's here. Looking to figure out how to get celebrities to help your nonprofit raise money? Yup, got that too.

CONCLUSION

The best job search, nonprofit or for-profit, is a targeted job search. Just as you once set your sights on your ideal job in the for-profit sector, this chapter was intended to help you hone the direction of your nonprofit job search. Keeping in mind your whole history, including the jobs you've been paid to do and the ones for which you have volunteered your time, you should now have a clearer sense of yourself as a nonprofit job candidate.

Now that we have identified the entire three-dimensionality of your nonprofit candidacy through a self-assessment process, networking and informational interviews, and additional sector knowledge gathering, it's time to put together a résumé that will act as your chief marketing piece. In the next chapter, we will shape your past into a document that sells your future as a serious nonprofit job candidate. We'll address which sections, formats, and language to include and which to avoid. Where you may find yourself lacking, we will introduce resources that will help you fill in any gaps of knowledge, skills, or experience.

CHAPTER 6

Building Your Nonprofit Résumé

When a headhunter or hiring manager advertises an open position, depending on the attractiveness of the job between 100 and 300 applications may cross the manager's desk. On average, the hirer may spend about eight seconds looking at each—more likely, fewer.

Pretty scary, huh? If you can't capture someone's interest in those eight seconds, you can kiss your chances to interview for your fairy-tale job goodbye. So how do you create a résumé that tells your story accurately and effectively, conveys the logic behind your transition to the nonprofit sector, and grabs the headhunter's or hiring manager's attention so that you'll get a longer read?

Neon green paper isn't the answer, tempting as it may sound. Nor is presenting your résumé as you did for each of the corporate jobs you've held. This change in your career, like any change in direction, requires a shift in presentation, marketing materials, and spin. It may also mean gathering more experience with, or intelligence about, nonprofits and nonprofit management through one of many available board positions, volunteer or consulting opportunities, or educational programs. In short, you must internalize that this change requires the development and rollout of a whole new product line: the nonprofit you! This chapter will discuss the elements of the nonprofit résumé and how you can fill in any gaps.

FOR-PROFIT RÉSUMÉS DIFFER FROM NONPROFIT RÉSUMÉS

The nonprofit sector isn't about buzzwords or keywords. It's about relevance. The first thing most hiring managers look at when they open your résumé is your current job and your current company. This will most likely be the first strike against you. The second thing is your education; if it is solely business related, it may be the second strike. Strike three may be a lack of numbers showing relevant scale or scope of your projects and accomplishments; a huge difference between what you've done and what you want to do, in either direction, won't make you look like a good fit for the position.

Rewriting your résumé to inoculate yourself against these strikes is key. This section will walk you through each of the important parts of a résumé, showing you how to expand them, how to highlight relevant data, and how to reflect accurately your achievements. Then we will look at format types and appropriate introductions that present you favorably.

Size Matters

One of the most common questions professional résumé writers hear is, "How can I present a 15-, 20-, or 30-year career in just one page of text?" The answer: you cannot, and if you do, you have not given your career the marketing it deserves.

Feel free to elaborate to the length of two or three pages, if you have the material to do so. A four-page résumé from a 19-year-old college student internship applicant is obnoxious. Yet if you are at a level where you are comfortable applying for a senior executive position, then a one-page résumé does you a disservice. While a recruiter will only spend a few moments looking at your résumé, you should provide enough material to communicate the full scope of your accomplishments. The recruiter will skip around to find the data needed to make a judgment about your candidacy. As such, length is less important than clarity of format and relevance of the information presented.

A good rule of thumb is that you should have one page of a résumé for every 10 years of experience. If you've been working for 25 years, you might have three pages to fill. If you've only been working for 9 years but have significant community volunteerism, you may be able to go to two pages and still have real content. If the résumé is getting too long but you still have significant publications, presentations, or other tangentially related work to include, keep yourself to a shorter résumé and include an addendum of selected materials.

Use Numbers

Let's go back to the imaginary hiring manager's desk stacked high with 300 résumés. Imagine further that each résumé is two pages and each cover letter is one page. That adds up to 900 pieces of paper. Throw in a few lists of references, reference letters, writing samples, or salary histories, and that quickly jumps to more than a thousand pieces of paper to muddle through. Knowing that at least 80 percent of these résumés are from unqualified candidates, the headhunter is going to speed through this pile.

The first thing most headhunters will look at is the résumé, not the cover letter. In fact, *cover letter* is hardly an accurate term, given that most hiring managers staple them to the back of the résumé. Most career changers fall back on their cover letter as the way to tell their story and do themselves a disservice by attaching their old, irrelevant for-profit résumé to their cover letter. (We discuss cover letters in more detail in Chapter 7.) Make sure your résumé tells your story—don't use the cover letter as a crutch. The résumé is, after all, what the headhunter sees first, only going back to read your cover letter if there is enough meat in your résumé.

Including specific numbers on your résumé allows a headhunter to quickly discern whether you have the required level of depth, breadth, and scope of experience for a particular position. Despite the fact that bottom-line numbers aren't the only things that affect the bottom line of a nonprofit, both the nonprofit and for-profit sectors are data driven. A headhunter may assume that if you have managed a budget of $200,000, you may be able to manage a budget of $500,000, or that if you've managed a budget of $5 million, you may be able to take the leap to $10 million. Yet the headhunter may also assume that if you have managed a budget of $200,000, you should take some steps between this and the $10 million corner-office job.

Specifically, list significant numerical data points that tell your story (e.g., revenue generated, alliances created, budgets reduced, staff managed, bottom-line growth, savings overall, speeches written, and press mentions secured). If you've done any nonprofit work or volunteer work, list numbers of dollars raised, staff managed, grants written, board members trained, and the like. But don't get too carried away.

Listing number of marathons run, number and ages of children, or your own age is too much information, and it potentially provides what is illegal for the headhunter to consider.

Be Specific

When was the last time your day-to-day job reflected that position description you agreed to years ago? If you are like most people, the answer is "not lately" or even "not ever."

Yet, most of us fall into the habit of reproducing the bullets of our job descriptions in our résumés, because it is the easiest starting point to explain what we do. However, your job description was probably poorly written to start with, and if you start with a poor outline, you'll end up with a worse résumé.

Your job description likely lists what you were supposed to do on a daily basis to fulfill the responsibilities of the job for which you were originally hired. It doesn't list your accomplishments—what you actually did—or how that work fit into the bigger picture of the corporation or organization. It certainly doesn't list all of the additional responsibilities you accumulated and for which you worked so hard. The nonprofit sector cares about the impact that you made in your for-profit life.

Fleshing out a short bullet-point item into a longer description will make your achievement both more understandable and more interesting. Below are some examples of ineffective bullets and their longer, more successful rewrites.

Space waster:	Secured donations from private corporations.
Attention grabber:	Raised $5 million in corporate donations through three $1 million major gifts, four community events, and the recruitment of two new board members.
Space waster:	Managed staff and budget in accordance with company policies.
Attention grabber:	Spearheaded a staff of 12 and a budget of $1 million, managing both day-to-day operations and the development and implementation of a year-long, departmentwide restructuring, which ultimately saved the company in excess of $200,000 per year.

Space waster: Acted as public liaison for company for all external inquiries.

Attention grabber: Led overall press strategy, weekly media outreach efforts, and the creation of collateral materials for a 14-partner coalition, resulting in coverage in print publications, including the *New York Times*, *Wall Street Journal*, and Associated Press, and on-air coverage in 843 radio and television stories.

Take Credit

The simple truth is that people don't always do what they were hired to do, and if they do, they don't often do it well. Your résumé should highlight not just what you did but how the overall outcome was different because *you* were part of the process. Ask yourself, "What wouldn't have happened but for the fact that I was there?" If you were part of a team, highlight your role and make sure you acknowledge the team, but take appropriate credit for your contributions as well.

Most résumés do not take enough credit for the work done. A résumé is no time to be a shrinking violet; if you don't show yourself off, the next candidate in the pile won't do it for you. As a for-profit candidate for a nonprofit job, you'll have to be extra diligent about showing off about what you've done that is relevant to where the nonprofit wants to go.

Think of your résumé as a talking point for your nonprofit hiring manager, most likely someone who doesn't understand where you have been. Rather than making them fumble through a foreign subject, spoon-feed them information in a way that allows them to understand where you have been and how your experience is relevant to their nonprofit. You can't do this without a bit of boasting.

Use Action Verbs

Verbs may take one of three distinct forms: occurrences (become, happen), states of being (are, seem, be) or actions (accomplish, strategize, bungee jump). Action verbs frame your experiences in terms of movement toward a goal and help you show off the results. Without action verbs, your résumé reads flat, and without a variety of them, your writing reads even flatter. Below are lists of action verbs appropriate for different types of skills you may list on your résumé.

Communications, Public Affairs, Public Relations, and Lobbying

acquainted
addressed
advocated
affected
aided
aired
answered
apprised
briefed
cast
communicated
controlled
conveyed
convinced
coordinated
corresponded

debated
defined
defused
dispatched
dispensed
dissuaded
distinguished
educated
effected
elaborated
elected
emphasized
expanded
explained
exploited
fielded

framed
handled
influenced
informed
interpreted
interviewed
introduced
lobbied
localized
marketed
mobilized
narrated
persuaded
phrased
profiled
promoted

provoked
publicized
quoted
represented
responded
reversed
spoke
sponsored
spread
targeted
taught
testified
thanked
translated
transmitted

Creative

advertised
choreographed
chose
circulated
coauthored
collaborated
collected
composed
condensed
conducted
conserved
contrived
copied

corrected
crafted
created
criticized
critiqued
customized
described
designed
detailed
displayed
drafted
drew
duplicated

edited
exhibited
fabricated
fashioned
illuminated
illustrated
imagined
improvised
modeled
named
noticed
photographed

printed
produced
published
revealed
showed
simulated
staged
substituted
tailored
traced
verbalized
wrote

Program Creation

adapted	devised	innovated	submitted
added	devoted	orchestrated	substantiated
admitted	diagnosed	originated	undertook
adopted	diagrammed	pioneered	visited
anticipated	directed	proposed	vitalized
chartered	established	reached	volunteered
commissioned	exceeded	reacted	won
complied	experimented	safeguarded	worked
conceived	founded	started	
conceptualized	inaugurated	steered	
demonstrated	initiated	stimulated	

Evaluation and Assessment

actuated	endorsed	observed	reviewed
analyzed	evaluated	patterned	suggested
appraised	examined	penalized	summarized
assessed	exposed	perceived	surveyed
audited	gauged	predicted	tabulated
averted	graded	probed	tested
competed	indexed	processed	tracked
contrasted	inventoried	projected	validated
correlated	investigated	ranked	valued
disclosed	judged	rated	viewed
discounted	measured	realized	weighed
discovered	monitored	redesigned	

Project Management and Leadership

absorbed	deferred	invented	serviced
accelerated	delegated	kindled	settled
accomplished	designated	litigated	shaped
appointed	determined	managed	signed
approved	disciplined	motivated	simplified
authorized	drove	oversaw	solved
began	earned	praised	sparked
broadened	elevated	presided	spearheaded
built	employed	prevailed	specialized
catapulted	enforced	prioritized	specified
chaired	excelled	pursued	succeeded
completed	governed	ran	surpassed
conferred	granted	rewarded	terminated
consolidated	implemented	selected	thrived
constructed	instilled	sent	
consulted	instituted	served	

KAPLAN

Organizational Development

achieved	diversified	lightened	staffed
acted	documented	organized	strategized
altered	doubled	performed	strengthened
amended	exchanged	permitted	stressed
augmented	excited	played	stretched
bargained	executed	preserved	superseded
challenged	finalized	protected	supervised
changed	focused	quadrupled	supplemented
channeled	formed	qualified	sustained
closed	headed	recruited	synchronized
committed	heightened	retained	synthesized
cut	hired	revised	trimmed
decided	induced	revitalized	tripled
decreased	inspired	revolutionized	witnessed
developed	led	stabilized	

Research and Analysis

applied	centralized	extracted	queried
ascertained	clarified	extrapolated	questioned
asked	classified	figured	read
assembled	cleared	hypothesized	requested
assigned	compiled	inferred	researched
assisted	concluded	inquired	searched
assumed	considered	located	speculated
authored	deduced	pinpointed	studied
carried	detected	polled	uncovered
cataloged	disproved	proved	unraveled
categorized	extended		

Data and Technical

automated	linked	planned	screened
checked	logged	programmed	segmented
combined	maintained	recorded	separated
compared	mapped	recovered	standardized
computed	minimized	reengineered	systematized
debugged	moved	repaired	updated
engineered	navigated	replaced	upgraded
entered	outlined	reported	used
isolated	overhauled	retrieved	utilized
issued	phased	revamped	verified
launched	placed	routed	

Operations and Finance

acquired	functioned	opened	renegotiated
bought	furnished	operated	reorganized
budgeted	grouped	operationalized	restored
calculated	guaranteed	ordered	restructured
charted	guarded	paid	resulted
compounded	incorporated	priced	scheduled
contracted	incurred	procured	secured
counted	inspected	prompted	shopped
decentralized	installed	purchased	shortened
depreciated	instigated	quantified	shrank
divested	insured	reconciled	streamlined
estimated	integrated	reduced	structured
exempted	juggled	registered	supplied
fit	kept	regulated	supported
followed	licensed	rejected	tightened
forecast	liquidated	related	transacted
formalized	merged	remedied	transferred
formulated	negotiated	remodeled	transformed
fulfilled	offset	rendered	

Capacity Building

activated	enabled	maximized	reshaped
advanced	encouraged	moderated	resolved
allocated	enhanced	modernized	salvaged
amplified	enlarged	modified	saved
awarded	explored	multiplied	took
balanced	familiarized	overcame	troubleshot
boosted	harnessed	participated	turned
brought	honed	practiced	unified
delighted	improved	prevented	united
dissembled	increased	rectified	
distributed	justified	refined	
eliminated	leveraged	regained	

Training and Technical Assistance

adhered	ensured	invested	prescribed
adjusted	exercised	lectured	presented
administered	expedited	mastered	provided
advised	facilitated	mediated	recommended
arbitrated	fortified	mentored	referred
arranged	guided	nurtured	rehabilitated
coached	helped	offered	reinforced
comforted	highlighted	oriented	reinstated
counseled	identified	passed	trained
disseminated	indoctrinated	prepared	tutored
engaged	instructed		

Fundraising, Community Relations, and Partnership Development

accessed	contributed	gave	raised
accompanied	converted	generated	received
approached	cooperated	greeted	recognized
attained	cultivated	grossed	sold
attended	delivered	hosted	solicited
attracted	eased	interested	tended
availed	elicited	interfaced	traded
borrowed	enlisted	invited	transported
called	enriched	involved	traveled
calmed	entertained	joined	treated
canvassed	financed	listened	welcomed
capitalized	fostered	merchandized	widened
captured	found	met	
catered	gained	netted	
contacted	gathered	obtained	

Use Appropriate Language

One of the biggest challenges you will face in telling your story is translating your for-profit experience into nonprofit speak. Simply put, the languages of the sectors are different. The nonprofit sector has stakeholders, not shareholders; donors, not investors; clients, not customers. To ensure that the person reviewing your résumé understands that you can make this shift, begin by incorporating the language of the nonprofit sector into your résumé. The following chart will help you to see how for-profit skills should be described on a nonprofit résumé.

For-profit employees...	Nonprofit employees . . .
...work for a company.	...work for an organization (or a cause).
...earn a profit.	...generate revenue.
...create an offering of stock or raise venture funding.	...solicit individuals for major gifts.
...achieve a return on investment.	...achieve impact from donated funds.
...sell a certain number of goods or services.	...serve a certain number of community members.
...make decisions that impact the bottom line.	...incorporate key organizational values into decisions.
...develop sales leads.	...research potential funders, stakeholders, and partners.
...create customer-focused marketing campaigns.	...advocate to impact social change.
...reduce governmental interference.	. . . capitalize on government grant opportunities.
...lobby for favorable policy change.	. . . educate stakeholders about effect of policies on issues.
...spearhead investor relations.	...achieve greater constituency buy-in.
...grow and develop customer base.	...manage and expand their constituency.
...rely upon staff.	...rely upon volunteers and champions.
...reduce tax liabilities for increased profits.	...balance budgets to retain tax-exempt status.

Like the for-profit sector, the nonprofit sector lives and dies by the bottom line. Yet in the nonprofit sector, quarterly earnings reports don't exist. Not everything that impacts the bottom line can be accounted for on a spreadsheet. In fact, some nonprofit employees will attest that the most important things they do cannot be accounted for at all. This is, of course, heresy to a corporate honcho but the bread and butter of the nonprofit sector. Understanding this difference allows you to determine which accomplishments, skills, and knowledge you want to put forward on your résumé. After all, putting a specific brand of milk in every refrigerator nationwide is different from making sure every child has milk to drink at lunch. Communicating that you have internalized this difference is essential, and shifting your résumé from a traditional for-profit résumé to one that can be read through a nonprofit lens is a great way to begin.

To get to know the language of the nonprofit sector, begin by reading it. The *Chronicle of Philanthropy* (*www.philanthropy.com*) is printed twice a month and is the major paper of those in the grant-seeking and grant-giving world. The *Nonprofit Times* (*www.nptimes.com*), distributed monthly, covers the business side of the nonprofit sector. The *Nonprofit Quarterly* (*www.nonprofitquarterly.org*), more of a journal, is printed four times a year with each edition focusing 80 or more pages on a particular topic of interest, and it often includes some of the best thinking happening in the sector today.

CHERRY MUSE   EXECUTIVE DIRECTOR, PUBLIC CONVERSATIONS PROJECT, WATERTOWN, MASSACHUSETTS

An attorney by training, Cherry was sworn in as a member of the Massachusetts Bar on the due date for her first child. Over the next five years, she and her husband had two other children, all the while balancing her role as an attorney with her role as a mother. She worked part-time, practicing law and developing a mediation practice. As her children started school, she became an active volunteer and, because of her legal background, was asked to serve on a number of committees and task forces that had a substantive impact on her town. "I found that I liked being a change agent," she says, "and discovered that most often I quickly became a leader wherever I served. This was a surprise, as I had never seen myself that way before." When her youngest child approached middle school age, Cherry decided to enter the nonprofit sector full-time.

Cherry's first job in the nonprofit sector was as associate program director for the Anti-Defamation League, a position that pulled together many of her volunteer activities—

building community, supporting human rights, strengthening education, and supporting the Jewish community. Eighteen months later, she became associate director of development. Cherry has also worked as director of development for YouthBuild USA and executive director of The Wellness Community—Greater Boston before becoming executive director of the Public Conversations Project. A good deal of her experience has been in founder-driven organizations.

How did the culture of the nonprofit sector comport with Cherry's work-life balance?

As a volunteer, Cherry had the luxury of picking and choosing her projects and activities. "I could set limits," she explains, "but that became considerably more difficult when I was a staff member." Cherry found that the nonprofit sector's self-selected population of mission-driven employees, especially her two founder-visionary bosses, made it difficult at first for her to establish boundaries and maintain a healthy work-life balance. "There have been times I felt myself getting competitive about who could work more and would find myself waking up earlier and earlier to get to the office first!" she remembers. "Fortunately, when my inner workaholic tried to emerge, my family helped me to set limits on myself."

What steps did Cherry take when she determined that she would find her next career in the nonprofit sector?

Cherry began collecting appealing newspaper help-wanted ads, even if she wasn't remotely qualified for the position. "After doing this for several months," she explains, "I went back and reread the ads to see what they told me about myself." When an ad appeared for a nonprofit whose mission she knew she could embrace, she jumped. Since then, Cherry's three subsequent nonprofit jobs have come through a combination of networking and responding to ads—this time on the Internet instead of the newspaper.

How did Cherry grow from a practicing mediation attorney into a nonprofit executive director?

Shortly after being hired for her first nonprofit job, it became clear to Cherry that to develop professionally, she would need fundraising experience. "I sought to become associate development director," she explains, "and my successive career moves were all possible because I added the fundraising component early on in my career." In addition, Cherry credits as part of her success the fact that she entered the nonprofit sector with career and volunteer experience behind her. Having served on multiple boards made her less intimidated by board members. "I had a clearer sense of what board members and volunteers wanted, because I had been a board member and volunteer myself."

Cherry's Key Lessons Learned:

- ■ "Being in the nonprofit field is no excuse for sloppiness, either in the workplace or in an interview. The same high standards for professionalism apply."

- ■ "Volunteering is an excellent way to get a sense of whether this is a world you'd like to enter."

- ■ "Get some fundraising experience, as a board member or just as a volunteer. The nonprofit will love you, you'll do some good in the world, and you'll be adding some valuable experience to your résumé."

Tell the Truth

According to a 2003 survey by the Society of Human Resource Management, 44 percent of 2.6 million respondents said they had fabricated at least one thing on their résumés. A 2004 report by the Federal Bureau of Investigation estimated that 500,000 people listed college degrees they didn't have. Some misrepresent themselves by glossing over the truth, perhaps listing a job that lasted from December of 2001 to January of 2002 as "2001–2002" on their résumés. Others outright lie, boasting a fantasized degree or expertise or claiming credit for work they never did—and couldn't do even if given the chance.

Nonprofits are stewards of public money and so have to answer to public scrutiny. Any good hiring manager or headhunter will run a credit, criminal, and educational check before considering you for a position. If you lie, you will get caught. Worse yet, you won't ever be viewed favorably again by that headhunter, that search firm, or that hiring manager. The best bet is always honesty; remember, the nonprofit sector is made up of many people just like you who changed course midstream. Tell them your tale, and they might just understand where you're coming from.

MAKING YOUR RÉSUMÉ WORK WITH SKILLS FROM YOUR FOR-PROFIT CAREER

A résumé is an opportunity to tell potential employers what you *can* do by showing them what you *have* done. This works well for those on a linear career path, where the next job is simply an increase in responsibility, scope, scale, or depth of current activities in the same general functional area or subject matter. For example, if you were looking to find a job selling commercial real estate in the greater Manhattan area, you would be well served by detailing what you have sold in Brooklyn in your current position. If you wanted to oversee brand marketing for an international corporation that sells luxury goods, you could bring forward your experience in brand marketing for an international corporation that sold high-end beauty products.

Nonprofit executives, hiring managers, and headhunters see too many résumés each day, however, to do the work for you, translating your experience in the for-profit sector into their needs in the nonprofit sector. As you make this transition into the nonprofit sector, detailing your commercial coups or your marketing victories won't be good enough. To help the résumé reader understand how you can translate the past into the future, write your résumé not as a description of where you have been but, rather, as a selling piece about where you are going.

Think Strategically about Your Skill Set

Think about your career change to the nonprofit sector in terms of functional expertise rather than subject area expertise. Certain nonprofit jobs demand a deep knowledge of the issue area itself and the universe in which its funders operate. Others do not. Those that do not are easier for corporate types to get.

Most nonprofits divide their work between management, communications, operations, programs, and fundraising. Positions requiring programmatic expertise fall under the program area almost exclusively. To write grants; have in-depth conversations with funders; and develop, implement, and evaluate programs, for example, you will need expertise in the subject matter. A communications director can always learn enough to go five or six questions deep with reporters, but more likely the person in that role will be running press releases, copy for annual reports, or other announcements by the program expert before sending them to the printer. The communications director will land the interview chair on a local news program, but the program director will actually take the seat.

Corporate transitioners are more likely to find success by focusing on nonprofit jobs that demand only a functional (or line management) expertise, including a mastery of functional skills but only minimal knowledge of the mission of the nonprofit. These positions include administrative, finance, and operations functions and often make for the easiest career changes from the for-profit sector. In most cases, these administrative, finance, and operations functions transfer smoothly across sectors: bookkeeping is bookkeeping and strategic planning is strategic planning. There are, however, some exceptions. Nonprofits are governed by a different set of tax principles, legal requirements, and public expectations. Accountants or lawyers looking to make the move should invest in additional education before claiming adequate expertise.

Let's look at a few examples of corporate types who transitioned by strategically transferring their skills from one sector to the other.

Rochelle, Customer Service Representative

- *For-profit.* Rochelle is a customer service representative at a mortgage company. She interacts with external and internal customers, mortgage brokers, and account executives, providing information in response to inquiries about products and services and handling and resolving complaints.
- *Nonprofit.* Rochelle would make an ideal nonprofit fundraiser or membership manager. Rochelle understands people and what gets them to yes. She has good listening skills and can be strategic in her timing in terms of what, when, and how she delivers information and asks for an investment in return.

Walter, IT Project Manager

- *For-profit.* Walter works as an IT project manager in a health care company, planning, directing, and coordinating activities of designated e-commerce projects. He follows formal project methodology; develops plans and goals; and determines staffing, strategy, scheduling, budgets, and risk assessment to meet targets set out by shareholders and senior management.
- *Nonprofit.* Like Rochelle, Walter has valuable skills to bring to the nonprofit sector. Nonprofit program directors use similar skills, providing leadership in developing program, organizational, and financial plans to fulfill the needs of donors, members, or community stakeholders. They look for ways to increase efficiency by incorporating the newest online resources and Web-based programming.

Leslie, Public Relations Executive

- *For-profit.* Leslie is a public relations executive whose portfolio consists mainly of cosmetics companies. She manages all account operations, from writing high-profile news releases, pitching and placing stories, and planning media launches. In addition, she is in charge of developing new business and delivering sales pitches. To do this, she must be both excellent at the execution of public relations work and an expert on trends in her population segment.
- *Nonprofit.* Leslie would be an attractive candidate to a women- and girls-focused organization in need of communications expertise or strategic corporate partnerships. Communications directors create, oversee, coordinate, and execute comprehensive communications and public relations plans, and they think strategically about positioning their organization as a leader in their fields. In addition, they are often tasked with overseeing major corporate partnerships; Leslie's background would make her a credible face for the organization with such partners.

Skills That Transfer Well from the For-Profit to the Nonprofit Sector

CompassPoint Nonprofit Services and the Meyer Foundation recently published "Daring to Lead 2006" in which they surveyed nearly 2,000 nonprofit executives in eight cities about the future of executive leadership in nonprofit organizations. Among their conclusions, they found that executives are placing new value on strategic planning, entrepreneurial concepts, and business development potential, because many of them do not have senior staff in charge of finance or development. In fact, their study showed that only 53 percent had a chief financial professional and 40 percent had a chief development professional. This held true for smaller organizations as well as others with more than 30 staff members.

Skills from the for-profit sector are proving more and more transferable as nonprofits are increasingly understanding their value. In tandem, as the face of philanthropy changes, donors are becoming venture focused, more hands-on, and exceptionally demanding of a return on their investment that maximizes capital, resources, and talent. To that end, nonprofits have opened up about what skills businesspeople can bring to the table.

Consider the following skills—many of which you may have honed in your corporate work—which are essential for the nonprofit leader of today.

Leadership and Influence

For-profit organizations use financial incentives to get the best out of their employees. Most nonprofits do not have such a luxury. Instead, those in the nonprofit sector are challenged to influence their employees in other ways, by constantly connecting daily outcomes to overarching goals, underscoring the importance of personal contributions to the team effort, and encouraging employees to continue to work toward a solution to sometimes overwhelming problems. Solving world hunger doesn't happen in a day, a week, a month, or even a year, but achieving specific goals along the way allows nonprofits to benchmark their successes to being part of the ultimate solution.

Managing Up, Down, and Sideways

The nonprofit sector is made up of team contributions, not individual trailblazers. It is true that nonprofits are founded by dynamic, focused, charismatic superstars, but they are run on a daily basis by those who can ultimately manage well in all directions: up to the senior staff or board; down to the staff; and sideways to constituents, funders, and other stakeholders. For-profit employees who come out of a culture where contributions are recognized and an investment is made in personal growth will find the transition to the nonprofit sector less foreign. While the nonprofit sector is often limited by its inability to fund expensive employee training and exotic corporate retreats, it can allow staff to try exciting things and develop themselves into better contributors.

Delegating with Kindness and Empathy While Demanding Accountability

No one is in the nonprofit sector for the high salaries or fancy perks. Employees aren't motivated by climbing the ladder one more rung or scoring the bonus on closing the deal. They are there because they believe in the mission of the organization and need to feel that their contributions matter. Managers who delegate with this in mind will likely have the most productive staff.

Adaptability, Flexibility, and Openness in Management and Communications

There is no cookie-cutter type of person working in a nonprofit. Similarly, each of the various internal or external stakeholders you might encounter on a daily basis is different from the next. Those with a desire and demonstrated ability to work respectfully and comfortably with families, community partners, elected officials, donors, media, individual citizens, and other culturally and socioeconomically diverse groups will transition most easily to the nonprofit sector.

Ability to Manage a Broad Portfolio of Responsibilities

Because nonprofits are small—again, many have a budget of less than $1 million—they often pool jobs together. Not all nonprofits can afford a director of development and a director of communications and, instead, hire a director of external relations. Similarly, vice presidents of finance and operations abound. The type of work being done remains the same, but more is asked of each staff member.

Knowing How to Get to Yes

Salespeople spend their days researching potential customers, determining their needs and their timelines, and pouncing at an opportune moment. Nonprofits do the same thing, except with donors, not customers. Knowing when and how to ask for resources, embodying an organization's mission, and understanding human nature is key to any nonprofit executive's success.

Managing Dotted-Line Relationships

Nonprofits rely on the kindness of others to accomplish their missions. Whether it be a large monetary donation or hosted office space, free services like printing, or loaned executives, nonprofits must "make nice" with partners and stakeholders to whom they are indebted. In addition, many nonprofits collaborate with other organizations to accomplish their mission, like a neighborhoodwide cleanup or a statewide reading drive. These stakeholder relationships are dotted, not straight lines. Keeping these partners not only happy but deeply invested is a challenge, and skill at doing this is attractive to the nonprofit sector.

Delivering Impressive Returns

Nonprofit employees are asked to do more with less. A proven track record of delivering results where the resources are limited and time is short facilitates the sector switch. Public dollars come with public scrutiny, and private dollars come with private scrutiny, but scrutiny is scrutiny. The ability to withstand it, and perform well against it, is key.

A Long-Term View

Nonprofits do not judge themselves by quarterly earnings reports. Often, the pace of change is slower. Being able to see the big picture and manage any setbacks along the way with renewed energy and idea, is an important skill for a nonprofit sector employee.

A Distinct Passion for the Work of the Nonprofit

Working in a nonprofit setting can be difficult. Some days it can feel almost impossible. However, a genuine and deep passion for the work, as well as an intense respect and love of the people being served, can sustain even the most disheartened.

CHRONOLOGICAL VERSUS FUNCTIONAL: WHICH RÉSUMÉ FORMAT IS FOR YOU?

The purpose of a résumé is to land an interview. Nothing more, nothing less. It need not exclaim to a potential employer why they must hire you this instant. Rather, it should help you to get your foot in the door so that you can tell that story yourself.

Résumé formats come in all shapes and sizes. The most common formats—outside of the academic curriculum vitae—are chronological or functional. Determining which one is right for you is as easy as deciding where you have been and where you wish to go next.

Résumé Format

When deciding which format to use, ask yourself these questions:

- Are you looking to change sectors, careers, focuses, or industries?
- Have you switched jobs too often?
- Have you not switched jobs often enough?
- Is your résumé opening enough interview doors?
- Are you a first-time job seeker?
- Are you seeking a promotion within your organization or a more senior position within your field at another?
- Are you just returning to the workplace from maternity, family, or medical leave?
- Are you relocating?
- Have you just finished a graduate degree or additional education?
- Are you applying to a more conservative human resources director?

First Things Last: Chronological Résumés

The most common format is the chronological résumé. It presents your work history in reverse chronological order, starting with your current position and working its way back to the job you landed with that navy blue interview suit you bought during your junior year of college.

Chronological résumés are most appropriate for candidates with stable, solid career progression through one or, at most, two fields. If you started off your career as a circus performer, this is probably not the format for you. If your career path has been somewhat more linear, then this format can work well.

The chronological résumé highlights growth and maturity throughout an organization or career. It is the format employers see most often, and it provides them with an easy-to-follow structure for interviews. On its face, it looks like the simplest to prepare, but like all résumés, it's a toughie. It can also be poison for candidates crossing into new fields, leaping sectors, or returning to the workforce after an extended leave.

Putting Your Best Foot Forward: Functional Résumés

Functional résumés allow you to flaunt the skills of your choice and the experiences of which you are proudest. This format gives you the luxury of combining a lifelong dedication to community service with your for-profit achievements when switching career tracks. It focuses attention on skills and achievements, rather than place of employment, which makes it ideal for midcareer changers or recent grads. As an added bonus, these résumés work well for candidates who want the world to forget about their brief professional dalliance with interpretive dance.

Lest you think this is the perfect format for you, beware. Many employers are immediately suspicious of these résumés because they are often used to hide spotty employment records, long absences from the workforce, or inconsistent performance. Some employers just aren't interested in taking the time necessary to put together a complete picture of you and will discard functional résumés without a second look.

The Best of Both Worlds

A better option for candidates who want the advantages of both the chronological and the functional résumés, without any of the detriments, is to combine them into one, using a functional introduction to a chronological work history. With a steady hand and an excellent editor nearby, these combination résumés can prove to be the right solution for those who want to spin their career history into easily digestible sound bites while expounding on their track record in a familiar, easy-to-read format. Most important, the combination format allows experienced for-profit employees to put their volunteer or board service up top, where it will be seen first.

THE NONPROFIT RÉSUMÉ: WHAT TO INCLUDE AND WHAT NOT TO INCLUDE

The for-profit résumé reflects results; the nonprofit résumé reflects results and contexts. Nonprofit résumés reveal more about the individual and allow some personality to come through. Figures 6.1 and 6.2 show two résumés for the same position, one in the for-profit world and the other for the nonprofit world.

The following nonprofit résumé outline reflects the "best of both worlds" format. It has an overview section, a chronological professional history, a listing of community involvement, education, and some various other sections you may wish to include. There is also a list of sections not to include.

Overview/Professional Achievements

Overview sections in traditional for-profit résumés list currently popular corporate-speak keywords targeted at computer scanning software. Nonprofit résumés don't need these words. For starters, most nonprofits can't afford this software. Further, corporate-speak isn't relevant. Listing your "P&L management" or "strategic mergers and acquisitions" or "global market identification" experience shows that you haven't internalized this sector change and that your transition may be bumpy. It screams to the hiring manager, "Proceed with caution!"

A better strategy is to use the "best of both worlds" résumé and write an introduction to yourself that brings together both your paid corporate work and your unpaid community service or professional leadership. The reader may still look at your current employment and job title but will do so through the lens of the skill set you are putting forward.

Change the title of the section from the vague "Overview," "Summary," or "Background" to something more action oriented like "Selected Career Highlights" or "Professional Achievements." This lets the reader know that you are actually putting forward a track record here, not a laundry list of management-speak, buzzwords, and fluff. Even if you talk mostly about the last four volunteer positions you held, you are still detailing the professional skills you bring to the table. Whether you got paid for the work or not, your experiences are still strengths and should be treated as such.

Figure 6.1 Communications For-Profit Résumé

Paula is applying for a job directing communications for a nonprofit that works with Russian orphanages to help improve conditions of the children living within them. This résumé, which she used for her last for-profit job search won't get her the job. Let's see why:

Paula D. JobSeeker

62 Main Street
Omaha, NE 68106

email: paula.jobseeker@email.com
tel.: (m) 402-555-7708; (h) 402-555-4632

SUMMARY
Professional communications background with comprehensive writing, advisory, publicity, and management expertise; particular experience in business, financial, and consumer technology; international work and study experience.

This summary section describes Paula as what she is today, and only in her corporate life.

EMPLOYMENT

Mainframe Computer Corporation (Omaha, NE)   2004-present
Director, Corporate Communications
- Wrote speeches, scripts, and presentations for CEO and CTO.
- Managed internal and external communications of company news.
- Managed public relations activities, supervising a team to plan and execute media relations.
- Managed vendor relationships and budgets.

Smith Public Relations Worldwide (Omaha, NE)   1998-2004
PR Account Director
- Served as public relations executive, conducting communications campaigns to support clients in technology industry; trained, mentored and directed professional development of junior staff.
- Assessed clients' public perception and developed plans to define and promote their brands, launch their products and services, and raise awareness and credibility among key constituencies.

Paula is relying too much on her job description to show what she is supposed to be doing. Nothing here shows the reader what she has accomplished.

Smith Public Relations Worldwide (Omaha, NE)   2000-2001
Supervisor
- Wrote communication collateral including company overview and market background pieces, press releases, product/service profiles, and customer case studies for distribution to key audiences.
- Led media training, message development, and engagement booking for client spokespersons.

Smith Public Relations Worldwide (Omaha, NE)   2000-2001
Supervisor
- Ghost wrote executive speeches and presentations, and contributed articles, including business profile supplement for trade press and advertorial published in *Business Week*.
- Edited and proofread all writing assignments produced by account teams for the clients.

This section worries the reader that Paula has jumped around a lot, when a closer inspection shows that she has had promotions within the same company.

Russian-U.S. Telephonica (Boston, MA)   1989-1998
Director and Founder
- Started consulting practice as U.S. agent to emerging Russian telecommunications provider.
- Taught seminars on emerging telecommunications technologies in both English and Russian.

Trade Resources USA (New York, NY)   1985-1989
Vice President
- Directed marketing and commerce initiatives for trade management and export consulting firm.
- Managed international purchasing projects including construction of colonial homes in Moscow, distribution of consumer electronics to retail outlets in Russia and supply of U.S. and European food and textiles to emerging privatized stores.
- Marketed U.S. and European high-technology products and services for export to the Soviet Union for international trading company.
- Oversaw contract fulfillment including distribution, delivery, implementation, and training.

None of these jobs make it clear to the reader why she would be qualified for the nonprofit sector.

Polar Trading Limited (Rockville, MD)   1982-1985
Contracts Manager
- Marketed U.S. and European high-technology products and services for export to the Soviet Union.
- Oversaw contract fulfillment including distribution, delivery, implementation, and training.
- Organized corporate exhibitions, designed marketing materials, developed client presentations.

EDUCATION
University of California, Berkeley Russian Studies major (BA 1982)

SKILLS
- Computer/technology proficiency: MS Word, Excel, PowerPoint, Internet
- Russian fluency: 10 years of academic study, extensive travel in Russia and business use of Russian
- Spanish proficiency: 11 years of academic study, including travel to Spain

Of course Paula knows how to use these basic computer programs. Listing this and listing it under "Skills," hides the deep linguistic background she has.

Figure 6.1 (continued) Communications Nonprofit Résumé

ADDITIONAL EMPLOYMENT EXPERIENCE

Russian-U.S. Telephonica (Boston, MA)   **1989-1998**
Director and Founder
- Started consulting practice as U.S. agent to emerging Russian telecommunications provider.
- Developed and managed strategic partnerships between U.S. and Russian equipment manufacturers, service providers and international distributors, establishing channel partnership for Motorola.
- Participated in seminars and conferences worldwide to assess emerging technologies and industry trends.
- Taught seminars on emerging telecommunications technologies in both English and Russian.

Trade Resources USA (New York, NY)   **1985-1989**
Vice President
- Directed marketing and commerce initiatives for trade management and export consulting firm.
- Managed international purchasing projects including construction of colonial homes in Moscow, distribution of consumer electronics to various retail outlets in Russia and supply of U.S. and European food and textiles to emerging privatized stores.

Polar Trading Limited (Rockville, MD)   **1982-1985**
Contracts Manager
- Marketed U.S. and European high-technology products and services for export to the Soviet Union.
- Oversaw contract fulfillment including distribution, delivery, implementation and training.
- Organized corporate exhibitions, designed marketing materials, developed presentations of client
- products and technologies to prospective buyers.

EDUCATION
- **University of California, Berkeley** Russian Studies major (BA 1982)
- **Moscow Energy Institute, Russia** Chosen by the American Council of Teachers of Russian for semester study and training program (Spring 1988)
- **Georgetown University** *Political and Economic Russian:* specialized language study (1992)
- **Yale University** Summer immersion program in advanced Russian (1987)

LANGUAGES
- **Russian fluency:** 10 years of academic study including semester in Moscow; 16 subsequent years of professional use of Russian with business associates, including multiple trips to Russia
- **Spanish proficiency:** 11 years of academic study, including travel to Spain

REFERENCES
Andrei Vladovsky, Board President, Russian-American Sister City Program, Omaha Affiliate, (402) 555-9756.
Jack Williams, Executive Director, Boys Club of New York, (212) 555-4752
Beatrice Derkach, Chief Communications Officer, Multicultural Alliance of Nebraska, (402) 555-8631

These positions are not communications-related. Paula can choose to separate them out, easily done because they follow chronologically. Otherwise, it would be ill-advised to muddy the waters here.

Not much needs to be done here since these jobs are, at first blush, somewhat irrelevant. What's important is that they show the international experience, and so Paula added in some diversity in the geography.

There was more to Paula's education than just her undergraduate work. This longer list adds flavor and dimension to her background in ways appreciated by nonprofit sector.

Paula highlighted her language since it was an important part of the job for which she was applying.

Paula is strategically listing her references, even though not required, to show her connections with the nonprofit sector.

Figure 6.2 Communications Nonprofit Résumé

> Paula expanded her résumé to two pages and added much of her volunteer work, thereby framing her background as directly applicable to the nonprofit sector.

Paula D. JobSeeker

62 Main Street
Omaha, NE 68106

email: paula.jobseeker@email.com
tel.: (m) 402-555-7708; (h) 402-555-4632

SELECTED CAREER HIGHLIGHTS

> This section brings Paula's paid and volunteer work right up front.

A seasoned external relations executive with a background in nonprofit, education, and corporate communications. Fluent in Russian and Spanish, and with comprehensive writing, advisory, publicity, and leadership expertise; experience managing relationships with senior executives, media, and external community; extensive track record in school admissions as communications liaison between college, alumni, and prospective students; international work and study experience. Selected accomplishments include:

> Note how much more broadly Paula describes herself in this summary. Instead of writing a description of her current corporate self or for-profit job, she describes her whole self, and pitches herself for the job she wants to have.

- *Marketing & Public Relations:* Created marketing public relations campaigns for corporations and nonprofits, both internationally and domestically, which increased awareness and raised capital, funds, and memberships.
- *Event Management:* Managed more than 50 events for local nonprofits, institutions of higher education, and *Fortune 50* CEOs and their shareholders. Events ranged from black-tie fundraising dinners to small meet-and-greet affairs.
- *Strategic Communications:* Developed strategic communications plans internally and externally, in corporations with offices around the globe, and locally for the Boys and Girls Clubs of Omaha.
- *Operational and Team Management:* Participated in agency operations and communications meetings to assess, plan and execute strategic objectives to ensure that best practices and highest quality standards were implemented agency wide.
- *Fundraising and Partnership Development:* Successfully raised $130,00 on behalf of the Boys and Girls Clubs of Omaha, and developed more than $10M in new business development internationally for Smith Public Relations.

> Here Paula really spoon-feeds her corporate and volunteer work to her reader.

EMPLOYMENT

Mainframe Computer Corporation (Omaha, NE)   2004-present
Director, Corporate Communications

> A little name drop here to make sure there is some concrete nonprofit work up front is always a nice touch.

- Developed and implemented communications initiatives, which increased awareness of this global, public software company and led to financial and industry success. Wrote and delivered speeches, scripts, and presentations for CEO and CTO, which educated and built confidence among customers and shareholders.
- Developed relationships with investor community, managing external communications of company news through press releases, Web site, conferences, quarterly and annual earnings reports, and investor tours. Oversaw 16 public relations activities per year attended by upwards of 25,000 shareholders.
- Raised employee morale and reduced staff turnover by aggressively increasing internal communications including development of letters from the CEO, internal news announcements, and employee newsletter.
- Managed more than 20 vendor relationships and budgets for corporate events, collateral production, and investor and public relations activities.

> Note how these four bullets say so much more about people than profits than the four bullets on Paula's for-profit résumé.

Smith Public Relations Worldwide (Omaha, NE)   1998-2004
PR Account Director (Mar'02-Feb'04); Supervisor (June'00-Mar'02); Senior Account-Executive (June'99-June'00)

> Each of Paula's bullets now show that her work was in pursuit of a greater mission, not just task-oriented.

- Served as public relations executive to a $10M portfolio of clients, including start ups, public companies, global enterprises, and nonprofits. Selected clients include: MCI WorldCom Advanced Networks, Project Oxygen, System Software Associates, UUNet, Vanguard Managed Solutions. Boys and Girls Clubs, and the Junior League.
- Ghost wrote executive speeches, presentations and contributed articles, including business profile supplement for Gartner report and advertorial published in *BusinessWeek*. Edited and proofread all writing assignments produced by account teams for the clients.
- Created growth opportunities for junior staff, led account team performance reviews, and mentored three account executives. Designed team project for interns, providing coaching and feedback. Hired two interns as FT employees.
- Wrote communication collateral including company overview and market background pieces, press releases, product/ service profiles, and customer case studies for distribution to key audiences.
- Led media training and message development workshops for client spokespersons and arranged speaking engagements at trade shows and conferences.

> These bullets show results, but results that are focused on both profits and people. Paula did her job, but she cared about the staff too.

COMMUNITY LEADERSHIP AND VOLUNTEER WORK

> Paula combined these jobs to show tenacity and upward mobility. She also added a section on the breadth and depth of her client portfolio, even noting a couple of nonprofits where she worked, even though they were limited engagements.

- **University of California, Berkeley College Alumni Volunteer Chairperson** (1998-present)
  Recruit alumni and lead volunteers in support of the off campus admissions efforts. Direct the program for the Omaha area, coordinating with alumni community to interview prospects and participate in college fairs. Serve as liaison between Admissions Office staff and alumni community to promote the college, oversee the interview and evaluation process, and ensure representation in area events. Plan and participate twice annual regional information workshops for prospects and receptions for accepted applicants.
- **University of California, Berkeley Alumni Admissions Volunteer** (1989-present)
  Conduct off-campus interviews with and write evaluations of high school applicants.
- **Boys Club of New York Mentor** (3 years)
  Coached group of 15 preteens in academic and recreation activities at Harlem Boys Club facility. Successfully raised $130,000 from corporation sponsors and individual donors to build a new playground structure.

> Because this wasn't Paula's main work, she doesn't put this at the top, but placing it here ensures that it is prominently displayed.

Because it is a summary of the entire document, you may want to consider writing this section of the résumé last. Once you have sorted out the rest of your résumé, this section becomes a longer version of your elevator speech. Start with a general statement about yourself and move into the details in full nonprofit-speak. Here are some examples of successful overview first sentences:

- *Example #1.* "A seasoned professional with more than ten years of experience managing high-level corporate activities and mission-driven nonprofit volunteer programs. Selected accomplishments include…."
- *Example #2.* "Dual JD/MBA with a track record of excellence within nonprofit and corporate environments. Career highlights include…."
- *Example #3.* "An up-and-coming star looking to dedicate energy, education, and experience to making a difference in the nonprofit sector. Initial successes include…."

Professional Experience

Your professional history outlines the paid jobs that you have held. It includes company name, title, location, and dates of service in the heading section, followed by details about accomplishments and achievements. For ease of reading, it is generally presented in bullet form rather than paragraph form. Because the nonprofit reader of your résumé may not know each of the businesses for which you've worked, you may also wish to include a sentence or two about the company's size, history, and focus.

This section should be written in reverse chronological order. Start with the most recent job and work your way back. Unless it is relevant to this job search, you don't need to go all the way back to the very first job you held 20 years ago.

Handling Current Unemployment

If you are unemployed, consider this a grand opportunity to "employ" yourself in the nonprofit sector, volunteering in an administrative or operational function (e.g., not just tutoring children but helping to run the tutoring program by creating and implementing a volunteer recruitment effort) or doing pro bono consulting for a nonprofit or two—or seven—of your choice. It's an excellent way to show dedication to the sector and, at the same time, have the first job on your résumé not read as "Corporate America." It is as easy as listing your new volunteer work as if it were your current job, assuming that you spend at least 20 hours a week at it, or creating your consulting firm of "Joe Smith Consulting" and bullet pointing actual assignments and projects as if they were paying clients. You should, of course, never lie about the status of this work, but it's perfectly fine to be spending 40 hours a week or more "working," even if it is unpaid.

Community Involvement

In the typical for-profit résumé, the community involvement section is almost an afterthought. There is usually only a line or two dedicated to the most current charitable activities. At most, it lists just the name of the organization and perhaps the title held, be it volunteer or board chair.

For the nonprofit résumé, consider this section a "Part B" to the "Professional Experience" section above it. Like the skills you gathered in the for-profit sector, the lessons learned in the nonprofit sector are arrows in your professional quiver. You have been drawing upon each in your corporate life and will continue to do so in your nonprofit life. Not listing this work, then, tells only half of your professional story.

Education

Like your professional history, education should be listed in reverse chronological order. Be sure to include the institution of higher education, your degree and major, as well as the date of graduation or years attended if you did not graduate. If you have gone through any additional continuing education that is relevant to this job search and better prepares you for the sector switch, list it here, too.

Grade Point Averages

Any honors, scholarships, impressive internships, or awards should be listed under the institutions at which they were awarded. Do not list your grade point average (GPA), even if it was a 4.0. You *can* say magna cum laude, cum laude, or Phi Beta Kappa, which communicates the point that you were a cut above the other students. At any other level, you risk additional and unnecessary judgment. Remember when you brought home a 98 in third-grade spelling and your dad asked where the other two points went? Nonprofits put high stakes on education and are often a bit snobby about it.

The exception to this rule is the "bootstrapping loophole": if you worked full-time while putting yourself through school and are exceptionally proud of your less-than-perfect but still impressive final GPA, make sure you note under your education that you "completed all class work while carrying both a full-time course load and working 40 hours per week to pay tuition." It's a nice story, and you should get credit for it.

Handling Ageism

Ageism is illegal, but everyone who looks at a résumé calculates age from the date of graduation. It might seem logical, then, to remove your date of graduation, but do so at your own risk. Whether or not you list your age, the hiring manager is still eventually going to meet you face-to-face. The best plastic surgeons in the world might not be able to make a young, gritty nonprofit staffed with 27-year-olds appreciate a 65-year-old corporate retiree; some might recognize the importance of "gray hair" for credibility and wisdom, but others won't. Instead of wasting their time and yours, be up front about your age at the start.

Additional Sections That May Be Relevant

Depending on your particular career history, there may be some additional sections that you want to include. For most, the details under each section are likely to fit into the basic sections already discussed. For others, however, it may be important to give more information.

Publications and Presentations

Publications and presentations are an ideal way to show subject matter expertise in a particular programmatic area. If your résumé is getting too long, consider writing a basic résumé with an addendum of "Selected Publications and Presentations." This approach will allow you to send in a short, focused résumé but also include the extra meat needed to make your case strongly.

Professional Affiliations

If you have professional affiliations, such as membership in the Association of Black Accountants, Home Decorators of America, or Society for Human Resource Management, list them here. If, in addition, you also have community involvement, such as in Kiwanis International, a parent-teacher association, or a neighborhood watch program, consider combining these sections under "Professional Affiliations and Community Leadership." This detailed affiliations and associations section will not only make your résumé less of a laundry list, it will also guide the eye to the important nonprofit work you have done.

Licensure and Certification

List any specific licensure or certification you have that is relevant to the job for which you are applying. For example, your bar membership always matters, but your certification as a real estate agent may not. Don't let yourself look as though you are all over the map (i.e., tried this, tried that, and now on to the nonprofit sector for career number seven).

Awards

Most awards you have received should fit into your professional chronology. For example, if you were awarded "Employee of the Month" six times running, that should be listed under the job where you received the accolade and even reference the work that led to such recognition. Awards for things not related to paid or unpaid professional achievements, like a softball championship, are entirely irrelevant in a résumé and may distract your reader.

Computer Skills

A hiring manager will assume that, in this day and age, you know how to use word processing and spreadsheet development software like Microsoft Word or Microsoft Excel, know how to perform basic research tasks on the Internet using any number of Web browsers, and have more than a passing understanding of Windows or Macintosh platforms. Stating that you are skilled at Microsoft Word is about as relevant as stating that you can read.

Some jobs require technology skills above and beyond basic computer functionality. These include fundraising software, presentation software, programming, or coding for the Internet. If you are applying for a job that requires such skills and you are comfortable using the computer program in question, list it on your résumé or in your cover letter. If not, don't list your computer expertise at all.

Technology and Ageism

Another reason some choose to list their computer expertise is because they feel they may be suffering from ageism and want to show that they aren't a relic when it comes to modern technology. By all means, if you are at all concerned about ageism, certainly don't list this technology to protect yourself from it. It will only serve to heighten any concern about whether you can keep up, get your hands dirty, or are current with the newest technologies if you seem defensive at all. Instead, let the rest of your great and active work speak for itself.

Sections to Avoid on Your Nonprofit Résumé

In all cases, use the doctrine of relevance to determine what belongs or does not belong on a résumé. Just because the nonprofit sector wants to get to know more of your personal side doesn't mean they want to see it in your résumé. Put less relevant facts, like your junior high school project saving cats, feeding the homeless, or joining the Girl Scouts, in the cover letter if they add some important dimension to your application, or bring them up in an interview if they don't impact your credentials but will help determine your personal fit. And you can always keep them to yourself.

Your reader is already spending a limited amount of time on your résumé. If you fill that time with irrelevant, confusing, or disturbing data, you've not spent your time wisely. Instead of distracting readers, leave out the following sections so they can focus on learning about your relevant achievements.

Objective

The "Objective" is a waste of space on your résumé: your objective is to get the job for which you've just applied. If a hiring manager is reading your résumé, then your objective is already apparent. Plus, if poorly written, it's the death knell of your career change. Saying that you want to find a job that uses your skills and provides you with career advancement is off-putting; the hiring manager doesn't want to know what the organization will do for you but what you will do for the organization.

Personal Interests

Listings of personal interests can be a wonderful way of showing *who* you are rather than *what* you are. You may be a stockbroker by day but a budding chef at night. Telling a recruiter that you are interested in "conversation," scuba diving, martial arts, marathon training, or juggling is interesting but possibly not relevant. If as a budding stockbroker, you want to get a job investing the endowment of a cooking school, that's another story. But be conscious of the message your personal interests might send: if you graduated on a needs-based scholarship from Yale and then were invited, all expenses paid, by your roommate's family on her graduation trip around the world, the combination of "Yale" and "world traveler" might paint a very different picture for your résumé reader than what you know to be reality.

Pictures

Do not include pictures on, or attached to, your résumé. It makes you look less serious and it incapacitates the résumé reader from being able to make a judgment about you based on your skills and your experience rather than your looks.

Health, Age, Marital Status, Children

It is not only irrelevant but actually illegal for a hiring manager to take into consideration your health, age, or marital status or the number of children, dogs, cats, birds, or monkeys you may have. Do not include this type of information in your résumé or cover letter. Disclosing that you are an "active, healthy, 57-year-old man" just worries them that you might not always have been active and healthy, or that you are threatening to sue for age discrimination if they don't hire you. Why play with fire? Let your accomplishments speak for themselves.

Handling Diversity

Federal and some state laws protect job candidates and employees from discrimination if they fall into a protected class. Protected classes include race, color, religion, creed, sex, nationality, age, disability, veteran status, and sexual orientation. Everyone belongs to at least one protected class; for example, you cannot be denied a job simply because you are a man or a woman.

One of the major differences between the for-profit world and the nonprofit world is that the nonprofit world not only wants to know what makes you different but will likely celebrate you for it. Your approach comes down to a question of personal comfort about putting your full self out there. If your extracurricular activities include memberships in, for example, the National Association of Asian American Professionals, the National Society of Hispanic MBAs, or the National Coalition of 100 Black Women, and you feel comfortable that the hiring manager knows your race from your paper application alone, make sure you list that information. Similarly, nonprofit employers are unlikely to bat an eyelash at job seekers who are members of the National Gay and Lesbian Law Association, the Jewish Community Center, or the American Gulf War Veterans Association.

It is by no means necessary that you list these things, but keep in mind that many nonprofits score big with funders, community members, and the media if they can show that they not only have a highly qualified staff but a diverse one, too, that represents the community they serve.

A Note on Political Correctness

Nonprofits, depending on their particular focus, tend to be politically correct to the extreme. There may be some cases where you opt not to include certain activities based on the particular focus of the nonprofit in question. For example, several years ago, the Boy Scouts of America got into some legal trouble for not allowing openly gay males become scouts or leaders. Most local chapters had nothing to do with this choice, and many rallied against it. However, if you are applying to an organization that works on behalf of civil rights and you lead your local Boy Scout troop, you may want to proceed with caution, lest you be judged unfairly as part of the problem. Instead of putting this activity on your résumé, if it was a watershed moment for you, shape your cover letter around it.

STEPS YOU CAN TAKE TO IMPROVE YOUR NEW NONPROFIT RÉSUMÉ

Now that you have begun to craft your résumé, you may have noticed that some pieces are missing. When looking at career changers, most hiring managers are looking for some sort of commitment to the sector leap. Does your résumé have this?

Showing a track record of forethought may be as easy as incorporating your current and past board work, community leadership, or relevant education on your résumé. For others, changing sectors is an ideal opportunity to get involved in new ways with issues about which you have passion—human rights, animals, equal representation, the environment—or with community organizations to which you are already tethered—a child's school, an institution of higher education you attended, a place of worship, or a political campaign, to name just a few. This career move is a perfect time to build a skill set through continuing education around a new career path, either enhancing what you already know or developing in a whole new direction. The experience and exposure you gain through board and volunteer work and continued education gives you both a growing network with which you can start your job search and the credibility to do it well, not to mention the perfect résumé bullet points.

Get on Board: Discover What You Can Do as a Board Member

Nonprofit boards are similar to corporate boards in many ways. They each provide oversight for a legal entity that has been incorporated with either a state or national government. They often recruit socially or strategically, depending on their size, history, and growth trajectories. Their sizes range from just a few members to a cast of dozens. The major difference is that nonprofit board directors do not receive any compensation for their service. Let's talk about why you should join a board and how you might go about doing so.

Ten Basic Responsibilities of Nonprofit Boards[1]

1. Determine the organization's mission and purposes.

2. Select the chief executive.

3. Support the chief executive and assess that person's performance.

4. Ensure effective organizational planning.

5. Ensure adequate resources.

6. Manage resources effectively.

7. Determine, monitor, and strengthen the organization's programs and services.

8. Enhance the organization's public standing.

9. Ensure legal and ethical integrity and maintain accountability.

10. Recruit and orient new board members and assess board performance.

What Can You Do for the Board?

Board members in the nonprofit sector are expected to fulfill the basic duties as outlined in the "Ten Basic Responsibilities of Nonprofit Boards." Above and beyond that, however, smart nonprofits grow their board strategically instead of socially. If you are invited to join a board, it is likely that you appealed to the chair as someone who could provide insight or energy around a current or planned initiative, whether that be a volunteer recognition event, a fundraising campaign, or a strategic planning process.

Whether explicitly stated or not, most boards today still work with the "4G model": Give, Get, Govern, or Get Off.

---

1   Richard T. Ingram, *Ten Basic Responsibilities of Nonprofit Boards*, (BoardSource, Washington, D.C.: 2003). This is an excellent resource for those interested in learning more about what nonprofit board service entails.

Give (Financial Investment) You will be expected to provide a financial donation; many nonprofits leave this to your discretion, but some phrase their expectations in such terms as "Give an amount that reflects your commitment to the cause," or "Please have this be the top philanthropic gift you'll make this year." Don't be disheartened by the financial aspect of board service. Remember, if all ten board members each give $5, this commitment of 100 percent shows an investment on behalf of the board much greater than if only 20 percent of the members gave a total of $50.

Get (Friend Investment) You will be expected to become a public champion of the cause, putting your name on the organization's letterhead and your friends and colleagues in their outreach database. At fundraising events, you might be expected to buy a table and sell tickets to your friends to foot that bill. When in-kind corporate donations, like computers or printing, are necessary, the nonprofit may look to your place of work as a resource. As the organization needs spokespeople to boast about successes or defend a crisis, they may look to you.

Govern (Time and Knowledge Investment) You will be expected to provide your time. Attendance at 75 percent of meetings is customary, so make sure you know when meetings are held so you can rearrange your schedule to attend. There likely will be at least one annual full-day (or longer) planning retreat and other volunteer events throughout the year that you must attend. In addition, you will be expected to serve on at least one of the standing committees, usually governance, fundraising, communications, human resources, evaluation, program, or finance. Then there are ad hoc committees, which exist for a sole purpose and have a beginning and an end. These committees can include, but are not limited to, audit, search, events, strategic planning, and fundraising campaigns.

Get Off (Stepping Down or Sideways) If you aren't quite ready to fulfill all the commitments of a board, choose to serve on an advisory council of an organization you enjoy. In some of the largest nonprofits, advisory councils exist as a group of impressive names that lend credibility or fundraising capacity to a nonprofit. In most smaller nonprofits—meaning most nonprofits—the advisory council can be a breeding ground for future board members, or it can be an off-ramp for board members who are no longer at their peak of service. In these nonprofits, advisory council seats usually come with a smaller expected financial commitment but with specific committee tasks and workload expectations. For example, you may be assigned to the technology committee to redesign the nonprofit's Web site or to the strategic planning committee for a one-time benchmarking project or to determine whether a revenue-generating enterprise is feasible.

Which Board Is Right for You?

Before you get yourself on a board, make sure it is the right board for you. Determining which board is right for you requires an honest assessment of your skills and interests as well as an understanding of what you can give.

Where is your passion? Just as you dissected the vast nonprofit sector to find the organizations that interested you, start by narrowing down the universe of nonprofits to boards you would like to join.

What kind of organization brings out your best? While the list of issue areas in the nonprofit sector is vast, the types of nonprofit boards are not. There are, essentially, three types of nonprofit boards: founding boards, working boards, and fundraising boards. Depending on where they are in their lifecycle, nonprofits will have one of these three types of boards.

What Can the Board Do for You?

Let talk about the obvious benefits you would reap if you were to join a board. First, the board oversees an organization whose mission is close to your heart. Second, the board will allow you to play a role you enjoy. Third, the board has expectations and needs around giving, getting, and governing that you can meet. But most important for you, the board will help you find a job in the nonprofit sector!

Your time, energy, intelligence, and financial resources—or connections to such—are worth something. Think strategically about what the board can do for you. In return for what you will be giving, you should be clear with yourself and others about what you are expecting in return. Use the board to build your knowledge of the nonprofit sector, a particular mission area, or a skill set, but also use it as a platform to show influential people in the nonprofit world your expertise and competence.

Skill Building Have you always been interested in animals and recently learned of the fascinating research being done in zoos across the country? Have social or business connections to those in the food industry? Never planned an event or done any traditional nonprofit fundraising? Introduce yourself to the board of a local zoo and volunteer to be on the fundraising committee for an annual event. Look, for example, at nonprofits like the National Zoo in Washington, D.C., which hosts ZooFari, an annual fundraising gala that has, each spring for more than 20 years, brought together 100 of the Washington, D.C., area's finest restaurants and vintners from around the country for an evening of gourmet foods, fine wines, fabulous entertainment, and dancing under the stars. This experience will bring together your skills and expertise, your connections and your knowledge, and your passion in a project squarely in the nonprofit sector.

Skill Marketing Fascinated by the new venture trends hitting the nonprofit sector? Spending your day job focused on developing market share for consumer goods? Determined to help the homeless learn job and life skills? Find a local nonprofit with a revenue-generating model that pays for such programming to take place. Look, for example, at nonprofits like Haley House in Boston, Massachusetts, whose Bakery Café creates economic sustainability for underemployed women and men and nurtures the local community. Through their bakery training program, at least ten underemployed, low-income women and men each year engage in a six-month training program. While being paid, these trainees—along with their trainers—prepare top-notch food for both the cafe and wholesale bakery. Once the trainees have successfully completed the program, Haley House helps them get jobs.

AUDE THIBAUT MAJOR DONOR DEVELOPMENT MANAGER, THE ROYAL OPERA HOUSE, COVENT GARDEN, LONDON, ENGLAND

One year after landing one of the most coveted finance jobs in her whole graduating MBA class, Aude realized that she was spending the majority of her waking hours doing things that didn't inspire her. While her career was mentally stimulating, it failed to move her soul. "It became apparent that my primary passion outside work was classical vocal music," she explains, "so I decided that I should try and find a job that would use my corporate skills not to make money but to make a difference and enjoy my day-to-day." What began as a simple line of questioning became a career in fundraising for the Royal Opera House in London.

Moving from banking into the arts provided quite a challenge for Aude. Because her previous experience seemed so unrelated to what she saw as her future career, applying for jobs through typical channels would lead only to her résumé being dismissed on sight. "Naively, I was surprised that human resources officers at arts organizations didn't read 'Goldman Sachs' and on my résumé and think, 'Wow, we must have her!'" With pedigrees from the Sorbonne, the London School of Economics, and Columbia Business School, Aude had an interesting dilemma on her hands.

What steps did Aude take to find her nonprofit job?

Aude had to translate her experience in banking into terms that could be understood by arts organizations. With the help of a specialized arts headhunter who helped her go over her résumé line by line, Aude repackaged herself for the search. "Quickly, it became apparent that the best fit for me would be in fundraising," she explains, "and so I did a voluntary, unpaid, three-month internship with an opera company in their fundraising department to show that I was committed to the mission and knew what I was getting myself into."

Aude found her position exclusively through networking with her contacts. "Fortunately," she found, "in the nonprofit sector, people are ready to meet with you very easily if you ask them for advice. One introduction—from a banker friend who had met a woman running a music festival on a plane to Boston—led to another, and I found myself in front of the development director of the opera company, who gave me an internship."

Will Aude's next position be in the nonprofit sector?

No. Aude feels that she has found the organization that she believes in. She enjoys what she does and feels compelled by the mission of the organization. For her, moving into the nonprofit sector was about following a specific passion rather than an overall sense of doing good. "If you go in with a purpose and a passion, you won't mind for a second any of the inefficiencies or necessary drudge work that comes even to the most qualified managers. I believe in the Royal Opera House and I wouldn't work for another nonprofit just because it is a nonprofit."

Aude's Key Lessons Learned:

- "Meet as many people as you can. Jump at any contact that is thrown at you. Meet them, get more contacts from them, and talk to more people. You will find that people are always ready to give their time to impart advice."

- "Use your networking time preciously. All the people you meet during your search will remain valuable contacts after it, but because you will be affiliated with an institution by then, your access and relationship may change."

- "Don't just 'work in nonprofit.' If you're passionate about the environment, then focus on it. If you are indignant about domestic abuse or the treatment of women, work for an organization that helps them. Don't go into the nonprofit sector like people go into the corporate sector, just because of some vague idea that draws you there. Follow your passion."

Networking Make sure you also think strategically about whom you want to meet through board service. As in the for-profit sector, nonprofits operate on word of mouth, personal connections, and social marketing. Most people who sit on nonprofit boards are also sitting on others or have sat on others in the past. If each nonprofit board averages around 8 members, your 7 board cohorts can connect you immediately to 56 other nonprofit decision makers.

Finding a Board Seat

The advent of the Internet has brought the board application and nomination process out of the country club and into the mainstream. Many Web sites exist where board-seat seekers can enter their profile and their interests and have board opportunities, both national and local, delivered to their in-box. Nonprofits can post their board needs and seek direct applications or look through a file of résumés for their perfect match.

Web Resources That Match Board Candidates and Nonprofit Boards

Web sites:

- boardnetUSA (*www.BoardnetUSA.org*)
- BoardSource (*www.BoardSource.org*)
- Bridgestar (*www.Bridgestar.org*)
- Volunteer Solutions (*https://volunteer.united-e-way.org/org/board/dir-A-1.html*)

Local nonprofit board fairs:

- National Council of Nonprofit Associations (*www.ncna.org*) lists state chapters that hold board fairs.
- The Council on Foundations (*www.cof.org/Locator*) hosts a listing of community foundations that will link to your local foundation.

Get Active: Work in the Sector as a Volunteer, Loaned Executive, or Retired Executive

There are many ways to volunteer in the nonprofit sector. You can work for free, for less than full pay, or for full pay by choosing from a variety of options and commitment levels. Independent Sector (*www.IndependentSector.org*) is the leadership forum for charities, foundations, and corporate-giving programs committed to advancing the common good in America and around the world. In 2001, it completed a landmark study of the state of volunteerism in America titled "Giving and Volunteering in the United States." Based on a national survey of more than 4,000 adults, this series of reports found that 44 percent of the adult population volunteered with a formal organization in 2000, amounting to 83.9 million adults. These adults volunteered approximately 15.5 billion hours of service in 2000 alone, at a value of $239.2 billion. According to Independent Sector, the current value of volunteer time is $18.04 per hour, so consider it real work!

Old-Fashioned Volunteering Made Current

When most of us think of volunteering, we imagine ourselves tutoring children or reading to the elderly. We see our parents leading our childhood scout troops. We remember the sick neighbor to whom we brought nourishing meals. None of that has changed, and all of that is still valuable. Joining a community environmental clean-up project or participating in your neighborhood watch group is important. You should do it, and you should do it often. But let's look at some other, new volunteering options available to you. Instead of spending one Saturday a year cleaning up your local park, get involved in the planning committee that runs clean-up days citywide. Instead of organizing your child's school's monthly bake sale, work with the administration to better track, spend, or invest the proceeds. Instead of spending five hours a month reading to the blind, use that time on a board committee that looks at ways to expand the program to reach more people.

To do this, you first must find an organization that needs what you bring to the table. This shouldn't be hard. As the government continues to cut back assistance and foundations become more selective about what they fund, the needs of nonprofits continue to grow. Set yourself up in a situation where you will be expected to donate at least 100 hours of your time over the course of many months. Most organizations, for-profit or nonprofit, have different focuses, workloads, and paces of action depending on the time of year; volunteering deeply will allow you to see the nonprofit sector and, in particular, your nonprofit of interest in its many seasons of development, growth, and change.

Second, ensure that you are not just working on the front lines but behind the scenes as well. Again, all volunteering is important, but not all volunteering strategically positions you to get a full-time job in the nonprofit sector. While providing direct service is fulfilling and heartwarming, only an in-depth view of the operations will tell you if this sector is right for you. Further, it will arm you with the right language to tell newly acquired, immediately relevant success stories in your interviews.

Web Resources to Help You Get Active

Find a volunteer opportunity:

- 1-800-Volunteer (*www.1-800-volunteer.org*)
- Hands On Network (*www.handsonnetwork.org*)
- Points of Light's Volunteer Centers (*www.pointsoflight.org/centers/find_center.cfm*)
- SERVENet (*www.servenet.org*)
- VolunteerMatch (*www.volunteermatch.org*)
- Volunteer Solutions (*www.volunteersolutions.org*)

Find a loaned executive placement:

- United Way's Loaned Executives (*http://national.unitedway.org*)
- Building Blocks International's Corporate Service Corps (*www.bblocks.org*)

Find a consulting project:

- Executive Service Corps Affiliate Network (*www.escus.org*)
- Taproot Foundation (*www.taprootfoundation.org*)

Become a Loaned Executive

Loaned executive programs offer corporate transitioners an opportunity to stick a toe in the nonprofit pond before jumping directly into the deep end. These programs allow business professionals to work on discreet projects, at the highest levels in nonprofit administration, for limited amounts of time. Corporations enjoy an enhanced community image, a reduction in internal training costs for high-performing staff, and an increase in the number of staff being groomed for executive leadership positions, while the loaned executive gets trained in fundraising and partnership development, learns up close how a nonprofit operates, and develops deeper insights into community needs and resources.

Corporate Voluntarism[2]

- 81.7 percent of corporations focus their employee volunteer programs on core business functions.

- One out of every two corporations stresses a commitment to community service in its corporate mission statement.

- 58 percent of corporations use their employee volunteer program for recruiting and retaining employees.

Become a Consultant

Another way to make the move into nonprofit work is to become a consultant, either paid or unpaid, as discussed in Chapter 3. Becoming a consultant allows you to become involved in important decision making at critical times in nonprofits you might like to join, as well as giving you valuable insider information about the type of organization, the way it goes about its business, and its approach to change.

Get Smart: Additional Education Comes in Handy

Taking time to earn a nonprofit management degree or attend a leadership program provides a natural segue into the sector. It demonstrates your dedication to move into a nonprofit career while stocking your career kit with the tools you will need to be successful once you've gotten there. Education can be gathered in an undergraduate or graduate university setting, through an executive education or extension course, or by attending one of the many local community leadership programs that exist nationwide.

Undergraduate and Graduate Degrees

Colleges and universities have responded to the growth of the nonprofit sector with expanded course and degree offerings in the nonprofit area. More than 255 colleges and universities offer degrees in nonprofit management, while others offer stand-alone, noncredit courses. These courses, which may be taught either at the undergraduate or graduate level, have titles like Fundraising, Governance, Strategic Planning, Human Resource Management, and Financial Management. More than a hundred institutions offer a graduate degree in nonprofit management.

A sample listing of these colleges, universities, and training organizations can be found in Appendix of this book.

---

2   *The Corporate Volunteer Program as a Strategic Resource: The Link Grows Stronger* (Washington, D.C.: Points of Light Foundation, 2000).

Business School As counterintuitive as it may seem, business school is a perfect way to transition from a corporate career into the nonprofit sector. Business schools understand that a nonprofit's very livelihood rests on its ability to operate effectively and efficiently like its corporate counterparts, and, recently, business schools have been attracting more applicants with a nonprofit career as a postgraduation goal. Some schools, like Harvard and Stanford, have even begun offering loan forgiveness programs to their graduates who enter the nonprofit sector after completing their education.

Women are also finding that business schools are using nonprofit degrees as a recruiting tool. Research studies repeatedly show that women more often than men opt for careers that ultimately make a contribution to society. Studies also show that they make graduate school choices, like medicine or law, that allow them to start their education immediately upon college graduation so that they can start a career before a family. New thinking in business schools, such as adjusting the required years of work experience for admission, has allowed women to pursue their MBA earlier, giving them the luxury of doing what was not an option for their mothers and grandmothers: flexibility while fulfilling their own personal and professional goals.

A list of the top nonprofit MBA programs can be found in the Appendix of this book.

Executive Education MBA programs are more and more often offering midcareer programs with specializations in nonprofit management. Harvard, Stanford, and Georgetown lead the list of highly ranked, competitive programs that have begun offering courses with names like the following:

- Governing for Nonprofit Excellence
- Performance Measurement for Effective Management of Nonprofit Organizations
- Public Leadership: Principles, Practices, and Realities
- Public Policy, Advocacy, and Social Change
- Strategic Perspectives in Nonprofit Management
- Philanthropy and Public Policy
- Strategy for Nonprofit Organizations

Most of these programs are offered in the evenings or on weekends, catering to a working professional's busy schedule. Participating in one of these programs offers deep and current knowledge, a ready-made network, and access to the university's graduate and continuing professional education career office.

A partial listing of these programs can be found in the Appendix of this book.

Leadership Programs

Many nonprofit organizations exist locally, statewide, or even regionally to bring together nonprofit and for-profit leaders around issues of pressing need. Through a carefully run application and acceptance process, they compile a diverse and dynamic annual "class" that comes together throughout a given year to discuss, learn, and cooperate around solutions to challenges. These programs make for exceptional educational and networking opportunities as well as lending a "seal of approval" to your résumé.

A partial listing of these programs can be found in the Appendix of this book.

Nonprofit Management Certificates and Specializations

More than 50 graduate schools nationwide offer nonprofit certificate programs for those without the time, energy, or resources to commit to an advanced degree in a university setting. Most of the certificates are in nonprofit management or leadership, with the balance covering specific areas like arts administration, fundraising, association management, and the like. Coursework in these programs is similar to topics covered more rigorously in graduate programs, and it often focuses specifically on best practices without delving deeply into the research and theory behind them.

A partial listing of these programs can be found in the Appendix of this book.

CONCLUSION

Writing a résumé often feels like cleaning out the attic. It seems like a good idea at first, but then halfway through, you begin to wonder why you ever started. Rest assured that the time and effort you put into writing and rewriting this vital marketing piece will make you a better networker and, ultimately, interviewee. In fact, it's likely to make you a better nonprofit employee as well.

The résumé is only part of your marketing package. You also need to worry about your cover letter, your interviewing style, and your references. Let's move on to those now.

CHAPTER 7

Cover Letters, Interviews, and References

While the résumé gets you noticed, cover letters, interviews, and references get you the job. They are part of the overall package you present and should be treated with as much importance as your résumé. In fact, these supporting materials, actions, and testimonials likely will set you apart from the other applicants in the pool, getting you greater consideration at decision-making time.

As a job seeker coming from the corporate sector, your cover letters, interviews, and references are your opportunity to show that you not only know the nonprofit sector and have a track record of dedication or success in a certain mission area but have thought strategically and deeply about what this transition will be like for you and the organization you ultimately serve. This chapter will walk you through how to write cover letters that resonate in the nonprofit sector, how to approach and master the nonprofit interview, and how to use your for-profit and nonprofit references strategically to get that dream job.

THE IMPORTANCE OF COVER LETTERS

As mentioned in Chapter 6, the biggest secret in headhunting is that recruiters read cover letters last. The word *cover* shouldn't even be included in *cover letter*, because most headhunters staple it to the back of a résumé once opened. In fact, when headhunters look at your cover letter, they feel you are at least somewhat qualified and want to know more.

Before you stop reading this chapter, remember that any materials that make it as far as a "hold" pile will be read, from cover letters to references to anything extra, like addendums of publications or presentations. It is then that cover letters matter most—more so for sector switchers—as they distinguish intriguing possibilities from average, everyday candidates. A cover letter adds another dimension to your application. It shows the recruiter that you can write and, most important for career changers, it answers the obvious questions: Why the nonprofit sector? Why this nonprofit in particular? And why now?

However, cover letters can be quicksand for candidates. From easy-to-catch mistakes like forgetting to change the name of the company in the address block or misspelling the hiring manager's name to larger issues of quantity, substance, and tone, a bad cover letter can torpedo your hopes of landing an interview and, ultimately, your nonprofit job.

Four-Paragraph Cover Letter Outline

Cover letters should be one page and run about three to four paragraphs, comprising your introduction, relevant passion, skills and qualifications, and any specific information about your current situation and contact information. Note that missing from this list—as they waste valuable space, may be illegal, and are certainly irrelevant, as discussed in Chapter 6—are references to age, height, weight, marital status, number and age of children, hobbies, race, religion, pets, or the results of your last physical. Just as with your résumé, do not, under any circumstances, ever attach your picture to the cover letter, unless you are responding to a call from the Barbizon School of Modeling and, even then, proceed with caution.

The following is a simple, four-paragraph outline that you can follow to take the guesswork out of writing your cover letter. Your first cover letter will be the hardest. After that, you will find that you can cut and paste a good deal to make the process more efficient.

Paragraph #1: An Introduction

Everyone reads the first paragraph of any letter they receive. Agonizing over this paragraph will further improve the "elevator speech" that you began developing in Chapter 5, because this is where you tell the reader what you are applying for and why, ever so briefly, you think you are the right candidate for the position. If you can't come up with something to say in this paragraph, take some time to consider if this is the right job for you. Perhaps you should be looking at jobs in organizations with missions closer to your heart or with different levels of seniority, responsibility, or expertise.

Make sure you are specific about the job in question, because most managers are hiring for more than one job at a time. Also, make sure to specify how you heard about the job. If you heard about it from an individual known to the staff, a recruiter, a hiring manager, or a job board, be sure to drop that name.

If you read about a position as an advertisement on a Web site or in a print publication, write that in your cover letter. After all, advertising costs money, and most nonprofits lack both a human resources department and a human resources budget. Being strapped for cash, they'll want to know which advertising brought them interesting candidates like you. In the interview, you'll get asked where you heard about this position, and if you can't remember or, worse, say that you "are applying for lots of jobs and must have seen it on one of the many Web sites," you simply won't sound smart—nor will the interviewer feel special. This is, after all, a wooing process. Better to hedge your bets and list it right up front in the cover letter.

A note on little white lies: If you get caught off guard when you are asked where you saw the job announcement and can't remember—probably because you did, in fact, see it on one of the many job Web sites you've researched—you can tell a teeny fib here and get away with it. The best answer in this situation is that you don't know where it was originally posted but that it was referred to you by a colleague who knows your work as well as your desire to work for this particular mission area and thought it would be a perfect match for your skills, expertise, and passion. Someone who knows your work and thinks that you would be right for this job is about as close to a pre-interview reference as you can get. In this situation, your answer sends the message that you have already passed a hurdle in a professional setting and raises your candidacy to the same level as that of other nonprofit candidates who have proven themselves in more familiar settings.

Sample Paragraph #1

Please find attached my résumé in application for the position of _____ _____ as posted on _____. My combination of _____ and _____, combined with my passion for _____, makes me an ideal candidate for this position.

This may be the only paragraph of your letter that is read. The aim of this paragraph is to tell the reader quickly for which position you wish to be considered and where you saw it advertised and to provide a quick sell.

Paragraph #2: A Little about Them

What is everyone's favorite subject of conversation? Themselves, of course. After you've told the reader what you are applying for and why, briefly, you would be the ideal candidate, tell a bit about what you know about the organization and its current needs. These paragraphs often start off something like, "The Nature Conservancy has long been a leader in . . ." or, "As times have changed, National Geographic has been able to . . ." and continue on to, "From reading your Web site, I was excited to learn about the new direction you are taking...."

Doing a little homework will separate you from the rest of the candidates. Of course, your reader already knows about the current challenges facing the organization, but the hirer doesn't know that *you* know—and doesn't know that you know it in the language of the nonprofit sector. The "Insert Job Here" cover letter won't work under normal circumstances, and it especially doesn't work for sector switchers. Talk about the organization's current work and segue back to how it blends with your career. This leads nicely into paragraph three, where you tell a little about how your skills dovetail with the organization's needs.

> Sample Paragraph #2
>
> The Good Foundation has long been a leader in _____, and I read with great excitement about the new direction your technology department is taking. I would greatly enjoy becoming a member of the team that will bring a better use of technology to your grantees. My experience to date has been in the area of digital divide issues as they affect organizations that....

Tell them a little about themselves to show that you've done some homework and understand where they are as an organization and where they want to be. Alternative phrases you can use in this paragraph include: "In my conversations with . . .", "From your Web site, I learned . . .", or, "In my work with . . .".

Paragraph #3: A Little about You

Now that you've told the hiring manager what you know about the organization and its current challenges, communicate what, specifically, you have done that qualifies you to get them to where they need to be. Pull from your paid and unpaid work your achievement skills that make you certain that you can be successful in this role. If the only relevant experience you've had has been as a volunteer, then lean heavily on this, but don't ignore that you've had paid work experience as well.

Don't feel you need to outline your entire professional history, as some of it will be irrelevant and most of it will be repetitive. Again, by the time the hiring manager has gotten to your cover letter, your résumé has already conveyed that you are at least in some way qualified. Now the hirer is trying to understand better why you are interested in this move at this time. Write up your professional history to read more like a strategic argument about why you should be interviewed rather than a rote recitation of your résumé.

> Sample Paragraph #3
>
> Specifically, as one of the first participants in the United Way's Corporate Technology Partners Program, I enabled _____ organization to _____. Prior to that, I....

And so on, specifically about how your skills and experience will help the organization meet the challenge at hand. By the time your interviewer has seen your résumé, she feels your experience at least merits further investigation; the hiring manager now wants to know why you are interested in this job. This will be the longest paragraph of your one-page cover letter, composed of four or five sentences, and should answer the questions: Why are you right for this position? and What skills do you bring that are relevant to the challenges we face?

Paragraph #4: Contact Information and Current Situation

Once you've made your quick pitch, shown your smarts, and tied your background to the organization's needs, all that's left is to tell the reader how to contact you. You are a great candidate, after all, and the organization needs to know this information. Nonprofits don't generally have lots of extra printers and faxes sitting around, so cover letters and second pages of résumés often find their way into other people's stacks of paper. If your cover letter looks great but your résumé didn't follow, or vice versa, some contact information in the letter will come in quite handy.

If you are currently leaving your job for a reason worth sharing with the hiring manager—perhaps a sickness in the family has meant that you can't travel as often as your job demands, but because of this, you are now interested in helping your prospective future employer cure this particular disease—this is the place to list it. Folks in the nonprofit sector will assume that you are making a change because of some form of enlightenment, and being up front about it will increase your chances of seeming real. Lists of corporate sector jobs aren't necessarily that interesting, but coupling them with a human touch is.

Sample Paragraph #4

I look forward to speaking to you soon about my qualifications and experiences. I can be reached at _____ during the day or _____ in the evenings.

Don't say that you look forward to learning more about the job or the organization; that's not your prospective employer's burden. Remember to create a letterhead with all of your contact information, including your e-mail address. Be sure to note if you are in a cubicle or have a public voice mail, or you risk letting your boss know about your job search before you are ready.

Make It Real to Them

One of the biggest frustrations that nonprofit hiring managers have with for-profit applicants is language that seems to go in circles, corporate-speak that doesn't seem ever to come down to telling what you actually accomplished at the end of the day. A nonprofit hiring manager will be impatient with all job seekers introducing themselves this way but especially with someone looking to transition out of corporate life. Already they may have a prejudice against sector switchers, having seen too many who believe that "nonprofits would be better off if they were run like for-profits." Starting off the cover letter in corporate-speak, or by saying how wonderful you and your corporate work have been, will only serve to deepen those prejudices.

Give your recruiter something relevant and substantial to chew on in the cover letter. Choose three or four key responsibilities from the position description and explain clearly and concisely where you have successfully managed projects or tasks of comparable size and complexity in your career. Be sure to tie your experience back to past or probable future success in the nonprofit arena. Here are some examples.

Prejudice Deepener #1:	While I was at The Great Corporation, we incorporated CQI into our new product rollout.
Prejudice Reliever #1:	Just as you are trying to do as you expand your program into five new cities, while at The Great Corporation, I spearheaded work to ensure that the quality of our product remained high while we entered new markets and sought out new customers.
Prejudice Deepener #2:	In my last start-up, I raised $50 million in venture capital seed funding.
Prejudice Reliever #2:	While most of my fundraising experience has been with venture capitalists, such as raising $50 million in seed funding for my last start-up, I believe that the skills I acquired to research prospects, develop relationships, and steward funders will translate well to the capital campaign on which you are about to embark.

Showing Your True Colors

Whether you have experience in a specific nonprofit field or are looking to shift into a new arena, explaining your passion in your cover letter can provide much-needed depth to your paper presentation. To paraphrase John F. Kennedy, "Ask not what your employer can do for you, but what you can do for your employer." The same is true for cover letters.

For example, no employer will get excited over the possibility of providing a "challenging and fulfilling opportunity where a generous salary can be earned while serving others." Most employers, on the other hand, will race to the phone to call a candidate who is "inspired by the opportunity to ensure adequate health care for underprivileged children while contributing to the long-term financial sustainability of the parent organization."

Nonprofits are excited about your interest in their universe. They are happy whenever anyone has realized that their issue area is critical and demands the dedication of anyone's full attention. Go bold! Tell them about your experiences as a child, as a mother, as a friend. Reveal your true colors, not as a corporate hack but as a warm-blooded, idealistic, passionate individual worth getting to know.

JENNIFER KEYS DIRECTOR OF HUMAN RESOURCES, INSTITUTE FOR SYSTEMS BIOLOGY, SEATTLE, WASHINGTON

Jennifer started her career working in marketing for a scientific instrument manufacturer, but something wasn't gelling. "One day my boss pulled me aside and told me, 'Jennifer, you're doing a good job, but this really just isn't for you.'" At her suggestion, Jennifer made a move into human resources. After relocating to Seattle, she landed a job in human resources at a biotechnology start-up. She stayed in the corporate world for six more years, and while she loved the substance of the work itself, she found the "hire, discipline, terminate, hire" grind was making her incredibly unhappy. When she saw an ad for a human resources position with the Girl Scouts, "This star lit up and the planets aligned, and I knew I had to have this job."

Still, Jennifer faced some difficulty in her transition. "When nonprofits have some extra money, they use it to hire another fundraiser or program person, not a human resources specialist," she explains. "While nonprofits are excellent at training staff and volunteers around certain activities," Jennifer found that "in other ways, human resources in many nonprofits is about 15 years behind. The culture is also completely alien to anyone raised in corporate America. There is a learning curve."

Jennifer left the Girl Scouts when she had done all she felt she could for the organization. However, she chose to find her next role in the nonprofit sector as well, this time for a larger nonprofit. She continues to enjoy the challenge and enjoyment, although she hasn't yet found a better work-life balance. "Employees in nonprofits are spread very thin," she explains. "Yet seeing a girl go camping for the first time or facilitating the hire of a scientist whose discovery will change the face of health care makes it all worthwhile."

How did Jennifer convince the Girl Scouts that she was driven by its mission?

Having been a Girl Scout for much of her youth, Jennifer dug out her old Girls Scouts sash and brought it to the interview. While she would never have done such a thing in the private sector, she gambled correctly that the Girl Scouts would love it. "Something like that," she explains, "is not only acceptable in the nonprofit world, it's encouraged!" Jennifer took a pay cut to work at the Girl Scouts but still considers it the best move of her career.

What differences did Jennifer find between human resources work in for-profit companies and nonprofit organizations?

Jennifer found that she had to change her focus completely when entering the nonprofit sector. "Employees are working for less than market rate and expect some other types of compensation," she explains. "I had to get used to consensus decision making, left-of-center employees, and conversations about things like disadvantaged groups under American imperialism. If you think you are a liberal, think again." Jennifer also had to get accustomed to employees who gave countless unpaid hours to the organization and, in return, expected her to overlook failings from time to time.

How did Jennifer acclimate to the more casual nonprofit culture?

In her previous corporate jobs, Jennifer did not experience the level of personal camaraderie found in the nonprofit sector. "My corporate background did not prepare me for the openness I found in this sector," she explains, "and so I had to learn to check some of my reserve at the door, lest my coworkers brand me as too politically correct or too corporate."

Jennifer's Key Lessons Learned:

- "Employees in the nonprofit sector demand transparency. If they are working for 30 percent less than market, they expect to have not just a say but a vote. Decisions are often based on relationships, not just facts and figures."

- "The culture has to fit you. While the eccentricities of some staff might make you a teeny bit crazy at times, it is part of the fabric that makes this sector so rich."

- "Be yourself, your whole self, in the interview. Read about the organization, be prepared to ask smart questions, and show them how your skills—and your passion—make you the right hire."

Applying via E-mail

The best and fastest way to apply, if given the opportunity, is via e-mail. It is the most direct method of communication and the least likely to get lost in a pile of papers on an overburdened hiring manager's desk. It makes it easy for a hiring manager to review your application while on the road, forward your résumé to superiors, and expedite the hiring process.

In this day and age of Internet viruses, the worst thing you can do is send a blank e-mail with your cover letter and résumé as attachments. Simply putting the words "See Attached" won't work either. Would you open an e-mail or its attachments from a total stranger? Given that hiring managers get attachments all day long and are extra vigilant about viruses, they'll likely not open yours, or they may just put off opening e-mails until they are distracted by another candidate and have forgotten all about you.

Instead, attach your résumé to the e-mail and insert the body of your cover letter in the text of the e-mail. Attaching your résumé preserves the formatting and style of your document, while inserting the cover letter allows you to make your pitch before the hiring manager makes a hasty judgment about a résumé filled with corporate work. It's highly possible that in the application instructions, you were asked to follow directions about the subject line of your e-mail, perhaps to insert the job title or your name; always follow those directions.

Top Ten Cover Letter Dos and Don'ts

1. **Do** keep it to one page.

2. **Don't** be so brief that the employer must go on safari to find information.

3. **Do** personalize each letter, making the case about this mission and this nonprofit.

4. **Don't** misspell the name of the human resources manager, headhunter, or organization.

5. **Do** craft each cover letter to the specific job and recruiter, mentioning the position and organization in the first sentence.

6. **Don't** load the letter with corporate jargon, acronyms, or the latest business guru's ideas.

7. **Do** match your skills, whether gained in paid work or through volunteerism, to the job responsibilities.

8. **Don't** include charts and tables.

9. **Do** set yourself out as unique among a potential applicant pool because of your track record and passion.

10. **Don't** distinguish yourself with paper so unique it detracts from the content of the cover letter and résumé.

Three Sample Cover Letters

Cover Letter Strategy #1: Wearing Your Heart on Your Sleeve

Jennifer Jobseeker
149 Main Street
Tallahassee, Florida
jennifer_jobseeker@email.com (904) 555-8594

April 17, 2007

Janice Searchchair
Search Committee Chair
415 Broadway
Somerville, Massachusetts 02144

Dear Ms. Searchchair:

I read with great interest the recent recruitment announcement for the position of executive director of the National Infertility Support Center on the Nonprofit Professionals Advisory Group Web site and would welcome the opportunity to explore it further.

Six million people in the United States suffer from infertility; I am one of them. I joined the National Infertility Support Center over ten years ago and found support and education through its exceptional services. I have often found myself telling both men and women to contact the National Infertility Support Center so that they, too, will not be alone while dealing with the difficult mental, emotional, and financial issues brought about because of infertility. More can be done, and through the National Infertility Support Center's comprehensive national network of chapters, the organization is extremely well positioned to transform the public's awareness of infertility and develop the financial resources to bring about change.

For the last 15 years, I have devoted myself to leading, managing, and increasing the influence of nonprofit organizations. Performing this function for the National Infertility Support Center, a highly respected national organization in whose mission I strongly believe, would be both challenging and exciting to me. It would be a culmination of my personal experience with, and passion for, infertility support and solutions, organizational leadership experience, and political expertise. I have spent my career in the nexus of public policy, advocacy, and change, all powered by the action and involvement of individuals wanting to make a difference. The passion behind the National Infertility Support Center is no different.

The specific qualifications noted in the job description correspond directly with my experience and the leadership roles that I have held, both in my corporate experience and a consultant to nonprofit organizations. These positions required extensive government and political acumen; the development and implementation of lobbying strategies on both a statewide and national level; direct support of highly engaged board members and volunteers; coalition building; fundraising through memberships, grants, and grassroots fundraising; the development of innovative programs; collaborations with a wide range of constituencies; and financial and staff management.

My expertise and abilities, coupled with my personal experience, make me an ideal candidate for this position. It would be my honor to assist the National Infertility Support Center in raising its voice, honing its programs and messages, and reaching its ultimate potential.

Thank you for your consideration.

Sincerely,

Jennifer JobSeeker

Cover Letter Strategy #2: Selling Your For-Profit Experience to a Nonprofit

Eugene JobSeeker
1304 Main Street
Cincinnati, Ohio 45205
bruce.jobseeker@email.com (513) 555-0885

April 21, 2007

Paul Headhunter
Williams Search Associates
6937 Main Street
Philadelphia, Pennsylvania 19131

Dear Mr. Headhunter,

Please find attached my résumé in response to your recent announcement for a finance director for the Young Charitable Foundation. My proven track record managing financial, administrative, human resources, legal, and tax matters for a company of similar size and complexity, combined with my deeply held desire to improve the capacity of our neighborhood youth service organizations, makes me an ideal candidate for this position.

Inner-city neighborhoods across the country are just turning the corner. The work of the Young Charitable Foundation to reward organizations doing good work with the opportunity to do more and better work has caught on, and foundations across the country are striving to emulate your success, while your benefactors are asking you to replicate and grow. It is a difficult but exciting place to be. As you navigate your expected growth trajectory, my experience may provide a valuable road map of success.

Since January of 1999, I have served as the director of administration and finance for the Northside Corporation. In this role, I designed and implemented all systems and infrastructure necessary for the efficient and smooth running of the organization. The organization experienced rapid and sizable growth soon after my tenure began, its asset base quadrupling and its needs for enhanced systems, space, and structures increasing. I have overseen or performed all duties required to turn a small group of staff members into a well-respected and well-oiled company, from setting up office space, hiring staff, and instituting and managing annual audits to searching for and interviewing more investment managers, investment advisors, attorneys, and various other consultants, as well as creating and implementing more complicated internal controls and policies. In addition, I have had the honor of working with the corporation's board, formalizing agendas and minutes, ensuring compliance with bylaws, and acquiring directors' and officers' insurance.

I am interested in joining the nonprofit sector full-time in a role that is both professionally demanding and personally fulfilling. My passion remains with neighborhood investment, and my skill set would be ideal for a foundation that is in the midst of early growth and change. My track record overseeing finance and investments throughout the past 25 years would allow me to contribute substantially. I look forward to speaking with you soon.

Thank you for your consideration.

Sincerely,

Eugene JobSeeker

Cover Letter Strategy #3: Bringing Your Nonprofit Volunteer Work Front and Center

Barbara JobSeeker
655 Norbury Drive
Austin, Texas
barjobseek@email.com (512) 555-9144

February 12, 2007

Kathryn HiringManager, PhD
Executive Director
Earth Friendly USA
Washington, DC
Via E-mail: *khm@email.org*

Dear Dr. HiringManager:

Mary Johnson recently told me about your search for a chief operating officer for Earth Friendly USA. My financial and administrative acumen and strategic management experience, combined with my experience working with mission-driven nonprofit organizations, make me an ideal candidate for this position.

I am particularly interested in your strategic use of volunteer opportunities and education to catalyze change. I served as a board member for Greener Group Texas, an organization that managed more than 2,300 volunteers annually and built its success on harnessing the power of volunteers to become effective advocates. We built our volunteer programs with the express purpose of developing a strong, educated response to rising oil prices as well as providing service and meaningful volunteer experiences. Our success in mobilizing volunteers and changing minds was inspiring and changed the course of fuel usage in this state. I witnessed, firsthand, how efficient and intelligent internal management can enable an organization to focus on building more effective programs and advocacy. I have spent my career at the crossroads where innovative management meets the creation of change, and I believe my skills and experience may be a good fit for Earth Friendly USA.

Specifically, as chair of the finance committee, I was responsible for the management of Greener Group Texas's financial and administrative operations and helped transform it from a small grassroots nonprofit with a budget of $4 million into a nationally recognized leader in the field of environmental advocacy with a budget of $11 million and a reserve in excess of $3 million. As we grew, I oversaw all day-to-day organizational management and short- and long-term business and strategic planning before we had a permanent staff in place. Eventually, I led the newly formed senior management team for finance, administration, human resources, development, programs, and advocacy.

At this point in my career, I am looking to work with a nonprofit advocacy organization where my management experience, ability to deliver strong operating results, sense of humor, and passion for mission can be of use. I can be reached at *barjobseek@email.com* or (512) 555-9144 to schedule a convenient time to meet and discuss my qualifications and interest in this position. Thank you for considering my application.

Sincerely,

Barbara JobSeeker

ANSWERING THE SALARY QUESTION

Application instructions often ask for salary history or salary expectations. This is one of the hardest directives to which a sector switcher must respond. Comparing your for-profit salary compensation package to your nonprofit compensation package is like comparing apples to oranges. Actually, it's more like comparing apples to hubcaps. The sectors' pay ranges have little in common, and the valuation of jobs is completely different. There are still, however, great opportunities to earn a living wage while getting more fulfillment, a nicer lifestyle, and more opportunities to lead change in return.

Many job announcements ask for you to respond with a résumé, cover letter, and salary history. Nonprofits do this because they don't know what they need to pay to get the right person in the job. Most haven't done a salary survey in years, if not decades, and many aren't aware of current market rates.

If you aren't asked in the cover letter, this question might come up at any stage of the job search cycle, and more often than not catches candidates—especially career changers—off guard. You may be asked up front, as you start an informational call, or the subject might not arise until you get to the offer stage. It could be slipped in anywhere, so you need to be prepared to deal with it. Mishandling this question will likely sound the death knell of your negotiating power or will certainly show your ignorance of the nonprofit sector. Let's look at several strategies to help deal with the salary question.

Avoiding the Question: Taking the Fifth

One option is to ignore the question, but you choose this option at your own risk. Remember, headhunters ask for this information because its something they need to know. Not telling them makes you look as though you are either avoiding the question, not following directions, or feel that the rules don't apply to you. Given that you are switching sectors, your knowledge and acceptance of the fact that nonprofits pay on a different scale, as discussed in the first half of this book, is key to getting an interview.

If you feel you must avoid the question, you ought at least to acknowledge that it was asked. At least this way, the headhunter knows you understand its importance but are choosing to put it off to another date. Say something like, "My salary history from the for-profit sector would make little sense in this context, as my skills and expertise were judged by an entirely different set of goals. This move into the nonprofit sector is not motivated by financial needs, although I would expect to be paid according to the level of skills and experiences sought in the position."

Polite Ways of Skirting a Salary Question When First Asked

- "I'd be happy to talk about that at the appropriate time. Why don't you tell me more about the job?"

- "Before we get to that, let me make sure I'm even in your ballpark. What is the salary range for this position?"

- "I'm not comfortable discussing salary at this stage. Perhaps we can do so when we meet in person?"

- "My current employer does not allow me to discuss the terms of my employment."

- "For the skills and experience you want, I'd expect that this position would not pay less than $_____. Correct?"

Be Prepared for These Pushy Responses

- "We don't have a salary range but would like to learn more about the market. What are you making now?"

- "I need to know because my boss/client will ask and won't consider anyone without a complete file."

- "I'm afraid I cannot consider your application without your complete history."

- "I understand that you may have taken a salary cut for this position, so give me your last few salaries as well."

- "I'd hate to waste your time. Let's make sure we can afford you before we get too far down the road."

Know When to Say When

The compensation negotiation is often seen as the last battle of a war, when in fact it is the homecoming dance of the courtship. For the relationship to lead to a happy marriage, neither side should leave the table with his or her pride hurt or feelings damaged. It is fine to push back when questioned about your current compensation, but know when to give in. If you don't, you risk coming off as entitled or unable to transition into the nonprofit sector. Remember, the employer has yet to pop the question, and there are still plenty more fish in the sea.

When you feel the time is right to disclose this information—and it's usually fairly obvious—remember that compensation includes more than just salary. A paycheck of $75,000 with benefits equaling $25,000 means that your next employer will need to compensate you in excess of $100,000 to make up the difference in benefits. That being said, the nonprofit sector can offer intangible but nonetheless valuable "compensation," such as title inflation, more flexible work hours, additional opportunity, and the chance to make a living doing something you really love. After all, being stressed out about the planning of logistics for an upcoming conference that will train youth workers to assist the homeless is a lot different from losing sleep over the same logistics for a conference telling a bunch of shareholders how much money the company made for them this quarter.

You Cannot Tell a Lie

At some point during the salary discussion, you may be tempted to enhance, exaggerate, expand, or just plain lie. Don't do it. Headhunters and human resources professionals are a crafty lot, and if they catch you in your lie, and they always will, you will lose credibility, lose the job opportunity, and probably lose every chance to be considered for any jobs with which they may be associated.

Remember that you can always tell them the context around which your salary was determined and what you know to be the true market value of your skills and experience.

Getting More Information about Salary Ranges in the Nonprofit Sector

Many factors affect what a nonprofit can and will pay, including the level of supervisory/managerial responsibility, the type of organization, the number of employees, the annual budget, the scope of the organization, and its geographic area. There are three ways to determine whether your financial needs are in the ballpark of the job for which you are applying.

First, you can look up the most recent tax return—Form 990—of the nonprofit at Guidestar (*www.GuideStar.org*). The salaries of the top five highest-paid employees and the outlays to the top five highest-paid consultants are listed on this tax return. If you are not applying for one of the top positions, you can still see the overall salary budget line to get a sense of the overall ranges from this information.

Second, you can get a more general sense of your likely salary by looking up the tax returns of the competitors of the organization, or of other local organizations with similar budgets, missions, and staff sizes. Looking up a three-person hospital foundation won't tell you anything about what the three-person American Heart Association of Providence will pay, but looking up the local American Cancer Society of neighboring Boston might.

Third, you can do some general homework about nonprofit salary averages across the country by reading the many annual salary surveys available. Two of the best include

1. the Nonprofit Times *(www.nptimes.com)*, which publishes a free annual salary survey every February.
2. *Abbott, Langer, and Associates (www.abbott-langer.com)*, which can run up to $375 but is exceptionally comprehensive. It surveys more than a hundred benchmark jobs and describes the highest-paid job characteristics, the national median total cash compensation, and the factors affecting salary rates.

MASTERING THE NONPROFIT INTERVIEW

Many job seekers coming from the for-profit sector come to the interview process thinking that they will do the nonprofit world a favor by bringing their corporate expertise into the social sector. As I discussed in Chapter 4, the interviewer on the other side of the table likely doesn't see it that way. You've heard the old expression: You never get a second chance to make a first impression. But what you haven't heard is that most interviewers will size you up within the first ten minutes of an interview. If you don't make a good impression immediately, or if you come across as interested only in putting your corporate stamp on their social mission, you risk spending the balance of your interview with a person who is smiling politely but mentally reviewing her grocery list.

Beat out "milk, cereal, eggs, bread . . ." by meticulously preparing for each phase of the interview. Wow them at the handshake and keep them engaged until "This way to your new office."

Remember, if you are being asked in for an interview, they have already decided that you are at least remotely interesting in some way. They wouldn't spend their time with you otherwise. All that is left for you to do is wow them with more of your hard work, preparation, and dedication to making a difference to the constituency they serve.

Phase One: Mind Your Appearance

Unlike many things in life, looking your best at an interview is entirely within your control. You know it's coming, you have time to prepare, and you can take full advantage of that. You'll likely look better than you do on a typical workday, and the interviewer knows it. Wear clean, pressed clothes, but keep in mind the type of non-profit with which you are interviewing. The navy blue, pinstriped suit will work with a foundation in New York City but might not mesh with a grassroots advocacy agency in Albuquerque, New Mexico.

On interview day, bring extra copies of your résumé, business cards, a pad, and pens. You never know when a one-on-one interview will turn into a series of interviews. Don't wear excessive jewelry, makeup, or cologne; this isn't a date. Remember that nonprofits will accept and even nurture your funkier side, but try not to be too funky, or you might distract your interviewers from the words coming out of your mouth. You can wear your horn-rimmed glasses, but leave your alligator skin attaché case at home.

Dealing with a More Sensitive Crowd

Get there early, or have the courtesy to call if you are running late. At best, an interviewer may be able to move other appointments to accommodate you. At worst, the interviewer will seethe through whatever time is left in the scheduled interview. A firm—and, please, dry—handshake is always appreciated. Don't bring stale smoke or—does it need to be said?—alcohol breath into an interview.

Keep your body language in mind. You don't want to come across as "too corporate" by sitting in a closed, tight, defensive position. Be sure to display enthusiasm and warmth, as well as an openness to what your nonprofit interviewer may see as your potential challenges in this career change. Upon seeing that you are open to required change, the interviewer will be more open to giving you a chance. When in doubt, mirror your interviewer, a seasoned nonprofit professional, and you'll come off as the same.

Another important tip: Be friendly to the voice on the other end of the phone when making an appointment. Candidates who abuse administrative staff get ratted out. They don't get second interviews, no matter how qualified they are. Remember, this is the nonprofit sector, where every voice counts and every vote is heard, from the executive director to the intern of three weeks. A receptionist is as likely to sink you as the vice president for development.

Examples of Positive and Negative Body Language

Openness and warmth:

- Smiling showing teeth
- Open hands with palms visible
- Open coat when seated
- Eye contact without intense staring
- Legs crossed at ankles, not knees
- Deep belly breathing
- Good posture standing and sitting

Confidence:

- Leaning forward in chair
- Chin up
- Interlaced fingers
- Hands joined behind back when standing
- Dry, firm handshake
- Maintaining one to two positions
- Articulation without much gesticulation

Nervousness:

- Whistling
- Fidgeting, constant shifting of position
- Jiggling pocket contents
- Running tongue along front of teeth
- Repeated clearing of throat
- Rubbing back of neck or running fingers through hair
- Wringing hands
- Tongue clicking or a dry mouth

Untrustworthiness or defensiveness:

- Frown or tight grin
- Squinting eyes
- Arms crossed in front of chest
- Pulling away
- Chin down
- Touching nose or face
- Darting eyes before or during answers
- Gestures with fists, chopping hands, or pointing fingers
- Clasping hands behind head while leaning back in the chair

Phase Two: Above All, Know Thyself, the Organization, and Its Needs

What has your past work experience done for your ability to help this organization get to where it wants to be? If you don't already know this, slowly step away from the interviewer's office and put your hands up. You aren't ready.

Think through how you wish to portray each job you have held, both the out-of-the-park successes and the sink-to-the-basement disasters. Rehearse your transitions between jobs. You will be asked about all of this, and while you shouldn't grumble about a previous employer, fudging through an obviously tough situation will make you look dishonest. Following are some examples of how to handle questions about past employment:

- *Backward-looking grumble.* My old boss wasn't too flexible about my personal needs. He just couldn't understand what was happening with my family, so I had to quit.
- *Forward-facing action step.* When my mother fell ill with cancer, I realized that my old position wouldn't allow me the flexibility I needed to take care of her at such an important time, so my boss and I agreed to part ways. Now that my mother has recovered, I have had time to reflect on my own priorities and what I could be doing with my skills and experience. At this point, coming to work for you to use my personal and professional background to help other families work through difficult illnesses and the stresses they bring to their households seems like where I really belong.

Research the organization and its senior management, where they have been and where they wish to go. When your interviewer or the assistant calls to schedule the interview, request an annual report, a strategic plan, or other material that will shed more light on the organization. Ask, "Is there anything that you can provide me, which I can't easily download from your Web site, that might give me more information about your organization and allow me to show you how I can best help you achieve your goals?" Having a thorough understanding of the organization will help you better assess and therefore better communicate in the language of the nonprofit sector how they will benefit by bringing you on staff.

ELLISE M. LAMOTTE   PROJECT DIRECTOR, WOMEN OF ETHNIC DIVERSITY INITIATIVE, THE COMMONWEALTH INSTITUTE, BOSTON, MASSACHUSETTS

Ellise landed in the nonprofit sector completely by accident. "I had gone to school and studied engineering," Ellise says, "and went right to work at New England Telecom, which then became Verizon, which spun off Genuity, and so the roller coaster went." By the time Verizon had decided against buying back Genuity, Ellise had already made contingency plans by getting her real estate license. When the layoff came, she was prepared. "I had set off on my real estate adventure," she says, "and after a couple of years, decided to have another adventure: motherhood."

Ellise settled into her new life but began to ask herself if she really wanted to stay home all day with her six-month-old baby. "I missed hearing people say, 'Job well done!' at the end of the day," she says, "but I knew I didn't want to go back into big corporate America again. If I was going to be away from my baby, I didn't want to be putting in a circuit for a telecom company, but doing something that really matters." That's when one of her friends sent Ellise an announcement for a position as project director for a nonprofit enabling diverse women entrepreneurs to grow their business ventures. "The job was networking and helping others succeed," she says, "which was what I had always enjoyed doing most in my professional and personal lives, plus it was working for a women's nonprofit, so I knew it would be family friendly."

What surprised Ellise most when she started her nonprofit job?

"I kind of knew that nonprofits were different," she says, "but I didn't know how different they were." Ellise quickly realized that nonprofits were less hierarchical than corporations, where "everyone does everything—from moving boxes to making coffee—and no one wastes money," she says. She was also impressed with the numbers of power players she was exposed to on her very first day. "The women I meet with on a daily basis are on the largest boards, run the most successful companies, and are elected to some of the highest offices in the state," she says. "It's amazing to sit in a room with several hundred million dollars of net worth, especially when they are all women!"

How has motherhood affected Ellise's professional life?

At the end of the day, Ellise realized that the difference in culture, acceptance, and access only added a layer to what was already a viable business plan. "Going back to work after having my baby was harder for me than the transition from for-profit to nonprofit," she says. "This is a nonprofit, but we still have revenue targets." That added layer, though, made all the difference for Ellise as a new mother. "This nonprofit is much friendlier to me as a mother than my corporate-America experience would have been," she says. "No one is giving me the evil eye when I have to leave early, and no one thinks twice when I have to work from home because my child is sick."

Ellise's Key Lessons Learned:

- "'Nonprofit' doesn't mean 'no money.' If you find the right nonprofit, it will be every bit as businesslike as you have come to enjoy in your corporate life but with the heart you didn't know you missed."

- "Network with the nonprofits where you want to work. If they are small, they might not have jobs when you first start looking, but as soon as a job opens up, you'll be the first one they call."

- "As you are interviewing, don't be afraid of having conversations about your personal schedule and how it might affect your work. You'll be surprised that nonprofits will understand where you are coming from and won't make you feel like you are begging for permission to have a life outside of the office."

Likely Nonprofit Interview Questions

Before you step over the threshold of an interviewer's office, you had better be prepared to impress the interviewer with well-thought-out answers to questions you haven't yet heard. Most of the questions can be anticipated, but you should always be prepared for the unexpected.

The Good…

Good interview questions are insightful, forward-thinking questions that allow you to tie prospective achievements to a proven track record. Here are some examples:

- "Why are you interested in raising money for the spotted owl?"
- "What did you do at General Electric that has prepared you for the job of communications around homeless issues?"
- "How did you raise internal corporate morale, and will those ideas transfer to the city library system?"

By the time you step into the interviewer's office, your work history as presented on your résumé has already at least minimally qualified you for the job. Good interview questions focus both on the projects and programs you have managed as well as your hopes, dreams, and desires in this new position in this new sector. Employers are as much interested in what you have accomplished as in what it will be like to work with you on a daily basis.

Answer questions thoroughly, but succinctly, through stories that detail both your experience and your personal style. You should always answer the interviewer's questions, but the direction you take your answers is up to you. Make a list of the points you want to get across in the interview—how you originally got interested in the field, why you are making this sector switch right now, how your background and specific projects have prepared you for the position, how your passion is in line with the organization's mission, and how this position fits into your future career goals—and thread them throughout the answers you give to questions. Make sure to underscore constantly your belief in the mission of the nonprofit and your understanding of how this sector will be different from the corporate world you wish to leave behind.

The Bad…

Invariably, the interviewer will roll around to a "bad" interview question, one that you feel a bit timid about answering. It could be because you were fired, had a bad relationship with your boss, or didn't quite succeed in a job. It could even be as simple as asking pointedly about your sector switch and its likely success or failure. Some such questions might include these:

- "So, you weren't in your last job for very long. What went wrong?"
- "You seem to move around a lot. Why?"
- "Tell me about a project that failed and your role in that failure?"

As much as you are tempted, jokes about poisoning your last boss aren't really funny, especially to someone who might be your next one. Everyone has spots on their résumé that don't shine as brightly as others. Don't attempt to cover them up. Making jokes or floundering through a long story will only make you look nervous or, worse, like you are lying. When confronted with a failure or a firing, just come clean.

Hit the incident head on. Say that you are glad that the interviewer brought it up. Relate that the situation was a difficult one, and stick to the facts when describing it. You might even be able to use it as the reason that you tired of the corporate rat race and want to move into an organization worth the fight. Give an accurate but overall positive assessment of what went wrong and what you learned from the situation. Never, ever bad mouth your former boss or old coworkers.

Finally, take blame where blame is due. Candidates who always point the finger anywhere but at themselves look as though they either cannot comprehend the problem or are covering up something. Turn the lens back onto yourself and use it as a chance to point out how you learn from your own mistakes. Nonprofits will appreciate your honesty and integrity and the fact that you can grow and change, because this sector switch will be a giant opportunity to succeed or fail doing just that.

. . . and the Ugly

Every so often an interviewer will stumble, whether intentionally or not, into illegal territory. Here are some ugly questions:

- "So are you a native New Yorker, or are you not from around here?"
- "Travilani, is that an Italian name? My grandmother was Italian."
- "Will it be difficult on your family for you to begin traveling for work?"

Do these sound like illegal questions or just small talk? Technically, they are illegal.

Illegal questions are questions related to your birthplace, nationality, native language or the ancestry of you, your spouse, your children, or your parents; your age; your sexual orientation or marital status; your race or color; your religion or the religious days or traditions you observe; any physical disabilities or handicaps you might have; an arrest record; your health or medical history; or your pregnancy or plans for pregnancy, birth control practices, and child care arrangements of yours or your significant other.

Although you aren't bound to answer these questions, you also do yourself a disservice by explaining to your interviewer the intricacies of employment law. Use your judgment before riding the politically correct bus out of town and away from your chances at a second interview. Most nonprofits can't afford to have a full-time human resources person interviewing all candidates, so your interviewer, while highly accomplished developing and implementing programs, is likely quite inexperienced and means no harm. A lecture from you only makes you appear rigid, possibly adding to the corporate stereotype. Instead, change the subject, and your green interviewer will get the picture. If, on the other hand, you sense that your interviewer is blatantly discriminating against you, you can and should call the interview to an end; it isn't a place you'd want to work anyway.

Ten Frequently Asked Nonprofit Interview Questions

1. What can you do for our organization?

2. Of which accomplishment are you most proud?

3. And of which are you least?

4. What was the last argument you won, and how?

5. What is the first thing you would do in this position if it were offered to you today?

6. Tell me about yourself and what brings you here today?

7. Why are you leaving the for-profit sector?

8. What do you do to relax in your spare time?

9. What will be your biggest challenge in this position? In coming to the nonprofit sector?

10. Why should we hire you instead of some of the others we are interviewing?

Speaking the Lingo

Before you head into the interview, review the section on language differences in Chapter 6. Take your cues from the nonprofit itself: some nonprofits are grassroots and old school in their approach, whereas others are social enterprise models with full staffs of MBAs. Using the job description, Web site, and other promotional materials, such as annual reports, direct mail pieces, or grant applications, you can discern the specific language of this particular nonprofit.

Examples of For-Profit Answers and Nonprofit Answers to the Same Question

Example #1: Have you had experience raising money?

- *For-profit answer.* Yes. I raised $10 million in venture capital for my last start-up endeavor. I see no reason why I can't raise the $2 million you need annually to run this program. Raising money is raising money, and I'm great at it.
- *Nonprofit answer.* Yes. I have had a great deal of experience raising capital in the for-profit sector, and I have many transferable skills that would help me be successful raising money in the nonprofit sector. I know, of course, that raising $10 million in venture funds isn't the same, because my investors expected to make a lot of money in return; and in the nonprofit sector, the donors will get a different type of return—a great feeling of doing a good thing. But let me tell you what skills it took to raise that $10 million. First, I had to research my prospective investors. Second, I had to begin a relationship with them and build trust in the fact that I would be stewarding their money. Third, I had to determine when, how, and where to ask and for how much. Finally, I had to stay in constant contact with them throughout the life of that "gift" to ensure that they were satisfied, continually engaged, and possibly interested in giving more at a later date.

Example #2: Are you willing to roll up your sleeves and get your hands dirty?

- *For-profit answer.* Sure. I'm not afraid of hard work. I am often in the office late at night and early in the morning. I do whatever is needed to get the job done.
- *Nonprofit answer.* Yes. In fact, I understand that this organization has less support staff that I am used to, but let me tell you that just yesterday, I was

the one changing the toner on the copier and refilling the paper trays. I feel no need to stand on ceremony because I am the boss. In fact, everyone in my shop pulls together to get the job done. We are all equal players when there is a task at hand or a deadline to be met.

Example #3: How have you determined whether a program or line of business is worth continuing?

- *For-profit answer.* Simply put, we have bottom-line goals. If the product is performing, we keep going. If not, we axe it and any staff who were responsible for its failure. I did that last month, making an example of the employee, and the rest of the staff have been working harder ever since.
- *Nonprofit answer.* Many factors go into a success or a failure, whether a lack of planning, poor execution, or a missed market. There are also different definitions of success. In August of last year, we had a product that was failing by our for-profit standards of bottom-line numbers. I took the staff member aside and privately asked why he thought the failure was occurring. He told me that he wasn't able to manage a piece of it adequately and felt responsible. Instead of firing him, I decided to reward his honesty with some additional training. The product isn't failing anymore, but it's also not a runaway success. That being said, this employee has now come back with three other great ideas that have been tremendous successes, and the other staff have followed his example. I'm always willing to lose a little money in one area to gain a better, stronger, more invested staff all around. Plus, at the end of the day, we're even more profitable.

Phase Three: Tag, You're It!

At some point in the interview, usually about three quarters of the way through, you will be asked if you have any questions. It may seem like the moment when you can finally let out a sigh of relief, sit back, and revel in the fact that the evaluation is over. Don't fall into that trap. As a candidate, and especially as someone new to the sector, you will be judged by your questions as well as your answers.

Whoever said that there are no stupid questions never sat in on a job interview. There are plenty of stupid questions, and the candidates who ask them don't get offered jobs. If you ask no questions, you will have lost a unique opportunity to learn about the organization, not to mention getting labeled as having no intellectual curiosity or enthusiasm about the position or the organization.

Be Prepared with Questions

Bring along good questions, albeit not too many. Three to four is a good number; ask five if you must. You will be judged both on your intellectual savvy and your etiquette. Don't make the committee late for the next interview because you can't take hints like eye rolls, seat shifts, heavy clock glances, and monosyllabic answers—all of these actions indicate that the interview is over. If the interviewer likes you, you will have all the time in the world to ask follow-up questions as the process unfolds.

Focus your questions on the future of the organization rather than the organizational chart or the salary range. Asking nitpicky questions will only make the interviewer think you are a small thinker; there will be time for the details later, like when you are reviewing an offer. Plus, an overwhelming concern about salary or benefits only underscores that your first career was for personal profit and not service to the community.

The Pre-Interview Checklist

✔ An interview cheat sheet with achievements and explanations organized by job and function, easily digestible by someone in another sector

✔ An appointment book to schedule a follow-up interview on the spot

✔ A working watch to ensure early arrival

✔ A folder with five extra résumés, business cards, pen or paper, and a notepad

✔ Tissues or a handkerchief

✔ Directions to the interview location, easily found online

✔ A portfolio of your creative work, strategic plans, or other proud accomplishments, preferably displaying anything you've done as a volunteer or board member

✔ A list of questions that show insight and research into the nonprofit sector and this particular organization and its challenges

✔ A silenced cell phone or beeper

✔ A copy of the job announcement, or notes taken about the position, to reread while you are waiting for the interview to begin. Circle nonprofit buzzwords to use throughout the interview.

✔ Breath mints

✔ A list of nonprofit references, if available, with current contact information and a brief explanation of their relationship to you or the project on which you worked together

✔ A sense of humor about yourself and humility about the challenges of switching sectors

✔ Letters of recommendation, preferably from nonprofit colleagues you've met along your journey

✔ A firm handshake, good eye contact, and a smile

Do Your Homework

Remember that brainy kid in junior high who asked questions like, "I did some extra reading and became curious. Can you tell me more about the crop rotation method of the early Mesopotamians?" We might not have learned our lesson then, but we can now. Curiosity and an active, lively intellect get attention. Every other student hated that kid, but the teacher always gave "the brain" an A+. By asking questions that show off your research or bring up strengths that the search committee might have overlooked, you can further impress a crowd that is still actively grading your performance.

Pull out the copy of the IRS Form 990 that you downloaded from the Internet (easily found and free at *www.guidestar.org*). Thumb through your dog-eared copy of the last annual report to discuss a program that you find particularly interesting. Mention something you saw in the last newsletter. Showing that you have taken the time to learn about the organization, whether by downloading information, discussing the organization with volunteers or board members, or through other research, will impress the search committee into believing that your sector switch is, indeed, motivated by all the right reasons.

Creativity Counts

By all means, ask questions on a variety of topics. Your search committee most likely has sat in the same chairs in the same room, listening to the same kind of candidates talk about the same sorts of subjects all day, and anything vaguely boring—like multiple questions on the same topic—will further lull them into a coma. Appearing somewhat knowledgeable but still intrigued about subjects interesting to each search committee member just might add that extra bit of enthusiasm necessary to catapult you ahead of One-Note Sally.

Good subjects to cover include the environment in which the organization operates, the management style employed by the top brass, obstacles and challenges that stand in the way of success, and the organization's view of its future. You can ask questions that highlight how you feel your for-profit background will meld with the hopes and dreams of their leadership.

Force Interesting Answers

Avoid questions with obvious or readily available answers—like ones in the job description, for example—or questions that can be answered simply with a yes or a no. You can ask your interviewer for clarification on a specific point, but don't ask for a repeat explanation of an entire subject, or you will risk coming across as the candidate without any listening comprehension skills. Stay away from such unsavory topics as salary, benefits, and vacation time. Similarly, questions about weekend assignments, tuition reimbursements, pay schedules, and Bring Your Dog to Work Day frequency should also be avoided. Asking such questions will paint your candidacy as more focused on what the organization can do for you than what you can do for it.

Great Questions That Show Your Understanding of the Nonprofit Sector

- What are the main objectives and responsibilities of the position? Is a strategic plan already in place to meet them?

- How involved is the board, and how would you characterize it?

- What challenges or obstacles are commonly encountered in reaching these objectives?

- What is the desired time frame for reaching the objectives?

- What resources are available internally, and what must be found or raised elsewhere to reach the objectives?

- How would you characterize the management philosophy of this organization? Of your department?

- What strengths and weaknesses currently exist in the staff that will report to me?

- How has this organization changed in the past, and where does it expect to go in the future?

- What is the top priority of the person who accepts this job? How will the successful candidate be judged in 6–12 months?

- What are the next steps in the selection process?

THE INTERVIEW'S OVER, NOW WHAT?

With an ounce of relief and a pound of pride, you step from your interviewer's office exhilarated that you have made it through yet another step of the job search process. But any good candidate knows that the job interview doesn't end with "Thanks, we'll be in touch." So what do you do now?

As you exit the interview, and undoubtedly throughout the ride home, you will begin to find yourself hounded by pesky thoughts of things you forgot to say. Resist the urge to pick up the phone and call your interviewer; until a decision has been made, everything you say can and will be held against you. You may come up with other things you wish to say, and calling each time will only make you look scatterbrained. But the nonprofit sector is a little kinder to mistakes and more forgiving of personal foibles. Returning to your interviewer with some thoughts about the interview is not only acceptable, it is encouraged—as long as you follow the right form.

Carefully debrief the interview. Think through the questions that were asked and the questions that were not asked. Review the list of points you expected to make and weigh them against what actually came out of your mouth. Judge your performance and think through what you could improve upon next time. Every performance can be improved, and until you accept a position, you should always assume there will be another.

Thank-You Notes Are Key

Regrettably, the art of the personalized thank-you note is a lost one. In the age of electronic communication, it's rare for hiring managers to get thank-you notes from candidates they have interviewed. When they do, it seems that most are quick notes jotted hastily, with typos throughout, and sent electronically without much effort or thought at all. Hiring managers would like to think that your interest in the job at hand, not to mention your respect for their time, warrants more than that.

A personalized thank-you note is not just polite, it's an opportunity for you to give one last sales pitch, and it's a chance to fill in the hiring manager on anything you realize you forgot to say in the interview. Yet most candidates forswear this golden opportunity. A good thank-you note doesn't gush; it expresses both appreciation for the hiring manager's time as well as a forgotten—or repeated—clarification of your skills and experiences as they relate to the organization's needs and challenges. A thank-you note gets the hirer's attention, and a good one gets placed in the résumé book and is ultimately read, and duly noted, by the search committee. As a sector switcher, this is the ideal moment for you to underscore your knowledge of this more touchy-feely world, showing how well you can and will fit into it.

Grace Jobseeker
123 Highway One
Newton, Massachusetts 02458
(617) 555-4658

Dear Jane Headmistress:

Thank you for spending time with me this afternoon discussing the exciting position at Newton Montessori School. As I explained, I feel that my skills and experiences crafting brands and marketing for The Major Corporation, combined with my ten years as a parent of Montessori children, will enable me to serve the school as an excellent director of admissions and recruiting.

I was extremely impressed with the work that the school has already done to position itself among its peers as a leader among other Montessori schools in the greater Boston area. As you know, I believe that what Newton Montessori needs at this time is to be "branded" with potential incoming parents of younger children as well as to neighborhood private schools for outgoing sixth graders. By becoming "the school from which the best kids graduate," Newton Montessori will have a waiting list in no time, making the job of selecting students a difficult but enviable task. As we discussed, my background in creating brands around education-based products, specifically for this age group and sector, make me an ideal candidate to develop the Newton Montessori brand.

In our interview, I told you a good deal about the work that I did on the communications committee of our parent guild. I forgot to mention, however, that the school that our sons attended is still, five years later, using the materials I helped develop and speaks of them with great acclaim. In creating them, I aimed for timelessness, knowing that the school wouldn't have the budget to re-create materials each year. It gives me great pleasure to know that what I created has been so effective.

Even though I understand that you will need to see other candidates, I want to be clear that I am actively seeking new employment and have several interviews scheduled for next week. This position is the one in which

I am most interested, however, and I will be checking back with you at the end of next week to see if you have made any determinations about your decision-making time line. I would consider it an honor and a privilege to be able to serve in this wonderful school.

Warm regards,

Grace JobSeeker

Post-Interview Reflections

After you leave the interview, it is essential to debrief about your performance. Answers to these questions will inform your thank-you note as well as future interview performance:

- Did you feel comfortable in the interview?
- Which questions could you have answered better?
- Where did you succeed? Where did you fail?
- Which topics led to awkward silences?
- Did you emphasize your understanding of the connection between the organization's needs and your skills and experiences?
- Did you create a conversational atmosphere?
- Did the interviewer ask questions for which you were not prepared?
- Did you understand and address the interviewer's concerns about your candidacy given your for-profit background?
- Did you forget to ask any questions about the job or organization that would inform your decision should the job be offered to you?
- What would you say or do differently next time?

Handling the Follow-up Call Well

Any conversation with a headhunter or hiring manager after an interview may contain an offer. Many will include reconnaissance questions necessary so that when an offer does come, it will be accepted. Like a proposal of marriage, a job offer is a question rarely asked without full knowledge of the response. Yet because your sector switch presents different issues around compensation, more questions likely will be asked of you than of other candidates.

Keep a list handy of any remaining questions you have about the position or the organization. You would need to satisfy any concerns before accepting a job anyway, so asking them during follow-up calls gives you more control over the conversation. Don't feel pressured into answering questions if you are surprised by the call. The headhunter doesn't know your schedule and can't see that you are sitting in your living room waiting all day for the air conditioner service technician. Put off the call with an excuse of a meeting currently in progress to give yourself time to catch your breath and call back when you are calm, collected, and, yes, cool.

STRATEGIC REFERENCES

Once you've mastered the interview, it's quickly on to the reference-checking stage of the search. You may be asked for these references at the interview or soon thereafter, so it's a good idea to have them prepped and ready.

Think of your references as an extension of your interview. Rather than your telling the search committee, again, how great you would be at this job, your references will do it for you. Be sure to choose references who can talk about the great work you've done with them in the context of your work in the nonprofit sector. If your references can only talk about your corporate prowess, they won't help you and may even hurt you. Because you'll need some references that can talk about your day job try, if possible, to pick people who have done some nonprofit volunteering—either with you or on their own—and can talk intelligently about how you would overcome any potential challenges.

Prepping Your References

Ask your references for permission before you list them. Prepare each by providing a current copy of your résumé, the job description, and some information about the organization. If appropriate, remind them about some of the exceptional things you did together that set you up for success in this new role.

Don't be too prescriptive about talking points, but remind them that this is a sector switch for you and they may get some specific questions about how you would make that leap. Make sure they know why you think you would be right in this new position. Allow your references to ask any questions they have so that they can process this move with you, not with the headhunter.

Handling a Likely Negative Reference

At some point in the process, a good hiring manager will ask if there is anyone they cannot call. These are the "off-list" references, and any one of them might dredge up some bad news. If you know that something is coming—perhaps you are quitting your current job because your boss is horrible and no one leaves the department well—make sure you are honest with the hiring manager. Hearing bad news from you will usually inoculate you against any issues that may arise; not hearing it from you will make you look as though you were purposefully evasive and lessen your credibility throughout the rest of the process.

If there is something more serious—a criminal record, a failed credit rating, or a college degree not actually earned, for example—fess up immediately. Because nonprofits steward public money, they are often under high levels of public scrutiny. To that end, many nonprofits insist on a criminal, credit, and educational background check by any number of private firms who do this sort of thing. They will find out what you are hoping to hide, and your only chance of inoculating yourself is to come out with it first and share the relevant context, rehabilitation, or remorse.

Thanking Your References

If you are searching for a job, your references most likely will get called several times at potentially inconvenient moments to laud your greatness. Keep them energized and engaged by actively appreciating them. Rather than sending an unnecessary gift, thank them with a note that updates them on your job search progress. Do not ask them if they were contacted—because they normally would be promised confidentiality by the recruiter—but they may still tell you. Either way, thank all of your references when the search ends, whether or not you get the job.

CONCLUSION

Writing a cover letter will seem, at first, like a daunting and overwhelming task. You'll need to learn a tone different from the one you've used in cover letters you've written throughout your corporate career. However, writing it in your own voice will become more comfortable with practice and eventually will seem like second nature. So, too, will your interview performance. As with anything else, practice makes perfect, so start talking to everyone and don't stop until you've landed your next job. Your references are a perfect sounding board, because they'll both need to know why you are making this move and why you think you are qualified to do so. They believe in you, have seen your career in action, and are willing to help. Let them—they'll thank you for it.

Epilogue

Throughout this book, you've read the stories of people who have made the transition from the for-profit to the nonprofit sector. Some came by accident; others were more purposeful. All are thrilled with their decision, and most wished they had done it sooner.

Undoubtedly you picked up *Change Your Career* because you were curious about what working in the nonprofit sector would mean for you, personally, professionally, and financially. This book endeavored to help answer those questions and inspire you on your journey. Now you are ready—go follow your dream!

Additional Resources

This abridged list should give you a sense of the resources at your disposal as you make this transition into the nonprofit sector. A longer, more detailed list may be found at http://www.nonprofitprofessionals.com.

Job Boards by Interest Area

General Nonprofit Job Websites

American Society of Association Executives –
http://www.asaecenter.org/

Bridgestar – *http://www.bridgestar.org*

CEO Update – *http://www.associationjobs.com*

Chronicle of Philanthropy –
http://philanthropy.com/jobs/

ExecSearches.com – *http://www.execsearches.com*

Guidestar – *http://www.guidestar.org*

Idealist – *http://www.idealist.org*

Nonprofit Oyster – *http://www.nonprofitoyster.com*

Nonprofit Times – *http://www.nptimes.com*

Opportunity NOCs –
http://www.opportunityNOCS.org

Academia, Teaching, and Higher Education

CASE – *http://www.case.org*

Chronicle of Higher Education –
http://www.chronicle.com

Council for Special Education –
http://www.specialedcareers.org/

Education Week – *http://www.agentk–12.org*

Higher Ed Jobs – *http://www.higheredjobs.com*

Animals and the Environment

American Zoo and Aquarium Association Positions –
http://www.aza.org/JobListings/

Environmental Careers and Opportunities –
http://www.ecojobs.com

EnviroJobs – *EnviroJobs@yahoogroups.com*

Environmental Jobs and Careers –
http://www.ejobs.org/

Green Dream Jobs –
http://www.sustainablebusiness.com/jobs/

Arts and Cultural

Arts Jobs – *http://www.artjob.org*

Arts Wire – *http://www.artswire.org*

Museum Jobs – *http://www.museumjobs.org*

Foundations and Philanthropy

Council on Foundations – *http://www.cof.org*

The Foundation Center with the Philanthropy News
Digest – *http://www.fdncenter.org*

On Philanthropy Job Bank –
http://www.dotorgjobs.com/rt/dojhome

PNN Online – *http://pnnonline.org/*

Health and Medical

Health Careers Online –
  http://www.healthcareers–online.com
Health Career Web – *http://www.healthcareerweb.com*
Public Health Employment Connection –
  http://cfusion.sph.emory.edu/PHEC/phec.cfm

International

International Jobs – *http://www.internationaljobs.org*
Overseas Jobs – *http://www.overseasjobs.org*
U.S. Foreign Service – *http://www.state.gov*

Legal

American Bar Associations – *http://www.abanet.org*
Emplawyer – *http://Emplawyer.net*
LawJobs – *http://www.LawJobs.com*

Lesbian, Gay, Bisexual and Transgender

Diversity Working – *http://www.diversityworking.com/
  career/Non_Profit/gay_lesbians.htm*
GLP Careers – *http://www.glpcareers.com/*
ProGayJobs – *http://www.progayjobs.com/nonprofit.php*
Queer Jobs Listserv – *queerjobs@yahoogroups.com*

National and Community Service

Community Career Center –
  http://www.nonprofitjobs.org
Idealist – *http://www.idealist.org*
Lifetime of Service (AmeriCorps Alums) –
  http://www.lifetimeofservice.org/networking/
VISTAnet – *listserv@listserv.icors.org*

Politics, Organizing and Government

Careers in Government –
  http://www.careersingovernment.com
National Organizers Alliance Job Bank –
  http://www.ultrabit.net/noa/jobbank.cfm
Opportunities in Public Affairs – *http://brubach.com*
Union Jobs Clearinghouse – *http://www.unionjobs.com*

Religious Organizations

Christian Jobs Listserv –
  christian-jobs@yahoogroups.com
Jewish Communal Jobs Clearinghouse –
  http://www.jewishjobs.com
Ministry Connect – *http://www.ministryconnect.org*
Work Ministry – *http://www.workministry.com*

Social Service

Coalition for Human Needs –
  http://www.chn.org/jobs/index.html
Jobs in Fair Housing – *http://www.fairhousing.com*
Social Service Jobs – *http://www.socialservice.com*
National Association of Social Workers JobLink –
  http://www.naswdc.org

Technology

Contract Employment Weekly, Jobs Online –
  http://www.cjhunter.com
Nonprofit Tech Jobs –
  http://groups.yahoo.com/group/Nonprofit_Tech_Jobs
Dice.com – *http://www.dice.com*

Women

Career Women – *http://www.careerwomen.com/*
Feminist Majority Career Center –
  http://www.feminist.org
Women's Information Network –
  http://www.winonline.org

Executive Search Firms Serving the Nonprofit Sector

Auerbach Associates – *http://www.auerbach–assc.com*
Commongood Careers – *http://www.cgcareers.org*
Development Resource Group – *http://www.drg.com*
Diversified Search – *http://www.divsearch.com*
Egmont and Associates –
  http://www.egmontassociates.com
Isaacson, Miller – *http://www.imsearch.com*
Kittleman & Associates, LLC – *http://www.kittleman.com*
Korn Ferry – *http://www.kornferry.com*
Lois Lindauer Searches – *http://www.lllsearches.com*
Morris & Berger – *http://www.morrisberger.com*
Nonprofit Professionals Advisory Group –
  http://www.nonprofitprofessionals.com
Russell Reynolds Associates, Inc. –
  http://www.russellreynolds.com
Slesinger Management –
  http://www.slesingermanagement.com
Spencer Stuart – *http://www.spencerstuart.com*

Temp/Staffing Agencies Making Placements in Nonprofits

Accounting Management Solutions –
http://www.amsolutions.net

Careers for Causes – *http://www.placementpros.com/*

First Source Staffing – *http://fssny.com*

Professionals for Nonprofits –
http://www.nonprofitstaffing.com

Nonprofit Staffing Solutions –
http://www.nonprofittemps.com/

Continued Reading

Books on Nonprofit Management

*The Nonprofit Sector: A Research Handbook, by Walter W. Powell and Richard Steinberg, Yale University Press; 2nd Edition (November 1, 2006)

*The Nature of the Nonprofit Sector by J. Steven Ott, Westview Press (October 1, 2000)

*Good to Great and the Social Sector: A Monograph to Accompany Good to Great, Jim Collins, HarperCollins (November 30, 2005)

*Love and Profit, James A. Autry, Harper Paperbacks; Reprint edition (September 1, 1992)

*Leadership in Nonprofit Organizations: Lessons from the Third Sector, Barry Dym and Harry Hutson, Sage Publications, Inc (January 12, 2005)

Books with Inspirational Stories

*The Cathedral Within, by Billy Shore, Random House Trade Paperbacks (November 1, 2001)

*Leaving Microsoft to Change the World, by John Wood, Collins (August 29, 2006)

**How to Change the World, by David Bornstein, Oxford University Press, USA (February 5, 2004)

*Be the Change! Change the World. Change Yourself. Edited by Michelle Nunn, Hundreds of Heads Books (November 1, 2006)

*Encore: How Baby Boomers Are Inventing the Next Stage of Work, by Marc Freedman, PublicAffairs (May 30, 2007)

Magazines, Periodicals, and Journals

Alliance Insight –
http://www.allianceonline.org/insights.ipage

Chronicle of Higher Education –
http://www.chronicle.com

Chronicle of Philanthropy –
http://www.philanthropy.com

Contributions Magazine –
http://www.contributionsmagazine.com

Exempt Magazine – *http://www.exemptmagazine.com/*

Fast Company – *http://www.fastcompany.com*

Generocrity – *http://www.generocitymag.com*

Good Magazine – *http://www.goodmagazine.com/*

Nonprofit Quarterly – *http://www.nonprofitquarterly.org/*

Nonprofit Times – *http://www.nptimes.com*

Stanford Social Innovation Review –
http://www.ssireview.org/

E–Newsletters

Bridgestar – *http://www.bridgestar.org*

Case Foundation – *http://www.casefoundation.org/about/contact/email–updates*

Charity Channel –
http://charitychannel.com/enewsletters/ncr/index.asp

Compass Point's Board Cafe –
http://www.compasspoint.org/boardcafe/index.php

Just Give – *http://www.justgive.org/html/nonprofits/npnewsletter.html*

Nonprofit About.com – *http://nonprofit.about.com/gi/pages/mmail.htm*

Nonprofit Legal Issues – *http://www.nonprofitissues.com/*

Nonprofit News Online – *http://news.gilbert.org/*

Nonprofit Policy News – *http://www.ncna.org/index.cfm?fuseaction=Page.viewPage&pageId=696*

Nonprofit Professionals Advisory Group –
http://www.nonprofitprofessionals.com

Omidyar Network – *http://www.omidyar.net/home/*

Skoll Foundation – *http://www.skollfoundation.org/*

Helpful Websites for Additional Research

Charity Navigator – *http://www.charitynavigator.org*

Guidestar – *http://www.guidestar.org*

National Center for Charitable Statistics –
http://nccs.urban.org

Network for Good – *http://www.networkforgood.org*

The Nonprofit FAQs – *http://www.nonprofits.org*

Educational Resources:
Degrees or Concentrations in Non-Profit

Graduate Programs (Graduate Degrees)

The following schools offer programs where you can earn your Master of Arts (MA), Master of Business Administration (MBA), Master of Nonprofit Administration, (MNA), Master of Public Administration (MPA), Master of Public Policy (MPP), Master of Science (MS), or Doctor of Philosophy (PhD) in nonprofit management.

Alabama

Auburn University at Montgomery, MPA with Concentration Nonprofit

Arizona

Arizona State University, MPA in Nonprofit Management

University of Arizona, MPA in Nonprofits and Government

California

University of San Francisco, MNA

University of California at Los Angeles, MPP in Nonprofit Policy

San Francisco State University, MPA in Nonprofit Administration

University of San Diego, MA in Nonprofit Leadership and Management Studies

University of Southern California, MPA and MPP with Concentrations in Nonprofit Management

Colorado

Regis University, MNA

University of Colorado at Denver, MPA, Doctor of Philosophy in Public Administration

Connecticut

University of Connecticut, MPA with Concentration in Nonprofit Management

Yale University, MBA with Concentration in Nonprofit Management

District Columbia

Georgetown University, MPA in Nonprofit Policy and Leadership

The George Washington University, MPA and MPP with Concentrations in Nonprofit Management

Delaware

University of Delaware, MA and MPA with Concentrations in Community Development and Nonprofit Leadership

Florida

Florida Atlantic University, MNA

Georgia

Georgia State University, MPA in Nonprofit Studies, MS in Urban Policy Studies in Nonprofit Studies

Kennesaw State University, MPA in Community Services/Nonprofit Administration

University of Georgia, MA in Nonprofit Organizations

Iowa

University of Northern Iowa, MA in Philanthropy and Nonprofit Development, MPP in Nonprofits

Illinois

DePaul University, MS in Public Service Management with Concentrations in Association and Management, MS in Public Service Management in Fundraising and Philanthropy, MS in Public Service Management in Nonprofit Administration

Northwestern University, Master of NonProfit Management

Southern Illinois University at Edwardsville, MPA

Illinois Institute of Technology, MPA in Nonprofit Management

Indiana

Indiana University at Bloomington, MPA and PhD with Concentrations in Nonprofit Management

Indiana University, Center on Philanthropy, MA in Philanthropic Studies, MPA in Nonprofit Management, PhD in Philanthropic Studies

Indiana University-Purdue University at Indianapolis, MPA in Nonprofit Management

University of Notre Dame, MS in Nonprofit Leadership

Louisiana

Louisiana State University at Shreveport, MS in Human Services Administration

Maine

Clark University, MPA in Nonprofit Administration

Maryland

College of Notre Dame of Maryland, MA in Nonprofit Management

Johns Hopkins University, MA in Policy Studies in Nonprofit Sector

University of Maryland, University College, MA in Management in Nonprofit Management

Massachusetts

Harvard University, MPP, MPA, PhD in Public Policy / Public Administration

Lesley College, MBA in Not-for-Profit Management

Tufts University, MA in Nonprofit Organizations

Worcester State College, MS in Nonprofit Management

Michigan

Oakland University, MPA in Nonprofit Organization and Management

University of Michigan, MSW, MPA, MPP with Concentrations in Nonprofit Management

Wayne State University, Master of Interdisciplinary Studies in Nonprofit Sectors

Western Michigan University, MPA in Nonprofit Management and Leadership

Minnesota

St. Cloud State University, MS in Public and Nonprofit Institutions

University of Minnesota, Humphrey Institute, Master of Public Affairs in Nonprofits, Master of Management in Nonprofits

Missouri

University of Missouri at Kansas City, MPA in Nonprofit Management, Doctor of Philosophy in Public Administration in Nonprofit Management

University of Missouri at St. Louis, MPP in Nonprofit Management and Leadership

North Carolina

High Point University, MPA in Nonprofit Organizations

University of North Carolina at Greensboro, Master of Public Affairs in Nonprofit Management

Nebraska

University of Nebraska at Omaha, MPA in Nonprofit, Doctor of Philosophy in Public Administration in Nonprofit

New Jersey

Seton Hall University, MPA in Nonprofit Management

Kean University, MPA in Nonprofit Management

New York

CUNY - Baruch College, MPA in Nonprofit Administration

Long Island University, MPA in Not-for-Profit Management

New School University, MS in Nonprofit Management

New York University - Wagner Graduate School, MPA and Doctor of Philosophy with Specializations in Public and Nonprofit Management and Policy, Management of International Public Service Organizations, and Nonprofit and NGOs

Ohio

Case Western Reserve University, MNA, Executive Doctor of Management

Cleveland State University, MA in Nonprofit Management, Doctor of Philosophy in Nonprofit Management

Kent State University, MBA in Nonprofit Management, MPA in Nonprofit Management

Ohio State University, Master of Social Work in Social Administration Practice

The Union Institute, MA in Nonprofit Management, PhD in Nonprofit Management

Oregon

Portland State University - Division of Public Administration, MPA in Nonprofit, Doctor of Philosophy in Public Administration and Policy in Nonprofit

University of Oregon, Master of Community & Regional Planning, MPA, Graduate Certificate in Not-for-Profit Management

Pennsylvania

Eastern University, MS in Nonprofit Management

Indiana University of Pennsylvania, Mater of Arts in Sociology in Administration & Evaluation and Human Services Administration, Doctor of Philosophy in Administration and Leadership Studies in Administration & Evaluation and Human Services Administration

Widener University, MPA in Nonprofit Administration

South Carolina

College of Charleston, MPA in Nonprofit Administration

South Dakota

University of South Dakota, MPA in Nonprofit Administration

Tennessee

University of Memphis, MPA in Nonprofit Administration

University of Tennessee, Chattanooga, MPA in Nonprofit Management

Texas

University of Houston – Victoria, MA in Interdisciplinary Studies in Nonprofit Leadership

University of Texas at Austin, Lyndon B. Johnson School of Public Affairs, MPA, PhD in Public Policy

University of Dallas, MBA in Nonprofit Management, MS in Management in Nonprofit Management

Virginia

George Mason University, MPA in Nonprofit Management

Virginia Commonwealth University, MPA in Nonprofit Management

Vermont

School for International Training, Program in Intercultural Service, Leadership, and Management (PIM) in Mission Driven Organizations

Washington

Seattle University, Executive Master of Not-For-Profit Leadership, MPA in Nonprofit Leadership

Wisconsin

University of Wisconsin – Milwaukee, MA, MBA, MPA in Nonprofit Management

Certificate Programs (Graduate Programs)

Alabama

Auburn University at Montgomery, Nonprofit Management and Leadership Certificate

University of Alabama at Birmingham, Graduate Certificate in Nonprofit Management

Arkansas

University of Arkansas at Little Rock, Graduate Certificate in Nonprofit Management

California

California State University – Hayward, Nonprofit Management Certificate

University of San Diego, Certificate in Nonprofit Leadership & Management

Calstate East Bay, Certificate in Nonprofit Management

Colorado

University of Colorado at Colorado Springs, Certificate in Nonprofit Management

Connecticut

University of Connecticut, Graduate Certificate in Nonprofit Management

District of Columbia

The George Washington University, Graduate Certificate in Nonprofit Management

Florida

Florida Atlantic University, Nonprofit Management Executive Certificate

Georgia

Georgia State University, Graduate Certificate in Nonprofit Management

University of Georgia, Graduate Certificate in Nonprofit Organizations

Illinois

DePaul University, Administrative Foundations Certificate, Nonprofit Leadership Certificate

Southern Illinois University at Edwardsville, Non-Profit Management Certificate

Illinois Institute of Technology, Certificate in Nonprofit Management

Loyola University Chicago, Certificate of Advanced Study in Philanthropy

Saint Xavier University, Certificate in Public and Non-Profit Management

Indiana

Indiana University – Bloomington, Nonprofit Management Certificate

Indiana University, Center on Philanthropy, Philanthropic Studies Certificate, Nonprofit Management Certificate

Purdue University, Certificate in Nonprofit Management

Perdue University North Central, Certificate in Nonprofit Management

Maryland

College of Notre Dame of Maryland, Certificate in Leadership of Nonprofit Organizations

Johns Hopkins University, Certificate in Nonprofit Studies

University of Maryland, University College, Nonprofit Financial Management Certificate

Massachusetts

Tufts University, Management of Community Organizations Certificate

Michigan

Oakland University, Post-Master's Certificate in Nonprofit Organization & Management

University of Michigan, Certificate in Nonprofit Management in Development

Ferris State University, Philanthropic Studies Certificate

Grand Valley State University, Graduate Certificate in Nonprofit Leadership

Lawrence Technological University, Graduate Certificate in Nonprofit Management and Leadership

Wayne State University, Master of Interdisciplinary Studies in Nonprofit Sectors

Western Michigan University, Nonprofit Leadership Certificate

Minnesota

University of Minnesota, Humphrey Institute, Nonprofit Management Certificate

Missouri

University of Missouri at Kansas City, Fund Raising Certificate

University of Missouri at St. Louis, Nonprofit Management and Leadership Certificate

New Jersey

Seton Hall University, Certificate in Nonprofit Organization Management

Rutgers University – Newark, Certificate in Nonprofit Management

New York

Roberts Wesleyan College, Certificate in Nonprofit Leadership

C.W. Post College, Nonprofit Management Advanced Certificate

SUNY College at Brockport, Certificate in Nonprofit Management

Nevada

University of Nevada, Certificate in Nonprofit Management

North Carolina

North Carolina State University, Graduate Certificate in Nonprofit Management

University of North Carolina – Greensboro, Nonprofit Management Certificate

University of North Carolina at Chapel Hill, Nonprofit Leadership Certificate

University of North Carolina at Chapel Hill, Social Work, Nonprofit Leadership Certificate

Ohio

Case Western Reserve University, Certificate in Nonprofit Management

Cleveland State University, Certificate in Nonprofit Management

University of Akron, Certificate in Nonprofit Management

Oregon

Portland State University - Division of Public Administration, Nonprofit Management Certificate, Nonprofit Development Certificate, Nonprofit Financial Management Certificate, Volunteer Management Certificate

University of Oregon, Graduate Certificate in Not-for-Profit Management

Pennsylvania

University of Pennsylvania, Certificate in Nonprofit Administration

University of Pittsburgh, Nonprofit Management Certificate

Widener University, Certificate of Advanced Graduate Studies in Nonprofit Management

Rhode Island

Rhode Island College, Certificate in Nonprofit Studies

Tennessee

University of Tennessee, Chattanooga, Certificate in Nonprofit Management

Texas

University of Dallas, Certificate for Not-for-Profit Management

University of North Texas, Graduate Academic Certificate in Volunteer and Community Resource Management

Virginia

George Mason University, Certificate in Nonprofit Management, Certificate in Association Management

Virginia Commonwealth University, Graduate Certificate in Nonprofit Management

Virginia Tech, Nonprofit and Nongovernmental Organization Management Certificate

Washington

University of Washington, Nonprofit Management Certificate

West Virginia

West Virginia University, Nonprofit Management Certificate

Wisconsin

University of Wisconsin – Milwaukee, Graduate Certificate in Nonprofit Management

Continuing Education (CEU)

Arizona

Arizona State University, Nonprofit Management

California

California State University at Hayward, Non-Profit Management

California State University at Fresno, Nonprofit Leadership and Management

California State University, Fullerton, Leadership for Public and Nonprofit Service

San Jose State University, Nonprofit Management

University of California at Irvine, Fundraising

University of San Francisco, Executive Nonprofit Management, Development Director

Florida

University of South Florida, Nonprofit Management

Indiana

Indiana University – Bloomington, Nonprofit Management

Indiana University, Center on Philanthropy, Fundraising Management

Maryland

Goucher College, Nonprofit Management

Michigan

Michigan State University, Excellence in Nonprofit Leadership & Management

Oakland University, Nonprofit Management

Minnesota

University of St. Thomas - Center for Nonprofit Management, Mini-MBA for Nonprofit Organizations

Missouri

University of Missouri at Kansas City, Fund Raising Management

Nebraska

University of Nebraska at Omaha, Fundraising Management

New York

New York University - School of Continuing & Professional Studies, Fundraising

The Union Institute, Certified Volunteer Manager

Oregon

Portland State University - Division of Public Administration, Nonprofit Management, Nonprofit Development, Nonprofit Financial Management, Volunteer Management

Pennsylvania

Bryn Mawr College, Executive Leadership

Marywood University, Program in Non-Profit Management

Texas

University of Texas at Austin - Thompson Conference Center, Management of Nonprofit Organizations

Virginia

University of Richmond, Philanthropy

Washington

Washington State University, Volunteer Management

West Virginia

West Virginia University, Nonprofit Management

Wisconsin

University of Wisconsin at Milwaukee, Professional Nonprofit Management

University of Wisconsin at Superior, Nonprofit Administration

Online

California State University, Long Beach, MPA

Capella University, MS, PhD in Human Services/ Management of Nonprofit

George Mason University, MPA, Certificate in Nonprofit Management, Certificate in Association Management

Indiana University-Purdue University-Indianapolis, Certificate in Nonprofit Management

Regis University, Master of Nonprofit Management

University of Colorado at Denver, MPA with Concentration in Nonprofit Organization Management

University of Illinois at Chicago, Certificate for Nonprofit Management, School of Public and Environmental Affairs (SPEA), Nonprofit Management Certificate

University of Maryland, Not-for-Profit Financial Management Graduate Certificate

University of San Francisco, Development Director Certificate

Walden University, MBA, MPA, PhD, Nonprofit Management and Leadership

INDEX

Index